Contents

To the Learner..3

Unit 1: Numbers and Operations

Whole Numbers 5

    Whole Number Concepts.........................5

    Estimating with Whole Numbers.............6

    Whole Numbers: Computation Practice..7

    GED Practice: Whole Numbers 8

    GED Practice: Whole Numbers II............9

    Steps For Solving Word Problems 11

    GED Practice: Solving Word Problems 12

    GED Practice: Solving Word Problems II..13

    Missing and Extraneous Information 14

    Missing and Extraneous Information
        Practice 15

    Order of Operations 16

    Set-Up Problems 17

    GED Practice: Set-Up Problems 18

Fractions...19

    GED Practice: Fractions 20

    GED Practice: Fractions II......................21

Decimals...22

    GED Practice: Decimals 23

    GED Practice: Decimals II......................24

Percents 25

    GED Practice: Percents 26

    GED Practice: Percents II 27

    Ratio and Proportion.............................28

    GED Practice: Ratio and Proportion.......29

GED Review: Numbers and Operations.........30

Unit 2: Measurement and Data Analysis

Data Analysis...33

    Mean, Median, and Number Series........33

    Probability 34

    GED Practice: Probability 35

Measurement 36

    GED Practice: Measurement..................37

Tables, Graphs, and Charts 38

    GED Practice: Tables 38

    GED Practice: Circle Graphs...................39

    GED Practice: Charts 40

    GED Practice: Line Graphs 42

    GED Practice: Bar Graphs......................43

    GED Practice: Mixed Practice.................45

GED Review: Measurement and
    Data Analysis 48

Unit 3: Algebra

    Introduction 51

    Powers and Roots of Numbers 52

    Simplifying Algebraic Expressions 53

    Evaluating Algebraic Expressions Using
        Substitution 54

    Solving One-Step Equations...................55

    Solving Two-Step Equations...................56

    Solving Multi-Step Equations.................57

    Solving Word Problems 58

    GED Practice: Solving Word Problems...59

    Formula Problems: Interest, Distance
        and Cost 60

Solving Inequalities 62

Factoring 63

Solving Quadratic Equations by
    Substitution 64

Coordinates 65

Graphing Linear Equations 66

Slope of a Line 67

Finding the Equation of a Line 68

Graphing Problems 69

GED Review: Algebra 71

Unit 4: Geometry

Angles and Lines 74

Triangles 75

Triangle Rules 76

Solving Geometric Figure Problems 77

Formula Problems: Perimeter,
    Circumference, Area, and Volume ...79

GED Practice: Geometry Word
    Problems 82

GED Review: Geometry 87

GED Math Test Handbook 90

Calculator 90

Using Special Formats 95

Simulated GED Test A 98

Analysis of Performance: Test A 115

Simulated GED Test B 116

Analysis of Performance: Test B 133

Answers and Explanations 134

Answer Sheets 171

The *Steck-Vaughn GED Mathematics Exercise Book* provides you with practice in answering the types of questions found on the actual GED Mathematics Test. It can be used with *Steck-Vaughn GED Mathematics* or *Steck-Vaughn Complete GED Preparation*. This exercise book contains both practice exercises and two complete simulated GED tests.

Practice Exercises

The GED Mathematics Test tests your math skills and problem-solving ability in four content areas. The practice exercises in this book are divided into four units that cover the skills in the four content areas:

Unit 1, Numbers and Operations, includes practice with problems that involve basic operations (addition, subtraction, multiplication, and division), order of operations, and numbers in a variety of equivalent forms (whole numbers, fractions, decimals, percents, exponents, and scientific notation). It also includes problems using ratio and proportion.

Unit 2, Measurement and Data Analysis, gives you practice in using basic math skills to solve problems about length, perimeter, circumference, area, volume, and time. These problems involve the customary U.S. measurement system, the metric system, and conversions within each system. Data analysis problems test your ability to locate and use information presented in tables, charts, and graphs. Also included are problems that involve finding the mean, median, mode, or range of a set of data and the probability that a given event will occur.

Unit 3, Algebra, includes practice with variables in tables, equations, and written descriptions as well as practice with using algebraic symbols and expressions to solve problems. Practice exercises also include solving for any variable within a formula, factoring, graphing equations, solving equations, and using exponential functions.

Unit 4, Geometry, includes practice in using basic operations to find the measures of angles and line segments in both common and irregular figures, using the Pythagorean Theorem, finding the slope of a line, and solving problems using the concepts of perpendicularity, parallelism, congruence, and similarity of geometric figures.

To prepare you for what you will find on the GED test, the units provide practice in setting up problems as well as solving them and practice in identifying missing and extraneous information. The practice exercises also present problems in real-world situations and in both written and graphic form. All the units include practice using the calculator to solve problems and practice answering multiple choice questions as well as alternate format questions.

Simulated Tests

The GED Mathematics Test is divided into two parts, each with 25 test questions that cover all four content areas. Part I of the test allows you to use a calculator, and Part II does not. Each part of the test contains both multiple choice questions, where you choose the correct answer, and alternate format questions, where you find the answer to a problem and enter that answer on a grid.

This exercise book contains two full-length Simulated GED Mathematics Tests. Each Simulated Test has the same two parts, the same number of questions, and the same types of questions that are on the actual GED Test.

Content Areas

The GED Mathematics Test covers four content areas: number operations and number sense; measurement and geometry; data analysis, statistics, and probability; algebra, functions, and patterns. Each content area accounts for approximately 25 percent of the questions on the test.

You will be asked to solve problems in all four content areas. Some problems will test your ability to do the basic operations—addition, subtraction, multiplication, and division—while other problems will test mathematical concepts such as ratio and proportion. Some problems will ask you how to set up a problem in order to solve it. You will also be asked to use formulas to solve problems. The formulas you need will be provided in each test.

Graphics

One half of the questions on the GED Mathematics Test relate to a graphic such as a drawing, chart, map, or graph. Practice with graphics is essential for developing the skills to interpret information presented on the GED Test. Always read all the information associated with the graphic before answering any questions based on it.

GED Math Test Handbook

The handbook on pages 90–97 of this book addresses two features of the GED Mathematics Test: the calculator and alternative answer formats. The CASIO *fx-260SOLAR* calculator is the official calculator for the GED Test. These pages include an illustration of this calculator and an explanation of its functions. The handbook also includes illustrations and explanations for the two types of alternate answer formats, the standard grid and the coordinate plane grid. If you are not familiar with the calculator and the grids used on the GED test, refer to this handbook before you begin using this book.

Analysis of Performance Charts

After each Simulated Test, an Analysis of Performance Chart will help you determine if you are ready to take the GED Mathematics Test. The charts give a breakdown of test questions by content area. By completing these charts, you can determine your own strengths and weaknesses as they relate to the mathematics area.

Correlation Chart

The following chart shows how the sections of this exercise book relate to the sections of other Steck-Vaughn GED preparation books. You can refer to these other books for further instruction or review.

CONTENT AREAS	Numbers and Operations	Measurement and Data Analysis	Algebra	Geometry
BOOK TITLES *Steck-Vaughn GED Mathematics Exercise Book*	Unit 1	Unit 2	Unit 3	Unit 4
Steck-Vaughn GED Mathematics	Unit 1	Unit 2	Unit 3	Unit 4
Steck-Vaughn Complete GED Preparation	Unit 6, Numbers and Operations	Unit 6, Measurement and Data Analysis	Unit 6, Algebra	Unit 6, Geometry

UNIT 1 Numbers and Operations

Whole Numbers Concepts

Directions: Compare the following numbers. Write >, <, or = between the numbers.

1. 324 _____ 432

2. 1,036 _____ 1,008

3. 12,992 _____ 12,991

4. 85,063 _____ 85,630

Directions: Write each set of numbers in order from smallest to largest.

5. 293; 392; 932; 923; 329 _____

6. 5,631; 6,531; 5,316; 6,315; 6,153 _____

7. 19,482; 9,842; 98,421; 18,429; 8,914 _____

Directions: Round each number to the given place.

8. Round 9,775 to the nearest hundred. _____

9. Round 6,998,546 to the nearest million. _____

10. Round 56,701 to the nearest ten thousand. _____

11. Round 11,324 to the nearest thousand. _____

Refer to the following chart to answer Questions 12–15.

Daily Sales Totals, Week Ending June 9	
Monday	$14,589
Tuesday	$12,556
Wednesday	$16,890
Thursday	$12,345
Friday	$10,098
Saturday	$22,776
Sunday	$11,231

12. Which day had higher sales, Thursday or Friday? _____

13. Which day had the lowest sales? _____

14. Which day had the highest sales?_____

15. Arrange the days on the chart in order from lowest sales to highest sales.

_____

You can use estimation to help find the answer to some multiple choice problems. First, round the numbers given in the problem. Then, use the rounded numbers to estimate the solution. Eliminate any of the choices that are not close to the estimated solution.

Example: Allen's weekly pay is $297. How much will he make in one year (52 weeks)?

(1) $ 1,485
(2) $10,544
(3) $13,824
(4) $15,444
(5) $18,324

Round $297 to $300. Round 52 weeks to 50 weeks. Multiply the rounded numbers. $300 × 50 = $15,000. Allen earns about $15,000 in one year. Option (4) is the only answer close to $15,000.

Directions: Estimate each answer. Eliminate any of the choices that are not close to the estimate. If there is more than one choice remaining, you may need to find the exact answer.

1. Last Friday night a local theater sold a total of 592 tickets at $6.00 each. How much money did the theater make on tickets last Friday night?

   (1) $3,000
   (2) $3,125
   (3) $3,552
   (4) $3,950
   (5) $9,472

2. Light travels at a rate of 186,282 miles per second. If it takes 11 seconds for light to travel from a certain star to Earth, about how many miles away is the star?

   (1)   18,600
   (2)   186,000
   (3)   1,860,000
   (4)   2,046,000
   (5) 20,460,000

3. A manufacturer of CDs finds that one out of every five hundred CDs produced in her factory is defective. If the factory produces 29,000 CDs in one day, about how many are defective?

   (1)   6
   (2)   60
   (3)   600
   (4)   6,000
   (5)   60,000

4. Two years ago in Bay City, 3,452 people took the GED test. Last year 2,807 took the test. What was the decrease in the number of people taking the GED test?

   (1) 1,655
   (2) 1,405
   (3)   745
   (4)   655
   (5)   645

<u>Directions</u>: Enter your answers to the following problems on the lines provided.

Example: What is the sum of 125 and 75? ___200___

1.   What is the product of 144 and 23? _____

2.   What is the difference between 24,593 and 10,638? _____

3.   What is the sum of 37,454; 41,345; 49,496; and 22,738? _____

4.   If you divide 896 by 32, what is the quotient? _____

5.   Find the product of 9,675 and 326. _____

6.   What does 90,000 minus 82,575 equal? _____

7.   What is the quotient of 230,400 divided by 36? _____

8.   What is the total of 861; 495; and 827? _____

9.   What is the product of 8,622 and 393? _____

 <u>Directions</u>: Use your calculator to solve these problems. Round to the nearest whole number. Remember that your calculator does not show a dollar sign. Enter your answers on the lines provided.

10.   Find the product of 16,774 and 19. _____

11.   Multiply $2,284 by 65. _____

12.   Divide 608,439 by 123. _____

13.   Divide 184,000 by 35. _____

14.   50,566 × 66 = _____

15.   325,666 ÷ 156 = _____

16.   What is the difference between 658,235 and 621,791? _____

17.   What is the sum of 7,478 and 9,757? _____

18.   Subtract seven thousand fifty-nine from eight thousand three hundred eleven.

_____

Directions: Choose the one best answer to each question.

1. On a word processing test, Lydia typed 694 words in 15 minutes. On that same test 6 days later, Lydia typed 753 words in 15 minutes. By how many words did Lydia's speed improve from the first test to the second test?

   (1) 49
   (2) 53
   (3) 59
   (4) 69
   (5) 71

2. Town and Country Video rents 3 video movies for $5.00. In one week Town and Country Video rented 675 videotapes. How much money did Town and Country Video record in rental receipts?

   (1) $ 225
   (2) $ 675
   (3) $ 725
   (4) $1,125
   (5) $1,500

3. The Appleton School District has 8 elementary schools and 2 senior high schools. The average enrollment at the elementary schools is 356 students per school, while the average enrollment at the high schools is 1,307 students per school. What is the total student enrollment in the Appleton School District?

   (1)   1,663
   (2)   2,614
   (3)   2,848
   (4)   5,462
   (5) 10,456

4. In 1985, the United States Patent Office granted 4,600,602 new patents. This is 641,197 fewer patents than the number of patents issued in 1980. How many patents were granted in 1980?

   (1) 3,205,985
   (2) 3,959,405
   (3) 4,600,602
   (4) 5,241,799
   (5) Not enough information is given.

5. In a recent school board presidential election for the Meadow Ridge School District, Agnes Hancock received 3,121 votes. Her opponent, Andrew Sawyer, received 2,374 votes. By how many votes did Hancock defeat Sawyer?

   (1) 447
   (2) 477
   (3) 497
   (4) 747
   (5) 774

Directions: Solve the following problem. Enter your answer on the grid provided.

6. In the month of July, which has 31 days, an average of 2,118 people visited the Museum of Science and Industry each day. The museum was open each day of the month. How many people visited the museum during July?

Directions: Choose the one best answer to each question. Most problems have more than one step. Use your calculator when indicated.

Questions 1 and 2 refer to the following passage.

A mail carrier recorded the number of pieces of mail she delivered during a one-week period. Her route covered 3 miles with 63 scheduled delivery stops. The mail carrier's record of deliveries by day was: Monday, 531 pieces; Tuesday, 116 pieces; Wednesday, 285 pieces; Thursday, 432 pieces; Friday, 157 pieces; and Saturday, 480 pieces.

1. What was the total number of pieces of mail delivered by the carrier for the week? Round your answer to the nearest hundred.

   (1) 1,900
   (2) 1,974
   (3) 2,000
   (4) 2,100
   (5) 2,200

2. What is the difference between the number of pieces of mail delivered on the heaviest delivery day and the sum of the two lightest delivery days?

   (1) 531
   (2) 415
   (3) 299
   (4) 258
   (5) 116

3. Four friends commute to work together. Each week the gas, parking, and tolls cost $134. If they split the costs equally, how much does each friend pay per week toward the commuting costs?

   (1) $18.75
   (2) $26.00
   (3) $33.50
   (4) $34.00
   (5) $36.25

Question 4 refers to the following diagram.

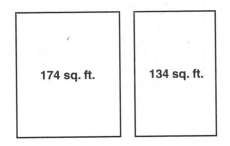

174 sq. ft.   134 sq. ft.

4. Carl is buying carpet for his office. The diagram shows the amount of carpeting needed for each of two rooms. What is the total square feet of carpet Carl needs?

   (1) 344
   (2) 324
   (3) 308
   (4) 298
   (5) 288

Question 5 refers to the following drawing.

Section A	?
Section B	36 in.
Section C	24 in.

72 in.

Note: Not drawn to scale

5. The magazine racks in the Freeport Library have adjustable shelves. If the shelves are inserted as indicated in the drawing, what is the height of section A?

   (1) 12 in.
   (2) 24 in.
   (3) 36 in.
   (4) 48 in.
   (5) 60 in.

Questions 6 through 9 refer to the following information.

Ms. Espinoza opened a savings account with $75 when she got a new job. The balances in her account for the first 6 months are:

Month	Deposit	End-of-Month Balance
April	$75	$ 75
May	5?	125
June	55	180
July	45	225
August	4?	265
September	75	340

6. In what month did Ms. Espinoza deposit the smallest amount of money?

(1) May
(2) June
(3) July
(4) August
(5) September

7. What was the total amount of money deposited in Ms. Espinoza's account for the 5 months after her initial deposit of $75?

(1) $265
(2) $253
(3) $221
(4) $202
(5) $201

8. In which month did Ms. Espinoza deposit the most money?

(1) May
(2) June
(3) July
(4) August
(5) September

9. In October, Ms. Espinoza withdrew $135. In November, she deposited $60. What was her balance at the end of November?

(1) $ 0
(2) $145
(3) $150
(4) $265
(5) $535

10. Joyce worked 84 hours in 3 weeks. She earns $6 per hour. How much did she earn in the three weeks?

(1) $ 14
(2) $ 28
(3) $ 252
(4) $ 504
(5) $1,344

11. On Stan's hiking map 1 inch equals 50 miles. How long will the actual trail be if the trail on the map is 3 inches long?

(1) 15 miles
(2) 50 miles
(3) 150 miles
(4) 300 miles

12. Each month Nadine pays $1,655 in rent for her office. Providing the rent does not increase, how much will she pay in office rent for three years?

(1) $ 4,965
(2) $19,860
(3) $39,720
(4) $59,580
(5) $65,655

Directions: Solve the following problem. Enter your answer on the grid provided.

13. Nathan's bank statement listed a balance of $455 in his savings account. Over the next three months he made deposits of $156, $344, and $25. What is the new balance in his savings account after these transactions?

Here are some steps that will help you solve word problems.

Step 1   Read the problem and decide what you are asked to find. Identify what information you need to solve the problem.

Step 2   Choose the operation (addition, subtraction, multiplication, or division) you will use to solve the problem.

Step 3   Estimate to find an approximate answer. This will give you an idea of the answer you're looking for.

Step 4   Solve the problem.

Step 5   Check your answer to make sure it makes sense. Does it answer the question posed by the problem? Does it seem reasonable? Compare your answer to your estimate.

Apply this strategy to the following problem.

Example: Beck's Bookstore bought 30 boxes of pocket dictionaries for $720. If there were 20 dictionaries in each box, how much did one dictionary cost?

   (1) $0.25

   (2) $1.20

   (3) $1.75

   (4) $2.20

   (5) $2.50

Step 1   You need to find the cost of one dictionary. You need the facts that 30 boxes of dictionaries cost $720 and that each box contains 20 dictionaries.

Step 2   To find the cost of one dictionary, first determine the total number of dictionaries by multiplying the number of boxes times the books per box. The second operation will be division because all the dictionaries are of equal value.

Step 3   Use estimation to determine that the dictionaries cost a little more than a dollar each because the total amount is $720 and the total number of dictionaries is 600.

Step 4   Solve the problem.

$$
\begin{array}{r}
30 \\
\times 20 \\
\hline
600
\end{array}
\begin{array}{l}
\text{boxes} \\
\text{dictionaries per box} \\
\text{dictionaries}
\end{array}
$$

$$
\begin{array}{r}
\$1.20 \\
600\overline{)\$720.00} \\
\underline{600} \\
1200 \\
\underline{1200}
\end{array}
$$

Step 5   Check your answer. Is it reasonable?
The answer $1.20 is close to the estimate of $1.00 per dictionary, so it is reasonable.

Option (2) $1.20 is correct. The cost of one dictionary is $1.20.

Directions: Solve the problems using the steps outlined on the preceding page. Choose the one best answer for each question. You MAY use your calculator when indicated.

Questions 1 and 2 refer to the following table.

Number of Books Checked Out of the Library	
May	5,679
June	7,432
July	9,204
August	9,677
September	6,340

1. What was the total number of books checked out of the library in July and August?

   (1) 19,891
   (2) 18,881
   (3) 16,636
   (4) 15,544
   (5) 15,356

2. How many more books were checked out in June than in May?

   (1) 473
   (2) 1772
   (3) 1753
   (4) 1853
   (5) 3337

3. A video recorder costs $259, and Ann pays $25 down on the purchase price. If Ann makes 6 equal payments after the down payment, what must she pay each month?

   (1) $49
   (2) $45
   (3) $43
   (4) $41
   (5) $39

4. Brian's car payment is $169 per month for 3 years. If Brian paid $750 down, what is the total cost of his car?

   (1) $3,096
   (2) $3,846
   (3) $6,834
   (4) $6,903
   (5) $8,112

5. On Saturday, the Wallingford Outlet had the following sales: 390 computers, 94 microwaves, 355 washing machines, 18 clothes dryers, 184 DVD players, and 189 cameras. What was the total number of items sold?

   (1) 952
   (2) 1130
   (3) 1230
   (4) 1330
   (5) 1383

Directions: Solve the following problem. Enter your answer on the grid provided.

6. Martha's weekly gross salary is $1,243. If $289 is taken out for taxes and $195 is taken out for other deductions, what is the amount of Martha's weekly net salary?

Directions: Solve the following problems using the steps for solving word problems outlined on page 11. Most problems have more than one step. Choose the one best answer to each question. You MAY use your calculator when indicated.

1. The Union Land Development Company divided a tract of land into 15 equally-valued lots to build homes in the Canterbury Subdivision. The tract of land was valued at $150,000. What was the value of each lot?

(1) $ 1,050
(2) $ 1,500
(3) $10,000
(4) $10,500
(5) $15,000

2. Regal Square Apartments has 14 floors. Each floor of the building has 4 apartments, and each apartment has 8 electrical outlets. How many outlets are there in the building?

(1)   26
(2)   32
(3)   112
(4)   448
(5)   512

Directions: Solve the following question and enter your answer on the grid provided.

3. The Wet Pet Shop ordered 475 goldfish for its annual giveaway. If each customer received 3 fish, how many fish were left after 105 customers visited the store?

Questions 4 and 5 refer to the following table.

Jefferson's Department Store	
Department	Net Sales
Toys	$78,598
Boys	$89,345
Girls	$46,969
Men's	$56,812
Women's	$64,001
Bed and Bath	$49,009

4. What was the total net sales for the departments listed?

(1) $281,043
(2) $288,756
(3) $384,734
(4) $394,823
(5) Not enough information given.

5. Combined net sales for the Men's Department and Women's Department were how much less than the combined net sales of the Boys' and Girls' Department?

(1)   7,189
(2)   9,843
(3)   15,501
(4)   15,901
(5)   16,501

Some problems cannot be solved because some piece of needed information is missing. Also, some problems include information you do not need to find the answer. Read each problem carefully to determine what information you need and whether it is provided.

Example 1: To wallpaper an entire bedroom, Jeff needs 880 square feet of wallpaper. If a roll of wallpaper covers 75 square feet, how much money does Jeff need to purchase the wallpaper for this room?

Using the steps for solving word problems on page 11, solve the problem above.

Step 1 Read the problem carefully and underline key words (*how much*).

Step 2 The facts are:
   A. 880 square feet of wallpaper are needed.
   B. One roll of wallpaper covers 75 square feet.

Step 3 You want to know:
   How much money is needed to purchase the wallpaper?

Step 4 Review your facts. This problem cannot be solved because you are not given an important piece of information: the selling price of the wallpaper per roll.

It is equally important to be able to recognize that some problems have too much information. Sometimes it is not necessary to use all the numbers that appear in word problems.

Example 2: The Booster Club sponsored a dinner dance to raise money to buy team uniforms. Eighty couples attended the dance at $28 per couple. After paying the expenses for the dance, the club was able to buy half of its team's uniforms which cost $15 per uniform. How much money was collected before expenses?

Follow the steps below.

Step 1 Read the problem carefully and underline key words (*how much*).

Step 2 The facts are:
   A. Eighty couples attended the dance.
   B. Each couple paid $28.
   C. Uniforms cost $15 each.
   D. The club could buy $\frac{1}{2}$ of the uniforms after expenses.

Step 3 You want to know: How much money was collected before expenses?

Step 4 Only one operation is necessary. Eighty couples attended and each paid $28. Multiply the price of the ticket by the number of couples attending the dance.

Step 5 Round $28 up to $30. The estimated answer is:
   $30 × 80 = $2,400.

Step 6 Carry out the operation to find the exact answer:
   $28 × 80 = $2,240

Step 7 Review your estimated answer against the exact answer.
   Those answers should be similar.

Two pieces of information are included in the problem that are not necessary to answer the question asked. The unnecessary information was the cost of the uniforms and the club's ability to buy half of the uniforms they needed.

<u>Directions</u>: Each problem below is missing information. On the lines below, write the missing information that is needed to solve each problem.

1. The city advisory council has 150 representatives. The representatives are Republicans, Democrats, and Independents. Forty-five of the representatives are Democrats. How many of the representatives are Independents?
   To determine the number of Independents, the missing piece of information is

   _____ .

2. An inheritance of $8,000 is to be shared equally by the members of the Marble family. What is each family member's share?
   To determine the dollar amount for each family member, the missing piece of information is

   _____ .

3. The Beverly Cycle Shop recorded sales of $4,567 for the total number of bicycles sold in June. What was the average cost per bicycle?
   To determine the average cost per bicycle, the missing piece of information is

   _____ .

<u>Directions</u>: Each problem below has too much information. Identify the extra information, and then solve the problem. Write your answers on the lines provided.

4. Norma applied for a new position at the hospital. Her annual salary is $15,750. The new position has an annual base salary of $18,750. Norma must pay $325 for union dues. What is the amount of the difference between the two salaries?

   The extra information is _____ .

   The answer is _____ .

5.

	Times	Tribune	USA Daily
Monday	523	288	151
Tuesday	536	254	79
Wednesday	511	352	87
Thursday	524	323	123
Friday	537	357	147
	2,631	1,574	587

   How many more *Times* were sold than *USA Daily* for the five days?

   The extra information is _____ .

   The answer is _____ .

Which solution gives you the correct answer for $6 + 4 \times 3$?

Solution A	Solution B
$6 + 4 \times 3 =$	$6 + 4 \times 3 =$
$10 \times 3 = 30$	$6 + 12 = 18$

Only Solution B gives you the correct answer. Because it is possible to solve the problem and calculate two different answers, mathematicians agree that rules are needed so everyone evaluates the problem the same way. The rules that follow are the rules for solving problems like these. The rules are called the Order of Operations.

Order of Operations
1. First, evaluate operations within parentheses.
2. Next, evaluate operations with powers and roots.
3. Perform multiplication and division operations from left to right.
4. Perform addition and subtraction operations from left to right.

Note: If the problems do not have parentheses or powers and roots, then start with the third rule.

Directions: Use the Order of Operations to solve the following problems. You may NOT use your calculator.

1. $3(7 + 4) - 18 \div 9$ _____

2. $\dfrac{5 \times 4 + 2}{17 - 2 \times 3}$ _____

3. $6(7 - 5) + 4$ _____

4. $14 + 28 \div 7$ _____

5. $\dfrac{5 \times 6 + 2}{12 - 4}$ _____

6. $8 + 4 \times 2$ _____

7. $\dfrac{(6 - 2)}{(3 + 1)}$ _____

8. $5 + 2 \times 4$ _____

9. $\dfrac{8}{2} + \dfrac{18}{6}$ _____

10. $6(3 + 7) - 4(4 - 2)$ _____

11. $\dfrac{21}{(5 - 2)}$ _____

12. $36 + \dfrac{12}{6}$ _____

Directions: Use the Order of Operations to solve the following problems. You MAY use your calculator.

13. $(5 \times 24) \div (14 \times 16)$ _____

14. $100 - 35 \times 24$ _____

15. $28 \div 4 + 45 \div 9$ _____

16. $\dfrac{(80 \times \$24)}{(80 \times \$12)}$ _____

17. $\$250 - (3 \times \$88) + (4 \times 22)$ _____

18. $(74 \times \$29) \times (44 \div 4)$ _____

19. $9 \times 18 \times 6 + 6 \div 12$ _____

20. $(8 + 9) \times (4 + 16)$ _____

21. $(\$156 + \$345) \times \$335$ _____

22. $(\$195 + \$185) \div 44$ _____

23. $\dfrac{(\$1900 - \$450)}{\$280}$ _____

24. $\$280 - \$45 - \$33$ _____

Often on the GED Mathematics Test, you will not have to solve a word problem—you will only have to decide the proper way to solve the problem by showing how to set up or write the expression for its solution.

Setting up a problem involves being able to write correct mathematical expressions when given written information. Study the following examples.

Written Information	Mathematical Expression
1. the amount earned after working 40 hours per week at $5 per hour for 10 weeks	$40 \times \$5 \times 10$
2. the average time worked per day if you worked 5 hours Monday, 7 hours Tuesday, and 6 hours Wednesday	$\dfrac{5 + 7 + 6}{3}$
3. the cost of 2 cans of tomatoes if they sell for 3 for $2	$\dfrac{\$2}{3} \times 2$

Example: Sam worked for 10 hours this week at $5.50 per hour, and also worked 8 hours at $6.00 per hour. Which of the following expressions describes Sam's earnings for the week?

(1) $10 + \$5.50 + 8 + \$6.00$

(2) $10(\$5.50 + \$6.00) + 8$

(3) $10(\$5.50) + 8(\$6.00)$

(4) $10(\$5.50) \times 8(\$6.00)$

(5) $10(\$5.50) \div 8(\$6.00)$

As you approach the problem, look first at the 10 hours of work. For this time period, the earnings are 10 times $5.50. Then look at the 8 hours of work. Multiplying 8 hours times the $6.00 rate gives these earnings. The correct choice is Option 3 or the sum of the two products. Since you are not asked to find the solution, stop after you find the correct set-up.

Directions: Write a numerical expression for each of the exercises below on the lines provided.

1. Steve earns $19,500 annually. Floyd earns $1,100 per month. Write a numerical expression that shows how much more per year Steve earns than Floyd.

   Numerical Expression: _____.

2. A sixty-minute television program has 5 commercial breaks. Each break lasts 2 minutes. Write a numerical expression that shows the actual length of the program.

   Numerical Expression: _____.

3. A bolt of fabric contained 30 yards of fabric. The store sold twenty-seven yards of the fabric at the regular price of $3 per yard. The rest was sold at the sale price of $1 per yard. Write a numerical expression that shows the total amount of money the store received for the fabric from the bolt.

   Numerical Expression: _____.

Directions: Choose the one best answer to each question.

1. Ernesto is paid $125 a week plus a $5 commission on each item that he sells in 28 days. Which numerical expression below determines the number of items he sold?

   (1) $125 + \frac{\$160}{\$5}$
   (2) $125 + $5(28)
   (3) $\frac{\$125}{(28)(\$5)}$
   (4) $125 − $5(28)
   (5) Not enough information is given.

2. Last year, the weekly cost of food for a family of four was $100. This year, the weekly cost is $110. Which of the following expressions shows the difference in the average cost per year for one family member?

   (1) $110 ÷ 4
   (2) ($110 − $100) ÷ 4
   (3) ($110 ÷ 4) + ($100 ÷ 4)
   (4) ($110 ÷ 4) + $100
   (5) 52($110 − $100) ÷ 4

Question 3 refers to the following diagram.

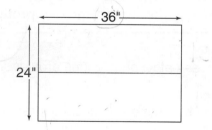

3. Which expression determines the number of books, each 2" thick, that will be needed to fill the two shelves of the bookcase in the diagram above?

   (1) 2 + (36 ÷ 2)
   (2) (36 ÷ 2) − 2
   (3) 2(36 ÷ 2)
   (4) (2 × 2) + 36
   (5) (2 × 2) ÷ 36

4. Which expression below determines the amount of each of Marcy's 24 monthly car payments if the total amount of her car loan is $6,096?

   (1) 24 + $6,096
   (2) $6,096 − 24
   (3) 24($6,096)
   (4) $\frac{\$6,096}{24}$
   (5) $12 \times \frac{\$6,096}{24}$

5. A postal carrier had three packages that had weights of 40 lb., 31 lb., and 51 lb. Which of the following expressions determines the average weight of the packages?

   (1) (40 + 31 + 51) ÷ 3
   (2) (40 + 31) + 51 ÷ 3
   (3) 40 + 31 ÷ 51 + 3
   (4) 3(40 + 31) + 51
   (5) 40 + 31 + 51(3)

6. Calvin drives 657 miles per week going to and from work. His car averages 18 miles per gallon of gas. Which expression below determines the total distance that Calvin travels in 3 weeks?

   (1) 3(657)
   (2) 657 + 3
   (3) 657 − 3
   (4) 657 ÷ 3
   (5) 657 ÷ 18 × 1.09

Fractions: Computation Practice

Review the rules for addition, subtraction, multiplication, and division of fractions in *Steck-Vaughn GED Mathematics* or *Steck-Vaughn Complete GED Preparation*.

<u>Directions</u>: Enter the answers on the lines provided.

1. What is the quotient when $\frac{1}{3}$ is divided by $\frac{3}{4}$? _____

2. What is the product of $\frac{3}{5}$ times 22? _____

3. If you multiply 32 times $\frac{13}{16}$, what is the product? _____

4. What is the difference between $22\frac{5}{9}$ and $14\frac{1}{5}$? _____

5. What is the sum of $\frac{7}{10}$ and $\frac{11}{30}$? _____

6. What is the sum of $6\frac{3}{5}$, $12\frac{1}{2}$, and $7\frac{3}{5}$? _____

7. If you divide 6 by $1\frac{1}{2}$, what is the quotient? _____

8. Divide $5\frac{1}{4}$ by $12\frac{1}{5}$. _____

9. Find the product of $2\frac{1}{3}$ times $1\frac{1}{5}$. _____

10. What is the difference between 8 and $7\frac{7}{8}$? _____

11. Add $12\frac{1}{4}$, $5\frac{13}{16}$, $4\frac{5}{8}$, and $3\frac{1}{2}$. _____

12. What does $15\frac{3}{7}$ minus $14\frac{5}{9}$ equal? _____

13. Find the product of $1\frac{3}{4}$ times 3. _____

14. What is the quotient of $3\frac{1}{2}$ divided by 4? _____

15. If you divide $\frac{3}{5}$ by 8, what is the quotient? _____

16. What is the total of $8\frac{9}{10}$, $12\frac{1}{2}$, and $4\frac{5}{12}$? _____

17. Find the difference between $9\frac{3}{8}$ and $5\frac{9}{16}$. _____

18. What is the sum of $18\frac{3}{4}$ and 8? _____

19. What is the product of 6 times $1\frac{1}{2}$ times $3\frac{3}{4}$? _____

20. What is the difference between $10\frac{2}{3}$ and $3\frac{3}{4}$? _____

21. Add $25\frac{3}{4}$ and $21\frac{5}{8}$. _____

22. Subtract $18\frac{1}{2}$ from 24. _____

23. Multiply $3\frac{2}{5}$ by $3\frac{1}{3}$. _____

24. Find the quotient of $4\frac{2}{3}$ divided by $2\frac{1}{3}$. _____

25. Find the sum of $2\frac{1}{2}$, $3\frac{1}{3}$, $4\frac{1}{4}$, and $5\frac{2}{5}$. _____

Directions: Choose the <u>one best answer</u> to each question. For <u>Question 1</u>, solve the problem and enter your answer on the grid provided.

1. A bolt of fabric contained 25 yards of fabric. Three pieces of fabric $3\frac{1}{2}$ yards long were cut from the bolt. Next, 5 pieces of fabric $1\frac{1}{4}$ yards long were cut. How many yards of fabric remained on the bolt?

2. A stack of books is $21\frac{7}{8}$ inches high. If each book is $\frac{5}{8}$ inch thick, how many books are in the stack?
   (1)   35
   (2)   40
   (3)   64
   (4)   175
   (5)   1,400

3. An architect's drawing was drawn so the scale of $\frac{1}{2}$ inch represented 6 feet. What was the actual height of a wall marked $4\frac{1}{2}$ inches high?
   (1)   9 ft.
   (2) 18 ft.
   (3) 27 ft.
   (4) 36 ft.
   (5) 54 ft.

4. If it takes $4\frac{3}{4}$ ounces of tint to mix one gallon of paint to the desired color, how many ounces of tint will be needed for 5 gallons?
   (1) 19
   (2) 20
   (3) 23
   (4) $23\frac{3}{4}$
   (5) 95

Questions 5 through 7 refer to the chart below.

Margorie Smith's Monthly Budget	
Expenses	Budget
Rent	$\frac{1}{3}$
Food	$\frac{1}{5}$
Savings	$\frac{1}{6}$
School Loans	$\frac{1}{5}$
Utilities	$\frac{1}{10}$

5. Which expense in Marjorie's budget receives the most money?

   (1) rent
   (2) food
   (3) savings
   (4) school loans
   (5) utilities

6. How much more of Marjorie's budget is being spent on rent than savings?

   (1) $\frac{1}{3}$
   (2) $\frac{1}{4}$
   (3) $\frac{1}{5}$
   (4) $\frac{1}{6}$
   (5) $\frac{1}{10}$

7. If Marjorie's monthly earnings are $2,375, how much does she spend on food?

   (1) $275
   (2) $325
   (3) $400
   (4) $475
   (5) $500

Directions: Choose the one best answer for each question. You MAY use your calculator when indicated. For Question 7, solve the problem and enter your answer on the grid provided.

Question 1 refers to the following diagram.

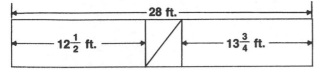

Note: Diagram is not drawn to scale.

1. Which statement determines the width of the gate in the diagram above?

   (1) $28 - 12\frac{1}{2}$
   (2) $28 - 13\frac{3}{4}$
   (3) $12\frac{1}{2} + 13\frac{3}{4}$
   (4) $28 - (12\frac{1}{2} + 13\frac{3}{4})$
   (5) $28 + (12\frac{1}{2} + 13\frac{3}{4})$

2. Poole Electronics makes 75 tape recorders per 8-hour shift. If the quality control inspectors rejected $\frac{1}{5}$ of the tape recorders made on one shift, how many tape recorders were acceptable?

   (1) 15
   (2) 25
   (3) 60
   (4) 65
   (5) 70

Question 3 refers to the following diagram.

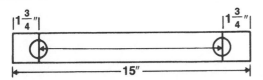

3. What is the distance between the center of the holes if 1 inch represents $4\frac{1}{2}$ feet?

   (1) $3\frac{1}{2}$ ft.
   (2) 11 ft.
   (3) $11\frac{1}{2}$ ft.
   (4) $13\frac{1}{4}$ ft.
   (5) $51\frac{3}{4}$ ft.

4. If Juan reads one page in $1\frac{1}{5}$ minutes, how many minutes will it take him to complete the last 125 pages?

   (1) 25
   (2) 50
   (3) 60
   (4) 100
   (5) 150

 5. Nancy runs at an average rate of $\frac{2}{15}$ mile per minute. At this rate, how many miles will she run in 55 minutes?

   (1) 2
   (2) 4
   (3) $5\frac{1}{2}$
   (4) $7\frac{1}{3}$
   (5) $15\frac{1}{2}$

 6. A tank holds 6,775 gallons of oil. How many containers of oil can be filled from the tank if each container holds $8\frac{1}{4}$ gallons?

   (1) 813
   (2) 812
   (3) 820
   (4) 821
   (5) Not enough information given.

7. Al needed 44 square feet of ceramic tile to remodel his home. If the average weight for each square foot of tile was $6\frac{1}{8}$ pounds, how much did the tile needed for the job weigh?

Decimals: Computation Practice

Review the rules for addition, subtraction, multiplication, and division of decimals in *Steck-Vaughn GED Mathematics* or *Steck-Vaughn Complete GED Preparation*.

Directions: Enter each answer on the lines provided. You may NOT use your calculator.

1. What is the product of 0.04 and 0.09? _____

2. Find the product of 0.368 times 0.62. _____

3. What is the difference between 0.7 and 0.35? _____

4. If you divide 0.8936 by 4, what is the quotient? _____

5. What is the difference between $50.00 and $25.25? _____

6. What is the difference between $700.00 and $446.58? _____

7. What does $14.59 minus $7.00 equal? _____

8. What is the product of $14.25 times 11? _____

9. Find the product of 0.8 times 0.007. _____

10. What is the quotient when 6.915 is divided by 15? _____

Directions: Enter each answer on the lines provided. You MAY use your calculator.

11. What is the sum of 2.33385 and 14.5323? _____

12. What is the quotient when 14.566 is divided by 4.9? _____

13. What is the sum of 2223.44 and 19.665. _____

14. Add 0.6877, 0.4, and 13.4. _____

15. If you multiply 59.67 by 0.089, what is the product? _____

16. If you divide 389.532 by 0.459, what is the quotient rounded to the nearest tenth? _____

17. What is the total of 0.999999, 5, and 9.89999? _____

18. Find the difference between 0.9 and 0.009. _____

19. What is the sum of $664.59 and $.49? _____

20. Find the quotient of 32.224 ÷ 22.3 rounded to the nearest tenth. _____

Directions: Use the steps for solving word problems. Choose the one best answer for each question. You MAY use your calculator when indicated.

Question 1 refers to the following chart.

Weekly Walk Record	
Day	Distance in Miles
Sunday	1.3
Monday	1.8
Tuesday	2.1
Wednesday	1.6
Thursday	1.5
Friday	1.1

1. Your goal is to walk 10 miles every week. The data shows the number of miles you have walked so far this week. How many more miles will you have to walk to complete your goal?

   (1)   0.6
   (2)   1.6
   (3)   6.6
   (4)   9.4
   (5)   9.6

2. The Busy Bee Nursery sells 150 potted plants to the local grocery store at the wholesale price of $7.95 each. When the same plants are sold retail, each plant costs $10.95. What is the difference between the wholesale and retail prices for 150 plants?

   (1) $ 150.00
   (2) $ 450.00
   (3) $ 450.50
   (4) $1,192.00
   (5) $1,642.00

3. A loan of $1,500 will be repaid in 36 installment payments of $57.75 each. What is the finance charge for the loan?

   (1) $ 173.25
   (2) $ 346.50
   (3) $ 579.00
   (4) $1,500.00
   (5) $2,079.00

4. Mr. and Mrs. Montgomery sold 150 shares of stock at $37.75. If they originally paid $25.85 for each share, what was their profit on the sale of the stock?

   (1) $ 129.25
   (2) $ 188.75
   (3) $1,785.00
   (4) $3,877.50
   (5) $5,662.50

Questions 5 and 6 refer to the following chart.

Degree	Hourly Pay
Engineering	$18.41
Business	$14.11
Chemistry	$16.41
Social Sciences	$12.07

5. What is the weekly pay for a social science graduate who works 40 hours per week?

   (1) $234.56
   (2) $253.60
   (3) $383.34
   (4) $482.80
   (5) $736.40

6. What is the difference between the weekly pay for an engineering graduate and a social sciences graduate, if they both work 40 hours per week?

   (1) $251.89
   (2) $253.60
   (3) $382.60
   (4) $392.60
   (5)   Not enough information is given.

Directions: Choose the one best answer to each question.

1. You make $1,200 each week. What is the amount of your paycheck after the following deductions?

Federal Income Tax	$121.53
Social Security Tax	$48.77
Medicare Tax	$25.41
State Income Tax	$84.66

(1) $719.47
(2) $757.57
(3) $819.57
(4) $919.63
(5) Not enough information is given.

2. A three-pound bag of apples can be purchased wholesale for $2.98. How many bags can a supermarket purchase for $149?

(1) 100
(2) 85
(3) 75
(4) 50
(5) 25

3. An order for 52 legal-size note pads costs $24.50. What is the cost per pad to the nearest cent?

(1) $.47
(2) $.48
(3) $.49
(4) $.50
(5) $.60

4. Leon bought the economy 15-pound package of flat-head nails at Kissel's Hardware for $.98 a pound. Which of the following statements gives the best estimate of the amount he will spend on the nails?

(1) $1.00(15)
(2) $1.00 + 15
(3) $1.00 − 15
(4) $1.00 ÷ 15
(5) 15 − $1.00

5. What is the total cost of six battery-operated screwdrivers for $19.98 each? Include the cost of 24 batteries that sell two for $1.79.

(1) $ 25.06
(2) $ 21.48
(3) $ 42.96
(4) $119.88
(5) $141.36

Directions: Solve the following problem. Enter your answer on the grid provided.

6. Kerry runs at a pace of 8.5 minutes per mile in a 26.2-mile marathon. How many minutes will it take her to finish the marathon?

Percents: Computation Practice

<u>Directions</u>: Complete the chart below of commonly used fractions, decimals, and percents. Enter each answer in the appropriate space in the chart.

	FRACTION	DECIMAL	PERCENT		FRACTION	DECIMAL	PERCENT
1.	$\frac{1}{8}$	0.125	12.5%	7.	$\frac{5}{8}$	_____	_____
2.	_____	_____	25%	8.	_____	_____	$66\frac{2}{3}\%$
3.	_____	0.333	_____	9.	_____	0.75	_____
4.	_____	_____	37.5%	10.	$\frac{4}{5}$	_____	_____
5.	$\frac{1}{2}$	_____	_____	11.	_____	0.875	_____
6.	_____	0.60	_____	12.	$\frac{9}{10}$	_____	_____

The percent formula is **base × rate = part.** The triangle shows the relationship of these three elements. Use this formula to find the missing element in a percent problem.

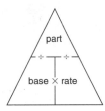

The percent increase or decrease is computed by subtracting the original amount from the new amount and dividing the difference by the original amount:

$$\frac{\text{new} - \text{original}}{\text{original}}$$

<u>Directions</u>: Enter your answers on the lines or grid provided. (Change a percent to a decimal to enter it on the grid.)

13. Find 125% of 90. _____

14. 3 is what percent of 5? _____

15. $\frac{1}{8}$% of 561 is what number? _____

16. 13 is what percent of 25? _____

17. 34% of what number is 306? _____

18. 45 is what percent of 90? _____

19. What number is 3% of 391? _____

20. 81 is 9% of what number? _____

21. 110% of what number is 22? _____

22. 99 is what percent of 396?

Directions: Use the steps for solving word problems. Choose the one best answer to each question. You MAY use your calculator when indicated.

1. Shoes sold at the Shoe Express are discounted 25% off the original price. If a pair of shoes originally cost $46, calculate the sale price of the shoes.

   (1) $11.50
   (2) $23.00
   (3) $34.50
   (4) $46.00
   (5) $57.50

2. As an apprentice carpenter, Grace earns $7.75 per hour. After her apprenticeship, her pay will increase to $11.75 per hour. By what percent of her current pay will her salary increase after she becomes a carpenter?

   (1) 40%
   (2) 45%
   (3) 51%
   (4) 52%
   (5) 60%

3. Mr. Wilfred drove his cab 26,500 miles last year for the Island Taxi Company. This was 80% of the number of miles he drove the year before. How many miles did he drive the year before?

   (1) 21,200
   (2) 22,083
   (3) 31,800
   (4) 33,125
   (5) 47,700

4. Yolanda earns $195 per week and pays 3% of her salary for health insurance. What does she pay annually for health insurance?

   (1) $195.00
   (2) $234.00
   (3) $304.20
   (4) $468.00
   (5) $585.00

5. A store charges 138% of its cost for sneakers. The store's cost is $28. How much does the store charge?

   (1) $17.36
   (2) $29.06
   (3) $38.64
   (4) $39.20
   (5) $41.54

6. Kara buys a stereo on sale. The sale price is $195, which is 75% of the original price. What is the original price of the stereo?

   (1) $146.25
   (2) $260.00
   (3) $270.00
   (4) $280.25
   (5) Not enough information is given.

Question 7 refers to the table below.

Number in set	10	25	100
Regular Price	$62.50	$156.25	$625
Discount	8%	18%	27%

7. Your company wants to order sets of calculators. The table shows the discounts the company will receive for ordering sets of 10, 25, or 100. What is the sale price for a set of 25?

   (1) $ 57.50
   (2) $128.12
   (3) $156.54
   (4) $184.44
   (5) Not enough information is given.

Directions: Choose the <u>one best answer</u> to each question. You MAY use your calculator when indicated.

1. Melvin spends $6\frac{1}{4}$% of his monthly salary on transportation. If his salary is $1,600 a month, how much does he spend on transportation?

   (1) $ 96
   (2) $100
   (3) $200
   (4) $400
   (5) $450

2. Ed Lee earned $200 a week plus a 15% commission on all sales greater than $1,000. If Mr. Lee's sales for one week were $2,500, what was his gross pay for that week?

   (1) $150
   (2) $325
   (3) $350
   (4) $425
   (5) $575

3. Canfield Health Insurance Company pays 80% on all medical expenses over the $275 deductible. What will Canfield pay on medical expenses of $2,750?

   (1) $ 550
   (2) $ 770
   (3) $1,980
   (4) $2,200
   (5) $2,475

4. Shirts in a store are on sale for 30% off. The sales tax is 7.25%. What is the total price of a shirt that has an original price of $29.95?

   (1) $20.53
   (2) $21.96
   (3) $22.41
   (4) $22.49
   (5) $26.48

Question 5 refers to the following table.

Letter Grade	A	B	C	D
Percent of Students	8%	18%	27%	10%

5. A group of junior college students took a test. The portion of the students who received each letter grade is shown in the table. How many students received a letter grade of B?

   (1)   5
   (2)   10
   (3)   15
   (4)   20
   (5)   Not enough information is given.

6. The sales tax rate where you live is 8.5%. You are buying a car for $28,540. What will be the total cost of the car?

   (1) $22,500.80
   (2) $28,650.89
   (3) $30,965.90
   (4) $31,865.90
   (5) $44,965.90

7. You are selling your house for $180,000. The realtor charges a commission of $5,000 plus 4.5% of the selling price. How much commission will the realtor earn?

   (1) $ 8,100
   (2) $13,100
   (3) $13,500
   (4) $14,500
   (5)   Not enough information is given.

Ratio and Proportion

Fractions are sometimes referred to as ratios. A <u>ratio</u> is defined as a comparison of two objects or numbers. In the illustration below, 4 of the 5 people voted while one person did not vote. A comparison of the number of voters to non-voters is expressed in a ratio of 4 to 1. The order in which you write the numbers of a ratio is extremely important. Review ratio and proportion in *Steck-Vaughn GED Mathematics* or *Steck-Vaughn Complete GED Preparation*.

Ratios can be written in three different ways.

As a Fraction	In Words	With a Colon
$\dfrac{4 \text{ voters}}{1 \text{ non-voter}}$	4 to 1	4:1
	voters to non-voters	voters:non-voters

Example 1: Each week, Janice gives a total of $15 in allowances to her two children in the ratio of 3 to 2. How much does each child get?

Let $3x$ = amount for one child and $2x$ = amount for the other child

$3x + 2x = \$15$

$5x = \$15$

$x = \$3$ One child gets $3x$ or $3(\$3) = \$9$ and the other gets $2(\$3)$ or $6.

A proportion is formed by putting an equal sign between two equal ratios.

$$\frac{1}{2} = \frac{2}{4} \qquad \frac{1}{2} \diagdown\!\!\!\!\!\times \frac{2}{4} \qquad \text{Cross multiply:} \quad 1 \cdot 4 = 2 \cdot 2$$

A proportion containing an unknown can be solved by using <u>cross multiplication</u>. You can solve many questions on the GED Mathematics Test by using the concepts of ratio and proportion.

Example 2: Solve for the unknown value in $\frac{x}{5} = \frac{80}{100}$.

$\frac{x}{5} = \frac{80}{100}$ The two ratios are equal and form a proportion.

$x \cdot 100 = 80 \cdot 5$ Cross multiply x times 100 and 80 times 5.

$100x = 400$

$\frac{100x}{100} = \frac{400}{100}$ Complete the process for solving for the unknown.

$x = 4$

To determine whether a word problem can be solved by using a proportion, look for two sets of related objects with three of the four elements given. The unknown is the missing element.

Example 3: Central Post Office processes 1,500 pieces of mail through the canceling machine in 3 hours. How many pieces of mail are processed during an eight-hour shift?

You have two sets of related objects: hours/pieces of mail = hours/pieces of mail.

You have three elements: 3 hours, 1,500 pieces, and 8 hours.

$\frac{3}{1,500} = \frac{8}{x}$ The pieces of mail in 8 hours is the missing element.

$3x = 12,000$

$\frac{3x}{3} = \frac{12,000}{3}$

$x = 4,000$

Directions: Use ratio or proportion to solve the following problems. Choose the one best answer to each question.

1. A cookie recipe required 3 ounces of margarine for every $3\frac{1}{2}$ cups of flour. If Bailey wanted to increase the recipe for a party, and he used 24 ounces of margarine, how many cups of flour will he need?

   (1) 8
   (2) $10\frac{1}{2}$
   (3) 28
   (4) 30
   (5) 84

2. Geraldine's rental car costs $35.95 for two days. How much will the car cost for 30 days?

   (1) $ 107.85
   (2) $ 539.25
   (3) $ 953.00
   (4) $ 976.25
   (5) $1,078.50

3. Avalon's phone bill was $375 for the first three months of the year. Assuming that this amount remains fairly constant for a three-month period, project how much the company will spend in a year.

   (1) $ 250
   (2) $ 375
   (3) $ 750
   (4) $1,125
   (5) $1,500

4. One of the life insurance policies at Kusay Insurance costs $.75 per month for each $1,000 of insurance. How much is the monthly premium for a $30,000 policy?

   (1) $18.75
   (2) $19.00
   (3) $19.75
   (4) $20.50
   (5) $22.50

5. Henry got 12 hits in the first 20 ball games of the year. If he were to continue hitting at the same pace, how many hits would he get in a 75-game season?

   (1) 25
   (2) 30
   (3) 45
   (4) 55
   (5) Not enough information is given.

6. Karen invested $600 in a stock portfolio. It paid her an income of $90 per year. If she had invested a total of $1,400 at the same rate, what would her yearly income have been?

   (1) $100
   (2) $110
   (3) $120
   (4) $210
   (5) $440

Directions: Solve the following problem. Enter your answer on the grid provided.

7. Carol types at a rate of 26 words per minute. How long will it take her to type a document containing 1,040 words?

Directions: Choose the <u>one best answer</u> to each question.

1. Which of the following equals $(9 - 3) \times 7$?

   (1) $9 - 3 \times 7$
   (2) $9 \times (7 - 3)$
   (3) $7 \times (9 - 3)$
   (4) $3 \times 7 - 9$
   (5) $(3 - 9) \times 7$

2. Which is an equal fraction, decimal, and percent?

   (1) $\frac{1}{2}$ 0.5   5%
   (2) $\frac{2}{5}$ 0.2   20%
   (3) $\frac{3}{4}$ 0.75   7.5%
   (4) $\frac{5}{8}$ 0.58   58%
   (5) $\frac{3}{10}$ 0.3   30%

3. Dunn Rite Car Rental Company owns 225 cars which it rents. Twenty-five of these cars are in the auto repair shop for maintenance. About what percent of the cars are still available to be rented?

   (1) 11%
   (2) 25%
   (3) 75%
   (4) 80%
   (5) 89%

4. A bill for repairing the brakes on the Johnsons' car was $125.25. If 20% of the bill was for parts and the rest for labor, how much were the Johnsons charged for labor?

   (1) $ 25.25
   (2) $ 45.25
   (3) $ 80.00
   (4) $100.20
   (5) $105.25

Directions: Solve the following problems. Enter your answers on the grids provided.

5. Ingall Hospital had 229 registered nurses on staff last year. Since then 15 nurses have retired, 3 nurses have been dismissed, and 16 new nurses have been hired. How many nurses are currently on staff at the hospital?

6. Last year enrollment at Cedar Creek Day Care increased by 25%. If enrollment at the beginning of the year was 84, what was enrollment at the end of the year?

7. Miranda made a dress which required 3 yards of fabric at $5.95 a yard. In addition to the fabric, she spent $5.19 for buttons and other notions. If she sold the dress for $45.00, how much did she profit from the sale? Round to the nearest dollar.

    (1) $22
    (2) $23
    (3) $24
    (4) $25
    (5) $26

8. A sporting goods store normally discounts all merchandise 16%. At a special sale, it is taking an additional $\frac{1}{5}$ off its discount price. During the special sale, how much would you expect to pay for a baseball glove with a list price of $56?

    (1) $47.04
    (2) $44.80
    (3) $37.63
    (4) $50.20
    (5) $35.84

Question 9 refers to the following chart.

Time	7:00	8:00	9:00
Distance	24 km	48 km	72 km

9. If a ship traveled away from port at a steady speed as shown in the table, how many kilometers from port was it at 8:35?

    (1) 56
    (2) 58
    (3) 60
    (4) 62
    (5) Not enough information is given.

10. Saul bought 4 CDs from Mike's Music Store when it had a "Going Out of Business" sale. Two CDs originally sold for $6.95 each. The other two sold for $8.95 each. Every CD was discounted by 30%. How much did Saul spend?

    (1) $21.30
    (2) $22.26
    (3) $31.80
    (4) $35.00
    (5) $25.32

Question 11 refers to the following chart.

Day	Hours
Monday	12
Tuesday	12
Wednesday	12
Thursday	12
Friday	12
Saturday	8
Sunday	4

11. Mary is paid $8.40 an hour for a 40-hour week and time-and-a-half for anything over 40 hours. How much was her gross pay for the week?

    (1) $436.80
    (2) $650.40
    (3) $736.80
    (4) $739.20
    (5) $840.00

12. Jenna wants to telephone a friend in Boston. The day rate is $.48 for the first minute and $.34 for each additional minute. The evening rate discounts the day rate by 35%. If Jenna is planning a 45-minute call, how much would she save if she called after 8:00 P.M.?

    (1) $5.40
    (2) $7.55
    (3) $5.25
    (4) $5.51
    (5) $6.30

Directions: Choose the one best answer to each question.

Question 13 refers to the following diagram.

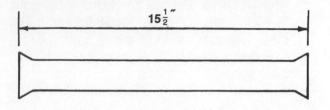

$15\frac{1}{2}''$

13. If you drill a line of holes $\frac{1}{8}$ inch apart (and $\frac{1}{8}$ inch from each end) in the metal plate, how many holes will you drill?

(1) 248
(2) 123
(3) 62
(4) $15\frac{5}{8}$
(5) $15\frac{3}{8}$

14. Which of the following pairs is equal?

(1) $\frac{1}{4}$ and 1.25
(2) $\frac{4}{5}$ and $\frac{88}{100}$
(3) $\frac{7}{8}$ and 0.375
(4) $1\frac{1}{7}$ and $\frac{8}{7}$
(5) $1\frac{2}{5}$ and 125%

15. Which of the following statements expresses a decrease?

(1) a $50 deposit in a checking account
(2) 12° above zero
(3) 100 feet above sea level
(4) 20 yard gain in football
(5) a loss of 25 pounds

16. Which expression represents 20% of 325?

(1) 325 ÷ 20
(2) 20 × 325
(3) 325 ÷ 0.20
(4) 325 − 0.20
(5) 0.20 × 325

17. On a map, 1 inch represents three miles. How many inches are needed to represent a road that is actually 171 miles long?

(1) 57 in.
(2) 55 in.
(3) 54 in.
(4) 51 in.
(5) 50 in.

Directions: Solve the following problems. Enter your answers on the grids provided.

18. A recipe for a party mix calls for $1\frac{1}{2}$ cups of peanuts, 3 cups of cereal, $4\frac{1}{2}$ cups each of pretzels and sesame sticks. How many cups of mix will this recipe make?

19. A baseball team had a roster of 11 players. Their batting averages were .220, .242, .204, .333, .514, .187, .442, .208, .318, .301, and .212. What was the team batting average?

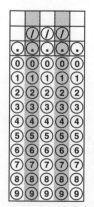

Data Analysis

Mean, Median, and Number Series

Some problems on the GED Mathematics Test will test your ability to determine the pattern of a number series, or the mean and median of a set of numbers. Each of these terms is defined below. Study the definitions and examples before completing the exercises.

Example 1: 2, 4, 6, 8, 10, __ , __
3, 6, 9, 12, 15, __ , __

The numbers 2, 4, 6, 8, and 10 form a number series or a special counting pattern. If you were asked to give the next two terms to this series, 12 and 14 would follow. The special counting pattern of this series is to increase each term by two. The numbers in the second number series increase by three.

To find the mean, or average, of a set of numbers, first determine the sum of the numbers. Then divide the sum by the number in the set.

Example 2: Find the mean of 4, 6, 8, 8, and 9.
Step 1 Add the amounts: $4 + 6 + 8 + 8 + 9 = 35$.
Step 2 Divide 35 by the numbers you added (5).
$35 \div 5 = 7$
The mean of the numbers in the set is 7.

The median is the middle number in the data when the numbers are arranged in order. If there is an odd number of values in the set, the median is the middle value. When the number of values is even, you can find the median by finding the mean of the two middle numbers.

Example 3: Find the median of 2, 6, 4, 3, 5, and 9.
Step 1 Arrange the numbers in order from least to greatest or from greatest to least.
2, 3, 4, 5, 6, 9   OR   9, 6, 5, 4, 3, 2
Step 2 Find the mean of the two middle numbers.
The two middle numbers are 4 and 5:
$(4 + 5) \div 2 = 4.5$
The median is 4.5.

Directions: Enter the answers on the lines provided.

1. What is the mean of the test scores? 97, 72, 89, 90, 90, and 87 _____

2. Determine the median of 53°, 56°, 57°, 58°, 59°, 61°, and 62°. _____

3. What is the next term in the series 48, 24, 12, 6? _____

4. Five houses on Elm Street cost $65,500, $56,000, $49,250, $32,750, and $43,600. What is the mean (average) cost of a house on Elm Street? _____

Probability

Probability is defined as the chance a given event or action will occur. The probability that an event will occur is the ratio of the number of favorable outcomes to the number of all possible outcomes that could happen at the same time or in the same place. The probability of an event, $P(E)$, can be expressed as a fraction, such as $\frac{1}{2}$.

Example 1: Before a football game, the referee tosses a two-sided coin. The team that wins the toss chooses whether its team will start the game by kicking or receiving the ball. When the referee tossed the coin, one team captain called heads.

There are two possible outcomes—heads or tails. Each outcome is equally likely to occur. There is only one favorable outcome for the team captain who called heads. The probability that the coin will land heads up is 1 out of 2, or $\frac{1}{2}$. So,

$$\text{Probability of Heads} = \frac{1}{2} = \frac{\text{number of favorable outcomes}}{\text{number of possible outcomes}}$$

Example 2: A used car lot has 12 cars in 5 different colors as shown below. If you choose one car at random, what is the probability that the car is red?

| blue | black | red | red | yellow | green |
| black | blue | yellow | green | red | red |

The total number of cars on the lot is 12. This is the number of possible outcomes. There are 4 red cars on the lot. This is the number of favorable outcomes. So,

$$P(E) = \frac{4 \text{ red cars}}{12 \text{ possible outcomes}} = \frac{4}{12} = \frac{1}{3}$$

Example 3: What is the probability of spinning an even number with this spinner?
List all the possible outcomes for spinning the spinner once.
There are 6 possible outcomes (1, 2, 3, 4, 5, 6).

Find how many chances are possible of spinning an even number on one spin. There are three favorable outcomes (2, 4, 6). So,

$$P(E) = \frac{3 \text{ even outcomes}}{6 \text{ possible outcomes}} = \frac{3}{6} = \frac{1}{2}$$

The probability of spinning an even number is one out of every two spins.

Directions: Choose the <u>one best answer</u> to each question. You may NOT use your calculator.

1. A flower vase of carnations contains 3 white, 4 blue, 2 yellow, and 6 red carnations. If one flower is randomly picked, what is the probability that it will be white?

   (1) $\frac{2}{15}$

   (2) $\frac{1}{5}$

   (3) $\frac{1}{3}$

   (4) $\frac{2}{5}$

   (5) $\frac{3}{5}$

2. Elena's shopping bag had 4 cans of soup, 3 cans of mixed vegetables, and 5 cans of corn. If she selects one can from the bag without looking, what is the probability that on the first pick Elena will choose a can of mixed vegetables?

   (1) $\frac{1}{5}$

   (2) $\frac{1}{4}$

   (3) $\frac{1}{3}$

   (4) $\frac{5}{12}$

   (5) $\frac{7}{12}$

3. Candy is packaged in a box that has 4 rows with 6 pieces per row. One row has nuts, another has creme fillings, another has jelly, and the last has cherries. When randomly selecting one candy, what is the probability of selecting a creme-filled piece of candy?

   (1) $\frac{4}{5}$

   (2) $\frac{3}{5}$

   (3) $\frac{1}{2}$

   (4) $\frac{2}{5}$

   (5) $\frac{1}{4}$

4. Juan has $1.50 in change in a mason jar. There are 15 nickels, 5 dimes, and 25 pennies. If Juan randomly selects one coin, what is the probability of selecting a dime on the first try?

   (1) $\frac{1}{9}$

   (2) $\frac{1}{3}$

   (3) $\frac{1}{2}$

   (4) $\frac{5}{9}$

   (5) $\frac{2}{3}$

5. The queen of hearts, clubs, spades, and diamonds were placed face down on a table. What is the probability that the queen of spades will be picked on the first random draw of one card?

   (1) $\frac{1}{2}$

   (2) $\frac{1}{3}$

   (3) $\frac{1}{4}$

   (4) $\frac{1}{5}$

   (5) $\frac{1}{6}$

6. In a gumball machine, there is a mixture of 50 red gumballs and 50 yellow gumballs. What is the probability of getting a red gumball if you place a coin in the machine and receive one gumball?

   (1) $\frac{1}{2}$

   (2) $\frac{1}{3}$

   (3) $\frac{1}{4}$

   (4) $\frac{1}{5}$

   (5) $\frac{1}{6}$

Measurement: Computation Practice

Some problems on the GED Mathematics Test have mixed measures that require you to convert units within the customary and metric systems.

Example 1: Margaret had three packages of ground beef. The first weighed 5 pounds, the second weighed 32 ounces, and the third weighed 6 pounds. What was the total number of pounds of ground beef she purchased?

Since the answer is required in pounds, the 32 ounces must be changed to 2 pounds. The next step is to add the three like measures.

$$5 \text{ pounds} + 2 \text{ pounds} + 6 \text{ pounds} = 13 \text{ pounds}$$

The metric system is based on powers of ten, such as 10, 100, 1000. Converting within the metric system is simple because it is easy to multiply and divide by powers of ten.

Example 2: The Danville Stroller Derby is 5 km long. How many meters is that?
The first unit is given in kilometers. To convert from kilometers to meters, multiply by 1000.
5 km × 1000 = 5000 m

Directions: Enter your answers on the lines below. You may NOT use your calculator.

1. 60 seconds = _____ minute

2. 52 weeks = _____ year

3. _____ hours = 1 day

4. _____ inches = 1 foot

5. _____ feet = 1 mile

6. 90 g = _____ kg

7. 7.88 ml = _____ l

8. 5.3 m = _____ mm

9. 18 cm = _____ m

10. 13.1 cm = _____ mm

11. Sue weighed 8 pounds 1 ounce at birth. Her brother weighed 17 ounces more than Sue. How much did Sue's brother weigh at birth? _____

12. Jan's truck can carry a 2-ton load of lumber. If the truck is loaded with 2,200 pounds at its first stop, how much can be added at the next stop? _____

13. If one gallon of milk costs $2, what is the cost per quart? _____

14. How many 10-inch pieces can be cut from a board that is 12 feet long?

    How much is left over? _____

15. A tornado typically moves about 64,400 meters in an hour.

    How many kilometers is this? _____

16. 108 grams of tea is how many kilograms? _____

Directions: Choose the one best answer to each question. You MAY use your calculator when indicated.

 1. A recycling drive collected 3 bags of 2-liter bottles. If each bag holds 50 bottles, how many milliliters can the collected bottles hold?

(1)   300
(2)   3,000
(3)   5,000
(4)   30,000
(5) 300,000

2. The bottling plant supervisor has to monitor the maximum weight of cans of soda being stored before distribution. If one case weighs 288 ounces and contains 24 cans, what is the maximum number of cases that can be stored in an area with a weight capacity of 3,456 pounds?

(1) 288
(2) 192
(3) 24
(4) 12
(5) 11

3. An international rowing club completed a race at a rate of 6.07 meters per second. How many kilometers per minute is this?

(1) 1.333 km/min
(2) 3.3 km/min
(3) 0.385 km/min
(4) 0.3642 km/min
(5) 0.3462 km/min

Directions: Solve the following problem. Enter your answer on the grid provided.

4. During the last week, Leonard spent the following time studying for the postal examination:

Mon. 2 hr. 15 min.
Tues. 3 hr.
Wed.   45 min.
Thurs. 1 hr. 40 min.
Fri.   2 hr. 20 min.

What was the average amount of minutes spent studying per day?

Question 5 refers to the following chart.

TOTAL POUNDS DELIVERED	SHIPPING CHARGE PER TIRE
100–499	$1.01
500–999	.97
1,000–1,499	.93
1,500–2,999	.89
3,000 +	.85

5. Patterson Tire received a delivery of 8 dozen tires. Each tire weighed 21 lb. 8 oz. According to the chart, what was the shipping charge for the tires received by Patterson Tire?

(1) $81.60
(2) $85.44
(3) $89.28
(4) $93.12
(5) $96.96

Directions: Choose the <u>one best answer</u> to each question. You may NOT use your calculator.

<u>Questions 1 through 5</u> refer to the following table.

Medal Count by Nation Summer Olympics 2000			
Country	Gold	Silver	Bronze
United States	39	25	33
Australia	16	25	17
Netherlands	12	9	4
Greece	4	6	3
Ukraine	3	10	10
Kuwait	0	0	1
Russia	32	28	28
France	13	14	11
China	28	16	15

1. The greatest number of medals was won by which country in the 2000 summer Olympics?

    (1) Australia
    (2) France
    (3) United States
    (4) China
    (5) Russia

2. How many more silver medals than gold medals did Australia win?

    (1) 2
    (2) 8
    (3) 9
    (4) 12
    (5) 13

3. How many more medals did China win than Greece?

    (1) 13
    (2) 26
    (3) 28
    (4) 46
    (5) 59

For <u>Questions 4 and 5</u>, enter your answers on the grids provided.

4. How many more gold medals than silver medals did the United States win in the 2000 summer Olympics?

5. What is the difference between the number of bronze medals won by France, Russia, and China and the number won by the United States, Kuwait, and Australia?

Directions: Use the information from the following circle graphs. Choose the <u>one best answer</u> to each question. You MAY use your calculator when indicated.

Questions 1 through 3 refer to the following chart.

Total Programming per Day

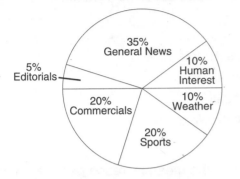

1. How many hours of human interest stories are scheduled daily?

   (1) 1.2
   (2) 2.4
   (3) 4.8
   (4) 8.4
   (5) 9.6

2. Which of the following represents 50% of the programming for the news network station?

   (1) editorials, commercials, and sports
   (2) commercials, sports, and weather
   (3) human interest, general news, and sports
   (4) general news, sports
   (5) human interest, weather, and editorials

3. Expressed as a fraction, what portion of the programming is devoted to editorials?

   (1) $\frac{1}{20}$
   (2) $\frac{1}{10}$
   (3) $\frac{1}{5}$
   (4) $\frac{1}{4}$
   (5) $\frac{7}{20}$

Questions 4 through 6 refer to the following chart.

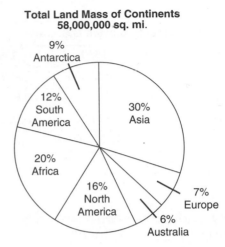

 4. Which continents have land masses greater than 9,000,000 square miles?

   (1) South America, Asia, and Australia
   (2) Europe, Africa, and Asia
   (3) North America, Asia, and Africa
   (4) Australia, Antarctica, and South America
   (5) Antarctica, Europe, and Africa

5. What is the approximate total square mileage of Antarctica and Australia?

   (1) 3,800,000
   (2) 5,300,000
   (3) 6,900,000
   (4) 8,700,000
   (5) 9,000,000

6. Which expression can be used to approximate the difference in the total square miles between the largest and the smallest continents?

   (1) 30% − 6%
   (2) (0.3 − 0.06) × 58,000,000
   (3) 0.3(58,000,000) − 0.06
   (4) 30% + 6% × 58,000,000
   (5) $\frac{58,000,000}{(0.3 + 0.06)}$

Directions: Choose the one best answer to each question. You MAY use your calculator when indicated.

Questions 1 through 6 refer to the following chart.

Five Most Populated U.S. Cities		
City	1990	1998
New York, NY	7,322,564	7,420,166
Los Angeles, CA	3,485,557	3,597,556
Chicago, IL	2,783,726	2,802,079
Houston, TX	1,637,859	1,786,691
Philadelphia, PA	1,585,577	1,436,287

1. How many more people lived in New York City in 1998 than in 1990?

   (1) 57,321
   (2) 71,722
   (3) 97,602
   (4) 134,974
   (5) 236,963

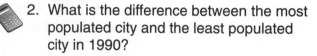

2. What is the difference between the most populated city and the least populated city in 1990?

   (1) 3,837,167
   (2) 4,538,837
   (3) 4,972,717
   (4) 5,421,277
   (5) 5,736,987

3. The population of which city decreased from 1990 to 1998?

   (1) New York
   (2) Los Angeles
   (3) Chicago
   (4) Houston
   (5) Philadelphia

4. The greatest population increase between 1990 and 1998 occurred in which city?

   (1) New York
   (2) Los Angeles
   (3) Chicago
   (4) Houston
   (5) Philadelphia

5. What was the mean increase per year over the eight-year period for New York? (Round to the nearest thousand.)

   (1) 2,000
   (2) 2,294
   (3) 2,500
   (4) 12,000
   (5) 18,353

6. What is the difference in population between the population of the most populated city and the least populated city in 1998?

   (1) 1,436,287
   (2) 1,585,577
   (3) 4,382,479
   (4) 5,983,879
   (5) 7,420,166

Questions 7 through 10 refer to the following chart.

Annual Health Care Spending per Person	
Age	Spending
0–5	$1,389
6–17	$ 730
18–44	$1,242
45–64	$2,402
65+	$4,840

7. For which age category is annual health care spending the lowest?

    (1)   0–5
    (2)   6–17
    (3)   18–44
    (4)   45–64
    (5)   65+

8. For which two age categories is annual health care spending about the same?

    (1)   0–5 and 6–17
    (2)   0–5 and 18–44
    (3)   0–5 and 45–64
    (4)   6–17 and 18–44
    (5)   18–44 and 45–64

9. For which age category is annual health care spending more than two times the spending of the previous category?

    (1)   6–17
    (2)   18–44
    (3)   45–64
    (4)   65+
    (5)   Not enough information is given.

10. What is the average amount spent on annual health care for the age categories 18–44 and 45–64?

    (1) $ 780.00
    (2) $1,059.50
    (3) $1,822.00
    (4) $3,041.00
    (5) $3,644.00

Questions 11 through 13 refer to the following chart.

Number of Attempts to Climb Mt. McKinley 1995 – 1999		
Year	Attempts	Successes
1995	928	546
1996	1,002	508
1997	994	535
1998	1,118	567
1999	1,035	421

11. In which year was the ratio of attempts to successes greater than 2 to 1?

    (1) 1999
    (2) 1998
    (3) 1997
    (4) 1996
    (5) 1995

12. In which year was the percent of successful climbs the greatest?

    (1) 1995
    (2) 1996
    (3) 1997
    (4) 1998
    (5) 1999

Directions: Solve the following problem. Enter your answer on the grid provided.

13. What was the average number of successful climbs for the period 1995 to 1999?

Questions 1 through 5 refer to the following line graph.

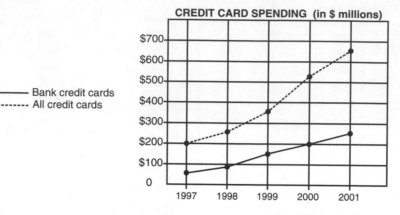

CREDIT CARD SPENDING (in $ millions)

—— Bank credit cards
------- All credit cards

1. About how many dollars were spent using all credit cards in 2001?

   (1) $250 million
   (2) $550 million
   (3) $650 million
   (4) $800 million
   (5) $900 million

2. During which time period was the increase in the dollars of bank credit card spending the greatest?

   (1) 1997–1998
   (2) 1998–1999
   (3) 1999–2000
   (4) 2000–2001
   (5) Not enough information is given.

3. Bank credit card spending represented what fraction of all credit card spending in 2001?

   (1) $\frac{1}{8}$
   (2) $\frac{1}{4}$
   (3) $\frac{2}{7}$
   (4) $\frac{5}{13}$
   (5) $\frac{7}{16}$

Directions: Solve the following problems. Enter your answers on the grids provided. (Change percents to decimals to enter them on the grids.)

4. What is the percent of increase in all credit card spending from 1997 to 2001?

5. What percent of all credit card spending in 1997 was from bank credit cards?

Directions: Choose the one best answer to each question. You may NOT use your calculator.

Questions 1 through 6 refer to the following bar graph.

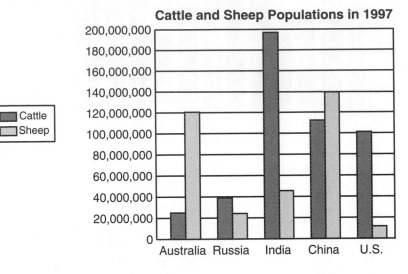

Cattle and Sheep Populations in 1997

1. Which two countries each had a population of more than 100,000,000 sheep in 1997?

   (1) Russia and India
   (2) Russia and China
   (3) India and United States
   (4) Australia and China
   (5) Russia and United States

2. Which country had the least number of cattle?

   (1) Australia
   (2) Russia
   (3) India
   (4) China
   (5) United States

3. In 1997, about how many more sheep were found in Australia than in the United States?

   (1)   10,000,000
   (2)   15,000,000
   (3)   20,000,000
   (4)   80,000,000
   (5)   110,000,000

4. In which two countries were fewer cattle than sheep found in 1997?

   (1) Australia and China
   (2) Australia and the United States
   (3) India and the United States
   (4) Russia and China
   (5) Australia and India

5. Which country had a cattle population of about 40,000,000 in 1997?

   (1) Australia
   (2) Russia
   (3) India
   (4) China
   (5) United States

6. What was the approximate difference between the sheep and cattle population in Australia in 1997?

   (1)   10,000,000
   (2)   20,000,000
   (3)   30,000,000
   (4)   80,000,000
   (5)   100,000,000

Questions 7 through 12 refer to the following bar graph.

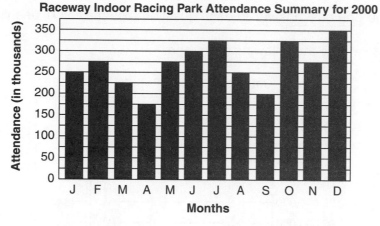

Raceway Indoor Racing Park Attendance Summary for 2000

7. What was the mean attendance at Raceway Park during the months of January, June, August, and September?

    (1) 125,000
    (2) 150,000
    (3) 175,000
    (4) 200,000
    (5) 250,000

8. To determine the total amount of proceeds (money taken in at the gate), what piece of information is needed?

    (1) the cost of maintenance of the park
    (2) the cost of the workers
    (3) the price of tickets for admission
    (4) the cost of parking
    (5) the cost of management

9. Which of the following expressions gives the average attendance for September, October, November, and December?

    (1) (200 + 325 + 275 + 350) ÷ 4
    (2) (200 + 325 + 275 + 350)
    (3) (250 + 275 + 225 + 175) ÷ 4
    (4) (250 + 275 + 225 + 175)
    (5) (400 + 325 + 250 + 200)

10. If tickets cost $5 per person, what was the amount of money taken in by Raceway Park during June of 2000?

    (1) $ 875,000
    (2) $1,125,000
    (3) $1,250,000
    (4) $1,500,000
    (5) $2,000,000

11. If $\frac{1}{3}$ of the tickets sold in June were senior citizens, about how many senior citizens attended the races in June?

    (1) 900,000
    (2) 600,000
    (3) 300,000
    (4) 200,000
    (5) 100,000

12. About what percent of the total yearly attendance was the attendance in December?

    (1)   8%
    (2) 10%
    (3) 11%
    (4) 13%
    (5) 18%

Directions: Choose the one best answer to each question. You MAY use your calculator.

Questions 1 and 2 refer to the following graph.

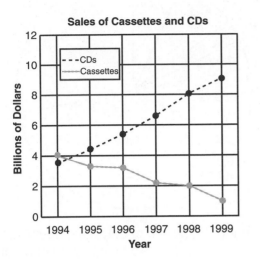

1. What was the difference between CD sales and cassette sales in 1995?

   (1) $1.1 billion
   (2) $2.1 billion
   (3) $3.2 billion
   (4) $4.5 billion
   (5) $8.5 billion

2. How much less were CD sales in 1998 than in 1999?

   (1) $1.0 billion
   (2) $2.0 billion
   (3) $3.0 billion
   (4) $4.0 billion
   (5) Not enough information is given.

Questions 3 and 4 refer to the following graph.

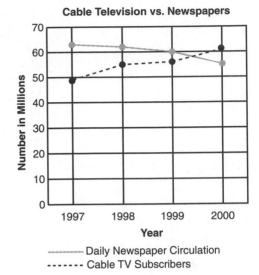

3. How many more people subscribed to daily newspapers in 1997 than to cable television?

   (1) 14,000,000
   (2) 10,000,000
   (3) 7,000,000
   (4) 22,000,000
   (5) 5,000,000

4. Which of the following describes a conclusion that can be drawn from the data shown for 1997–2000?

   (1) Daily newspaper circulation steadily increased.
   (2) Daily newspaper circulation always exceeded cable TV subscribers.
   (3) Cable TV subscribers steadily increased.
   (4) Cable TV subscribers steadily decreased.
   (5) Not enough information is given.

Questions 5 through 7 refer to the following graph.

Questions 8 through 10 refer to the following diagram.

Sales of Cellular Phones

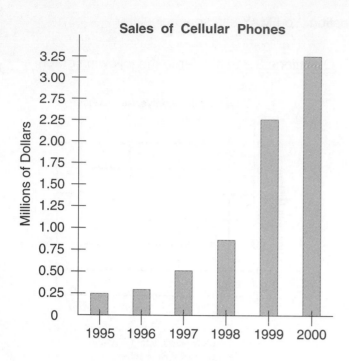

July Production of Automobiles
121,000 cars

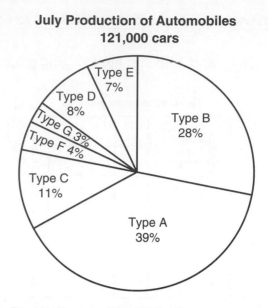

5. In which year was the greatest number of cellular phones sold?

   (1) 1996
   (2) 1997
   (3) 1998
   (4) 1999
   (5) 2000

6. Estimate the overall increase in sales from 1995 to 2000.

   (1) $2.0 million
   (2) $2.5 million
   (3) $2.7 million
   (4) $3.0 million
   (5) $3.4 million

7. Which expression below could be used to estimate the average sales per year for 1995, 1996, and 1997?

   (1) 0.25 + 0.3 + 0.5 ÷ 3
   (2) (0.25 + 0.3 + 0.5) ÷ 3
   (3) (0.25 + 0.3 + 0.5) × 3
   (4) (0.25 + 0.3 + 0.5) + 3
   (5) 0.25 + 0.3 + 0.5 − 3

8. During the month of July, how many Type E cars were produced by this auto company?

   (1) 3,630
   (2) 4,840
   (3) 8,470
   (4) 9,680
   (5) 13,310

9. Which type of car was the least-produced car by this company?

   (1) Type C
   (2) Type D
   (3) Type E
   (4) Type F
   (5) Type G

10. Express as a fraction the number of Type F cars produced during the month to the total number of cars produced?

   (1) $\frac{1}{2}$
   (2) $\frac{1}{5}$
   (3) $\frac{1}{16}$
   (4) $\frac{1}{20}$
   (5) $\frac{1}{25}$

Questions 11 through 17 refer to the following chart.

1998 Enlisted Personnel in Armed Services

	Women	Men
Air Force	53,542	251,390
Army	60,787	313,646
Navy	42,261	281,113
Marines	8,928	135,292

11. How many more men were enlisted personnel in the Navy than in the Marines in 1998?

    (1)   33,693
    (2) 145,821
    (3) 249,421
    (4) 333,933
    (5) 470, 278

12. What was the total number of enlisted personnel in the Air Force in 1998?

    (1) 269,832
    (2) 304,932
    (3) 456,925
    (4) 514,631
    (5) 717,340

13. Which expression can be used to determine the percent of the total enlisted personnel in the Air Force who were women?

    (1)   53,542 ÷ 251,390
    (2) (53,542 + 251,390) ÷ 53,542
    (3)   53,542 ÷ (53,542 + 251,390)
    (4) (251,390 − 53,542) ÷ 2
    (5)   251,390 − 53,542

14. Which branch of the Armed Services had the largest percent of women in 1998?

    (1) Air Force
    (2) Army
    (3) Navy
    (4) Marines
    (5) Not enough information is given.

Directions: Solve the following problems. Enter your answers on the grids provided.

15. How many more women were enlisted personnel in the Army than in the Air Force?

16. What was the average number of women enlisted personnel in the Air Force, Army, and Navy in 1998? Round the answer to the nearest hundred.

17. How many more men are in the Navy than in the Air Force?

Directions: Choose the one best answer to each question. You MAY use your calculator when indicated.

1. Which are the next two numbers in the series 5, 13, 21, 29, 37?

   (1) 45 and 54
   (2) 45 and 53
   (3) 44 and 52
   (4) 43 and 49
   (5) 42 and 48

2. A regular deck of 52 cards has 13 diamonds. If you select one card from the deck, what is the probability of drawing a diamond?

   (1) $\frac{1}{4}$
   (2) $\frac{4}{1}$
   (3) $\frac{3}{4}$
   (4) $\frac{4}{3}$
   (5) $\frac{2}{1}$

Question 3 refers to the following diagram.

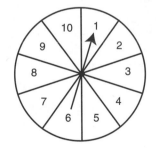

3. What is the probability of spinning an 8 on the first spin?

   (1) $\frac{1}{10}$
   (2) $\frac{1}{5}$
   (3) $\frac{3}{10}$
   (4) $\frac{5}{1}$
   (5) $\frac{10}{1}$

4. Which number series follows the pattern $\frac{x}{1}, \frac{x}{2}, \frac{x}{4}, \frac{x}{8}, \frac{x}{16}$?

   (1) 1, 2, 4, 8, 16
   (2) 16, 8, 4, 2, 1
   (3) 0, 2, 4, 6, 8
   (4) 10, 5, $2\frac{1}{2}$, $1\frac{1}{4}$, 1
   (5) 0.1, 0.2, 0.4, 0.8, 0.16

Questions 5 and 6 refer to the following passage.

Ms. Ashley is manager for the Discount Center. She recorded total sales for six months: January, $4,270; February, $2,675; March, $2,751; April, $3,734; May, $2,683; June, $4,671.

5. What was the median dollar of sales figures for the Discount Center?

   (1) $2,683.00
   (2) $3,242.50
   (3) $3,742.50
   (4) $4,270.00
   (5) $4,671.00

Directions: Solve the following problem. Enter your answer on the grid provided.

6. What was the mean dollar of sales for the six months at the Discount Center?

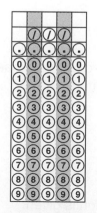

Directions: Solve the following problems. Enter your answer on the grid provided.

Question 7 refers to the following chart.

Miles Per Gallon of Gasoline

6-Cylinder Cars	mpg
Subcompact	25
Compact	23
Mid-size	20

7. If an owner of each of the cars listed above drove 20,000 miles last year and paid $1.25 per gallon of gasoline, how much less was spent on gas by the owner of the subcompact size car than by the owner of the mid-size car?

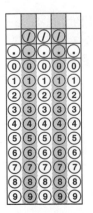

8. Don monitored the daily high temperature on a Fahrenheit thermometer for 7 days during January. Those temperatures were: Monday, −7°; Tuesday, +3°; Wednesday, −10°; Thursday, 0°; Friday, +5°; Saturday, −15°; Sunday, +3°. What was the difference between the highest and lowest temperatures?

9. A case of tuna contains 24 6-ounce cans. How many pounds of tuna are in $1\frac{1}{2}$ cases?

(1) 10.5
(2) 13.5
(3) 18
(4) 24.5
(5) 27

10. A city's annual rainfall over the past four years has been 29.86, 28.32, 25.21, and 27.36 inches. What is the amount of rainfall needed this year so that the average over the five years is 28 inches?

(1) 30.25
(2) 29.25
(3) 28.95
(4) 28.5
(5) 27.8

Question 11 refers to the chart below.

Company Salaries		
Position	**Number**	**Annual Salary**
President	1	$125,000
Vice President	1	$85,000
Manager	1	$56,000
Sales Agents	2	$46,400
Stock Clerks	3	$24,000

11. The chart shows the salaries of all the employees in a small company. What is the mean of the salaries?

(1) $ 56,000
(2) $336,400
(3) $ 67,280
(4) $ 70,500
(5) $ 53,850

Daily Feeding Guidelines
1 can = 13.2 oz.

	Dog's Weight	Up to 5 lbs.	Up to 10 lbs.	Up to 20 lbs.	Up to 50 lbs.	Up to 90 lbs.	Over 90 lbs.
A M O U N T T O F E E D	Less Active Dog	up to $\frac{3}{4}$ can	up to $1\frac{1}{4}$ can	up to 2 cans	up to 4 cans	up to 6 cans	6 cans plus 1 can for each 16 lbs. over 90 lbs.
	To Lose Weight	up to $\frac{1}{2}$ can	up to $\frac{3}{4}$ can	up to $1\frac{1}{2}$ can	up to 3 cans	up to $4\frac{1}{2}$ can	$4\frac{1}{2}$ cans plus 1 can for each 21 lbs. over 90 lbs.

Directions: Solve the following problem. Enter your answer on the grid provided.

12. Mr. Estrada has a dog that weighs 88 pounds. The veterinarian advises Mr. Estrada to put the dog on a diet because it is overweight. What is the maximum amount of canned food Mr. Estrada should feed his dog, in ounces?

13. Reyna's dog weighs 122 pounds. Since the dog is old and not as active as it used to be, Rayna wants to make sure her dog doesn't gain more weight. How many cans of dog food should Reyna feed her dog each day?

(1) $4\frac{1}{2}$
(2) $5\frac{1}{2}$
(3) 6
(4) 7
(5) 8

Tax Rate on Taxable Income

Less than $5,000..3% of the taxable income

At least-	But less than-		
$5000	$12,500.....$150.00 plus 4%	of excess over $5000
$12,500	$20,000.....$450.00 plus 4.5%	of excess over $12,500
$20,000	$30,000.....$787.50 plus 6%	of excess

14. Last year you had taxable income of $28,000. What is the amount of tax that you owe?

(1) $1,150.00
(2) $1,187.50
(3) $1,267.50
(4) $1,275.00
(5) $1,287.00

15. A carton contains 25 cards, each marked with a different number from 26 to 50. If a card is chosen at random, what is the probability that it is marked with a number greater than 45?

(1) $\frac{1}{8}$
(2) $\frac{1}{5}$
(3) $\frac{1}{4}$
(4) $\frac{1}{3}$
(5) $\frac{2}{5}$

16. Melissa bought 14 yds. of fabric. She cut it into 8-inch pieces to make a quilt. How many 8-inch pieces does she have?

(1) $1\frac{3}{4}$
(2) 6
(3) 20
(4) 63
(5) 112

UNIT 3 Algebra

Introduction

In algebra, you add, subtract, multiply, and divide according to the same rules and order of operations, but you can use letters to represent one or more numbers. When a letter is used to represent a range of numbers, it is called a <u>variable</u>.

An <u>algebraic expression</u> consists of constants, variables, and operations.

Examples:

Algebraic Expression	Meaning	Operation Indicated
$8y$, $8 \bullet y$, $(8)(y)$	8 times y	Multiplication
$\frac{16}{b}$, $16 \div b$	16 divided by b	Division
$4 + s$	4 plus s	Addition
$9 - x$	9 minus x	Subtraction

The multiplication symbol $\times$ is usually not used in algebra because of its possible confusion with the variable x.

To use algebra to solve problems, you may need to translate words, phrases, and sentences into mathematical symbols. To do this, it helps to look for words that indicate operations.

Examples:

Verbal Phrase	Algebraic Expression
The sum of 5 and a number	$5 + x$
Ten less than a number	$y - 10$
A number multiplied by five	$5n$
A number divided by 11	$\frac{y}{11}$

<u>Directions</u>: Write the phrases as algebraic expressions on the lines provided. Let x represent the number.

1. A number is decreased by 3

_____

2. Product of 4 and a number

_____

3. If b and h represent two numbers, write the sum.

_____

4. Represent algebraically the number of inches in y yards.

_____

5. 50 divided by a number

_____

6. 15 increased by a number

_____

7. Twice a number is increased by one.

_____

8. Represent algebraically the number of weeks in d days.

_____

Reading and Writing Powers

A <u>power</u> is a number with a base and an exponent, such as 2^3. In this case, 2 is the base and 3 is the exponent. The exponent tells how many times the base is used as a factor. $2^3 = 2 \times 2 \times 2 = 8$.

Example 1:

Exponential Form	Rule
$1^3 = 1 \times 1 \times 1 = 1$	One to any power is always one.
$5^1 = 5$	A number raised to the first power is always the same number.
$3^0 = 1$	Any number to the zero power (except 0) is always 1.

Finding Square Roots

When you understand powers, you also understand roots. A root is an inverse of a power. The square root is one of a number's two equal factors. The sign for square root is $\sqrt{\ }$.

Example 2: Find the square root of 36. The square root of 0.25 is what number?

$\sqrt{36} = 6$ because $6^2 = 6 \times 6 = 36$

$\sqrt{0.25} = 0.5$ because $0.5^2 = 0.5 \times 0.5 = 0.25$

Writing Numbers in Scientific Notation

You can use <u>scientific notation</u> to write very large or very small numbers. To write a number in scientific notation, write it as a product of two factors: (a decimal greater than or equal to 1 but less than 10) × (a power of 10).

Example 3:

Decimal Form	Product Form	Scientific Notation
73,000,000	$7.3 \times 10,000,000$	7.3×10^7
0.00923	9.23×0.001	9.23×10^{-3}

<u>Directions</u>: Evaluate the following expressions. Write your answers on the lines provided.

1. 8^2 _____

2. 1^5 _____

3. 2^3 _____

4. 5^3 _____

5. $\sqrt{16}$ _____

6. $\sqrt{25}$ _____

7. $\sqrt{100}$ _____

8. $\sqrt{121}$ _____

9. 3^4 _____

10. 12^2 _____

11. $\sqrt{169}$ _____

12. $\sqrt{225}$ _____

<u>Directions</u>: Write the following in scientific notation. Write your answers on the lines provided.

13. 3,500 _____

14. 29,000 _____

15. 85,700 _____

16. 26,410 _____

17. 2,100 _____

18. 0.005 _____

19. 0.0024 _____

20. 0.012 _____

21. 0.035 _____

22. 0.221 _____

When you combine like terms or use properties to make algebraic expressions easier to work with, you are simplifying the expression. An expression is simplified if it has no grouping symbols and all the like terms have been combined.

Combining Like Terms

Like terms are terms in an expression that have the same variable raised to the same power. For example, $8x$ and $3x$ are like terms. The terms x^2 and x, however, are not like terms.

Example 1: Simplify $3x^2 - 3 - x^2 + 2x + 5 - 5x$.
Group like terms together. $3x^2 - x^2 + 2x - 5x - 3 + 5$
Add or subtract like terms. $2x^2 - 3x + 2$

Using Properties to Simplify Expressions

Using the distributive property allows you to combine like terms by adding their coefficients.

Example 2: Simplify $4(2x + 6) - 5(x + 2)$.
Multiply using the distributive property. Use parentheses to show that $5x + 10$ is being subtracted. $\qquad$ $8x + 24 - (5x + 10) =$

To remove the parentheses, multiply by -1. $\qquad$ $8x + 24 - 5x - 10 =$

Combine like terms. $\qquad$ $8x - 5x + 24 - 10 = 3x + 14$

Directions: Simplify each expression. Write your answers on the lines provided. You may NOT use your calculator.

1. $5x^2 + 7 - 3x^2 - 8$ _____

2. $-2(y - 3)$ _____

3. $3(4p + 1) - 3(p - 1)$ _____

4. $-2z^2 + 11 - 3z^2 - 6$ _____

5. $\dfrac{(-12r - 9)}{3}$ _____

6. $5(x^2 + 7) - 3x^2 - 8$ _____

7. $-(2y - 6) - 5(7 - y)$ _____

8. $-3(3y)$ _____

9. $\dfrac{40st}{4}$ _____

10. $\dfrac{(4 - 16a)}{4}$ _____

11. $(22x - 12) - (-13x + 2)$ _____

12. $-2(-5p^2)$ _____

13. $(5p^2 - pq - 3q^2) - (3p^2 - 4pq + 7q^2)$ _____

Substituting numerical values in algebraic expressions, and later in geometric formulas, is a very important skill that will help you on the GED Mathematics Test. The examples and exercise that follow require you to recall all the rules and skills that you have learned about positive and negative numbers, order of operations, and powers and roots. Study each example carefully.

Example 1: Find the value of $x + y$ if $x = 15$ and $y = 12$.
    1. Write the expression. $x + y$
    2. Substitute 15 for x and 12 for y. $15 + 12$
    3. Perform the operation of addition. $15 + 12 = 27$

Example 2: If $a = 3$ and $b = -5$, find the value of $a - b$.
    1. Write the expression. $a - b$
    2. Substitute 3 for a and -5 for b. $3 - (-5)$
    3. Perform the operation. $3 + 5 = 8$

Example 3: What does the value of $\frac{ab + c}{2}$ equal when $a = 2$, $b = 6$, and $c = 8$?
    1. Write the expression. $\dfrac{ab + c}{2}$

    2. Substitute 2 for a, 6 for b, and 8 for c. $\dfrac{(2)(6) + 8}{2}$

    3. Perform the operations. $\dfrac{12 + 8}{2} = \dfrac{20}{2} = 10$

    In step two, parentheses are used to separate the 2 and 6 to indicate the operation to be performed.

Example 4: Find the value of $\frac{a}{b}$ if $a = 15$ and $b = 24$.
    1. Write the expression. $\dfrac{a}{b}$

    2. Substitute 15 for a, and 24 for b. $\dfrac{15}{24}$

    3. Perform the operation. $\dfrac{15}{24} = 0.625$

    In this example, the answer is a decimal.

Directions: Evaluate each of the following expressions if $a = 3$, $b = 5$, $c = 6$, $d = 1$, $x = -1$, $y = 2$, and $z = -4$. Write your answers on the lines provided.

1. $bc - ad$ _____

2. $\dfrac{(xy - yz)}{xyz}$ _____

3. $\dfrac{b^3}{b^2}$ _____

4. $x^3 + (y - 2z)$ _____

5. $\dfrac{10cd}{abc}$ _____

6. $\dfrac{3(x + z)}{x}$ _____

7. $a^3 - b^3$ _____

8. $ay + by$ _____

9. $(5x - 5z) + ab$ _____

10. $3a^2b - 6$ _____

11. $3x(xy - b)$ _____

12. $\dfrac{y}{x} + yz$ _____

13. $a(7 - a)^2$ _____

14. $\dfrac{bc - 5a}{b}$ _____

15. $\dfrac{3(y + z)}{x}$ _____

16. $\dfrac{a}{b} + \dfrac{b}{c}$ _____

Solving One-Step Equations

You can solve an equation by writing an equivalent equation that has the variable isolated on one side. Two operations that undo each other, such as addition and subtraction, are called inverse operations. Inverse operations can help you to isolate the variable on one side of an equation.

Example 1: Solve $8 = n + 4$.

This is an addition equation. Use the inverse operation (subtraction) to undo the addition.

$8 = n + 4$ Original equation

$8 - 4 = n + 4 - 4$ Subtract 4 from each side to undo the addition.

$4 = n$ Simplify both sides. Check this solution in the original equation.

Example 2: Solve $x - 5 = -13$.

This is a subtraction equation. Use the inverse operation (addition) to undo the subtraction.

$x - 5 = -13$ Original equation

$x - 5 + 5 = -13 + 5$ Add 5 to each side to undo the subtraction.

$x = -8$ Simplify both sides.

To check the solution, substitute -8 for x in the original equation.

Example 3: Solve $-4x = 1$.

This is a multiplication equation. Use the inverse operation (division) to undo the multiplication.

$-4x = 1$ Original equation

$\frac{-4x}{-4} = -\frac{1}{4}$ Divide each side by -4 to undo the multiplication.

$x = -\frac{1}{4}$ Simplify. Check this solution in the original equation.

Example 4: Solve $\frac{x}{5} = -30$.

This is a division equation. Use the inverse operation (multiplication) to undo the division.

$\frac{x}{5} = -30$ Original equation

$5(\frac{x}{5}) = 5(-30)$ Multiply each side by 5 to undo the division.

$x = -150$ Simplify. Check this solution in the original equation.

<u>Directions</u> Solve the following one-step equations. For questions 9 through 12, use *n* for each unknown number. Write your answers on the lines provided.

1. $x + 9 = 18$ _____

2. $y + 12 = -12$ _____

3. $60 = 5x$ _____

4. $\frac{r}{3} = 11$ _____

5. $m - 20 = 45$ _____

6. $34 + x = 10$ _____

7. $-3x = -9$ _____

8. $\frac{n}{4} = -2$ _____

9. Twelve times a certain number is thirty-six. _____

10. A number added to ten equals eighty. _____

11. Six less than some number equals two. _____

12. A certain number decreased by 13 is equal to 39. _____

Solving Two-Step Equations

Solving some equations requires two steps—that is, performing two different operations—to both sides of the equation.

Example 1: Solve $2x + 5 = 9$.

$$2x + 5 = 9$$
$$2x + 5 - 5 = 9 - 5$$
$$2x = 4$$
$$\frac{2x}{2} = \frac{4}{2}$$
$$x = 2$$

Check:
$$2(2) + 5 = 9$$
$$4 + 5 = 9$$
$$9 = 9$$

Subtract 5 from both sides of the equal sign. Divide both sides by 2. The solution is $x = 2$. To check the solution, substitute 2 for x in the original equation.

Example 2: Solve $-3x - 9 = 12$.

$$-3x - 9 = 12$$
$$-3x - 9 + 9 = 12 + 9$$
$$-3x = 21$$
$$\frac{-3x}{-3} = \frac{21}{-3}$$
$$x = -7$$

Check: $-3(-7) - 9 = 12$
$$21 - 9 = 12$$
$$12 = 12$$

Add 9 to both sides. Divide both sides by -3. The solution is $x = -7$. Check by substituting the solution into the original equation.

Example 3: Solve $\frac{x}{5} + 6 = 1$.

$$\frac{x}{5} + 6 = 1$$
$$\frac{x}{5} + 6 - 6 = 1 - 6$$
$$\frac{x}{5} = -5$$
$$5\left(\frac{x}{5}\right) = 5(-5)$$
$$x = -25$$

Check:
$$\frac{-25}{5} + 6 = 1$$
$$-5 + 6 = 1$$
$$1 = 1$$

Subtract 6 from both sides. Multiply both sides by 5. The solution is $x = -25$. Check by substituting the solution into the original equation.

<u>Directions</u>: Solve the following two-step equations. Write your answers on the lines provided.

1. $4x + 7 = 11$ _____

2. $6x - 13 = 17$ _____

3. $\frac{x}{8} + 9 = 10$ _____

4. $\frac{x}{2} - 6 = 2$ _____

5. $-8x + 12 = 36$ _____

6. $\frac{-x}{9} - 7 = 3$ _____

7. $3x + 4 = 10$ _____

8. $-2x + 7 = -25$ _____

9. $5 - 5x = -10$ _____

10. $14 + \frac{x}{4} = -2$ _____

11. $25 + 10x = 75$ _____

12. $-8 - 2x = -4$ _____

13. $-1 + \frac{x}{3} = 2$ _____

14. $17 - \frac{x}{10} = 5$ _____

15. $8 - 3x = 17$ _____

16. $\frac{x}{4} - 3 = 7$ _____

Solving Multi-Step Equations

Use a combination of inverse operations to solve multi-step equations.

Example 1: Solve $2x - 9 = x + 10$.

To solve this equation, identify an unknown side of the equation. You want the unknowns on one side and the numbers on the other side.

Unknown	Numerical	Check:

$$2x - 9 = x + 10$$
$$2x - x - 9 + 9 = x - x + 10 + 9$$
$$x = 19$$

Check:
$$2x - 9 = x + 10$$
$$2(19) - 9 = 19 + 10$$
$$38 - 9 = 19 + 10$$
$$29 = 29$$

Move -9 from the unknown side to the numerical side by addition. The unknown x is moved from the numerical side by subtraction. The like terms are collected on both sides so that the unknown side is equal to the numerical side. Check your solution. Substitute into the original equation.

Example 2: Solve $7x - 2 = 11x - 1 + 15$.

Before any solution can be found, you must simplify the right-hand side of the equation by combining like terms, -1 and $+15$.

Numerical Unknown
$$7x - 2 = 11x - 1 + 15$$
$$7x - 2 = 11x + 14$$
$$7x - 7x - 2 - 14 = 11x - 7x + 14 - 14$$
$$-16 = 4x$$
$$\frac{-16}{4} = \frac{4x}{4}$$
$$-4 = x$$

Check:
$$7x - 2 = 11x - 1 + 15$$
$$7(-4) - 2 = 11(-4) - 1 + 15$$
$$-28 - 2 = -44 - 1 + 15$$
$$-30 = -30$$

Directions: Solve each equation using inverse operations. Write your answers on the lines provided.

1. $100 + 7x = 250 - 18x$ _____

2. $5n - 6 = 4n + 2$ _____

3. $3(x - 4) - 2(x - 8) = 1$ _____

4. $14x - x + 1 = 14$ _____

5. $5x + 8 = 4x - 12$ _____

6. $5x - 75 = 3x + 7$ _____

7. $10(x - 3) - 7x = 0$ _____

8. $16 + 3x = x + 32$ _____

9. $3x + 1 = 25 - x$ _____

10. $36 = 18x - 12x + 6$ _____

Directions: On a separate sheet of paper, write and then solve an equation for each of the following. Use x as the unknown.

11. The sum of four times a number and four equals twenty.

12. Six is subtracted from nine times a number. The difference equals forty-eight.

13. The sum of two times a number and ten equals fourteen plus three times the same number.

14. Five times a number is decreased by four and equals four plus three times the same number.

15. Five times the sum of a number and three is equal to the sum of that number and fifteen.

Solving Word Problems

Use the rules that you learned in solving one-step, two-step, and multi-step equations to solve algebraic word problems. Study the format for organizing information in the examples below.

Example 1: The sum of three consecutive numbers is 48. Find the numbers.

Step 1 Read the problem carefully. Be sure you understand the information you are given and what you are being asked to find.

Step 2 Assign a variable to the unknown term or terms: Let x = 1st consecutive number; $x + 1$ = 2nd consecutive number; and $x + 2$ = 3rd consecutive number

Step 3 Write the equation and solve for the unknown.

$$(x) + (x + 1) + (x + 2) = 48 \qquad 3x = 45$$
$$3x + 3 = 48 \qquad \frac{3x}{3} = \frac{45}{3}$$
$$3x + 3 - 3 = 48 - 3 \qquad x = 15$$

Step 4 Substitute 15 as the value of x for each of the variables in Step 2.

1st consecutive number = x = 15
2nd consecutive number = $x + 1$ or $15 + 1 = 16$
3rd consecutive number = $x + 2$ or $15 + 2 = 17$

The three consecutive numbers are 15, 16, and 17: $15 + 16 + 17 = 48$.

Example 2: Claude's savings are two times Rene's savings. Together their savings total $6,000. How much has Claude saved?

Step 1 Read the problem carefully. Note that you are being asked to find <u>Claude's</u> savings.

Step 2 Assign a variable to the unknown term.

Let x = Rene's savings and $2x$ = Claude's savings.

Step 3 Write the equation and solve for the unknown.

$$2x + x = \$6,000$$
$$\frac{3x}{3} = \frac{\$6,000}{3}$$
$$x = \$2,000$$

Step 4 Substitute $2,000 as the value of x, the variable in Step 2: Rene's savings = x = $2,000 and Claude's savings = $2x$ = $2($2,000$) = $4,000

<u>Directions</u>: On a separate sheet of paper, set up and solve the following word problems. Use n as the unknown.

1. The sum of two consecutive numbers is 111. Find the two numbers.

2. Marion is 4 years older than Pam. The sum of their ages is 32 years. How old are Marion and Pam?

3. One hundred eighty is divided into two parts so one part will be three times the other part. What is the larger part?

4. Riley and Jessica spent a total of $300 at the mall. Riley spent twice as much as Jessica. How much did each spend?

5. The sum of two numbers is 98. If one number is six times the other, find the two numbers.

6. Evelyn and Eleanor worked a total of 36 hours. If Evelyn worked 10 hours longer than Eleanor, how many hours did each woman work?

Directions: Set up and solve the following word problems. Choose the one best answer to each question. You MAY use your calculator when indicated.

1. Twelve times the sum of a number and 2 is equal to 36. What is the number?

    (1) 24
    (2) 12
    (3) 6
    (4) 1
    (5) 0

2. Jerry swam twice as many laps as his younger brother Bill. If Jerry and Bill swam a total of 60 laps, how many laps did Jerry swim?

    (1) 50
    (2) 40
    (3) 30
    (4) 20
    (5) 10

3. The sum of three consecutive numbers is 24. What is the largest number?

    (1) 6
    (2) 7
    (3) 8
    (4) 9
    (5) 10

4. Twice the product of 3 and a number exceeds the sum of the number and 80 by 10. What is the number?

    (1) 10
    (2) 12
    (3) 18
    (4) 22
    (5) 24

5. A certain number is subtracted from 20. The result multiplied by 3 is equal to 45. What is the number?

    (1) 3
    (2) 5
    (3) 10
    (4) 15
    (5) 45

6. The sum of three consecutive even numbers is equal to two times the largest number. What is the largest number?

    (1) 2
    (2) 4
    (3) 6
    (4) 8
    (5) 10

7. Joan has 16 coins in her pocket. She has the same number of quarters as nickels and she has twice as many dimes as quarters. How many dimes does she have?

    (1) 4
    (2) 5
    (3) 6
    (4) 8
    (5) 12

8. A vending machine operator is counting the change taken in from a single candy machine. He finds that he has 43 quarters, twice as many nickels, and 4 more than 3 times as many dimes as nickels. How much money was in the machine?

    (1) $23.44
    (2) $35.87
    (3) $41.25
    (4) $44.25
    (5) $51.25

Formula Problems: Interest, Distance, and Cost

Since you know how to substitute numerical values into algebraic expressions and how to solve equations, you can apply the same rules to solve problems involving formulas. The formulas that you will need on the GED Mathematics Test will be provided for you in your test booklet. Those formulas are on page 101 of this book.

<u>Directions</u>: Select and use one of the formulas to solve each of the following questions. Choose the <u>one best answer</u> to each question. You MAY use your calculator when indicated.

Interest:	$i = prt$	$r = \dfrac{i}{pt}$	$t = \dfrac{i}{pr}$	$p = \dfrac{i}{rt}$
Distance:	$d = rt$	$r = \dfrac{d}{t}$	$t = \dfrac{d}{r}$	
Cost:	$c = nr$	$r = \dfrac{c}{n}$	$n = \dfrac{c}{r}$	

1. Marion deposited $800 in a savings account. One year later, the teller posted $56 in her savings book. At what rate of interest was she paid on her savings?

   (1) 5%
   (2) 6%
   (3) $6\frac{1}{2}$%
   (4) 7%
   (5) $7\frac{1}{2}$%

2. Mr. and Mrs. Kennedy borrowed $1,200 from their family for 9 months to invest in a small business venture. If they agreed to pay $8\frac{1}{2}$% interest annually, how much must they repay?

   (1) $ 72.00
   (2) $ 76.50
   (3) $1,176.50
   (4) $1,276.50
   (5) $1,806.00

3. McCory's Bookstore received a shipment of novels costing $2.95 each. If there were 550 novels in the shipment, what was the total cost of the shipment?

   (1) $1,295.00
   (2) $1,375.00
   (3) $1,550.00
   (4) $1,622.50
   (5) $1,650.00

4. Midwestern Airway's flight #403 from Springfield to Cincinnati takes $1\frac{3}{4}$ hours. If the rate of speed is 124 miles per hour, what is the distance from Springfield to Cincinnati?

   (1) 864 miles
   (2) 432 miles
   (3) 217 miles
   (4) 216 miles
   (5) 213 miles

5. Mrs. Avers deposited $3,000 in her credit union savings account. What amount of interest will she receive on her deposit if she leaves the money in the account for one year at $8\frac{1}{2}$% interest?

   (1) $250
   (2) $255
   (3) $300
   (4) $350
   (5) $400

6. A truck traveled 390 miles in 6 hours. What was the average rate of speed for the truck?

   (1) 50 mph
   (2) 55 mph
   (3) 60 mph
   (4) 65 mph
   (5) Not enough information is given.

7. Wayne drove 160 miles to Stockton in 4 hours and another 146 miles beyond Stockton in 2 hours. What was Wayne's average speed for the total time that he drove?

(1) 40 mph
(2) 45 mph
(3) 51 mph
(4) 73 mph
(5) 80 mph

11. A case of 32-ounce bottles of general purpose cleaner costs $25. If one bottle of cleaner costs $2.50, how many bottles of cleaner are in the case?

(1) 5
(2) 10
(3) 15
(4) 20
(5) 25

8. Elinor borrowed money from the credit union to purchase a piece of property to build her own child care center. The loan was for 2 years and the annual interest rate was 8%. If Elinor paid $370 interest in the first year, what was the amount of money she borrowed?

(1) $8,000
(2) $7,000
(3) $6,500
(4) $5,500
(5) $4,625

12. Margaret O'Connor received $120 interest from First Home Bank on her savings account balance of $2,400 in one year. What was the simple annual rate of interest?

(1) 5%
(2) 10%
(3) 12%
(4) 15%
(5) 20%

9. A car and a truck left LaPointe at 1:15 P.M. traveling in opposite directions. If the driver of the car drove 55 miles per hour, and the truck averaged 50.5 miles per hour, how many miles apart will they be at 4:15 P.M.?

(1) 151.5
(2) 165
(3) 316.5
(4) 415
(5) 540

13. How long will it take Danette to travel 90 miles if she drives at an average speed of 50 mph for 25 miles and at an average speed of 65 mph the rest of the way?

(1) $\frac{1}{2}$ hour
(2) 1 hour
(3) $1\frac{1}{2}$ hours
(4) 2 hours
(5) $2\frac{1}{2}$ hours

10. Ron sells fresh pineapples at his fruit stand. How much should Ron charge for each pineapple if he pays $10.80 a dozen and wants to make a profit of $.75 each?

(1) $ .90
(2) $1.08
(3) $1.50
(4) $1.65
(5) $2.00

14. Elaine's Style Shop received an order of 250 swimsuits from Swimsuits, Inc. If the owner of the shop paid $6.95 for each swimsuit, what was the total amount of money to be sent to Swimsuits, Inc.?

(1) $ 690.00
(2) $ 695.00
(3) $1,600.00
(4) $1,737.00
(5) $1,737.50

Solving Inequalities

An <u>inequality</u> is an algebraic statement used to show quantities that are not equal. The graph of an inequality is the set of points on a number line that represent all solutions of the inequality. If a point on the graph is part of the solution, a solid dot is used. An open circle indicates that the number at that point is <u>not</u> part of the solution.

<u>Example 1</u>:

Inequality	Verbal Phrase	Graph
$x < 2$	All real numbers less than 2	
$x > -2$	All real numbers greater than -2	
$x \leq 1$	All real numbers less than or equal to 1	
$x \geq 0$	All real numbers greater than or equal to 0	

In an inequality one side of the statement has a greater value than the other side. It is <u>not</u> an equation because the sides are not equal. To solve an inequality, use the same steps as you would to solve an equation, with one exception. If you multiply or divide by a negative number, you must <u>reverse</u> the direction of the inequality symbol (see Example 2). When an inequality is solved, more than one number satisfies the inequality.

<u>Example 2</u>: Solve $5 - 3x < 2$ and graph the solution.

$$5 - 3x < 2$$
$$5 - 5 - 3x < 2 - 5$$
$$-3x < -3$$
$$x > 1$$

Check by substitution.
For $x = 2$: $5 - 3(2) < 2$
$$5 - 6 < 2$$
$$-1 < 2$$

Notice that the "less than" inequality sign is reversed (changed to "greater than") because you divided by -3. The value used to check, $x = 2$, is shown on the graph as included in the solution of all numbers greater than 1.

<u>Directions</u>: Solve each inequality and graph the solution.

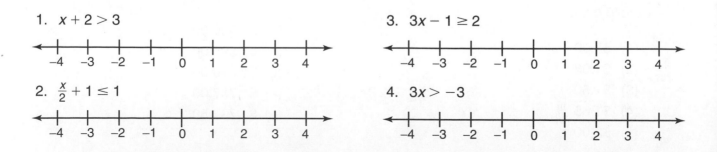

1. $x + 2 > 3$

2. $\frac{x}{2} + 1 \leq 1$

3. $3x - 1 \geq 2$

4. $3x > -3$

Factoring

Factors are numbers that are multiplied together. In the algebraic term $4x$, 4 and x are factors. To factor an expression, find a number and/or variable that divides evenly into each term of the expression.

Example 1: Factor $2x + 8$.

Find a factor that divides evenly into both terms.	Both $2x$ and 8 can be divided evenly by 2.
Divide to find the other factor.	$\frac{2x+8}{2} = (x + 4)$
Check by multiplying the factors.	$2(x + 4) = 2x + 8$

Example 2: Factor $x^2 + 4x$.

Find a factor that divides evenly into both terms.	The factor x divides evenly into both terms.
Divide to find the other factor.	$\frac{x^2 + 4x}{x} = (x + 4)$
Check by multiplying the two factors.	$x(x + 4) = x^2 + 4x$

A quadratic expression is one that contains a variable raised to the second power, like $x^2 + x$. Both factors of quadratic expressions will always contain the variable. In the case of $x^2 + x$, both terms divide evenly by x, giving the factors x and $x + 1$.

A quadratic expression in this form, $x^2 - 11x - 12$, as in the example below, results when you multiply two expressions, each with a variable and a constant. Because the third term in the example is negative, you need to find factors with different signs.

Example 3: Factor $x^2 - 11x - 12$.

Find all the possible factors for the third term.	(1)(–12), (12)(–1), (–2)(6), (–6)(2), (–3)(4), (–4)(3)
Find the two factors that when added give the integer part of the middle term.	The numbers you need are 1 and –12.
Write the two factors using the variable as the first term in each factor and the integers as the second term.	$(x + 1)(x - 12)$
Check your answer by multiplying.	$(x + 1)(x - 12) = x^2 - 11x - 12$

Directions: Factor each expression. Write your answers on the lines provided.

1. $10x + 60$ _____

2. $16x - 4$ _____

3. $4x^2 + 12x$ _____

4. $6x^2 + 12x$ _____

5. $8x^2 + 16x$ _____

6. $10x^2 + 20x$ _____

7. $x^2 - 5x + 4$ _____

8. $x^2 - 8x + 7$ _____

9. $x^2 - 3x - 10$ _____

10. $x^2 - x - 6$ _____

11. $x^2 + 8x - 20$ _____

12. $x^2 + 3x - 10$ _____

Solving Quadratic Equations by Substitution

These statements, $x^2 - 16 = 0$ and $y^2 = 6y - 5$, are examples of quadratic equations. If you encounter an equation like this on the GED Mathematics Test, use substitution to help in selecting your answer choice.

Example: Which of the following is the solution for $x^2 - 16 = 0$?

    (1)   4 and −4
    (2)   4 and −2
    (3)   2 and −4
    (4) −4 and −2
    (5) −4 and −1

By substituting the answers listed from the options, you can solve the equation. Use the rules for positive and negative numbers, and remember the order of operations. Option 1 has the two numbers that will satisfy this equation.

Let x = 4
$$x^2 - 16 = 0$$
$$(4)^2 - 16 = 0$$
$$(4)(4) - 16 = 0$$
$$16 - 16 = 0$$

Let x = −4
$$x^2 - 16 = 0$$
$$(-4)^2 - 16 = 0$$
$$(-4)(-4) - 16 = 0$$
$$+16 - 16 = 0$$

Directions: Use substitution to determine the solution to each of the following problems. Choose the one best answer to each problem.

1. Which of the following pairs satisfies the equation $x^2 - 9x + 14 = 0$?

    (1) −7 and −2
    (2)   7 and 2
    (3)   2 and −7
    (4) −2 and 7
    (5) Not enough information is given.

2. Which of the following pairs satisfies the equation $x^2 - 8x + 12 = 0$?

    (1) −2 and −6
    (2) −2 and 6
    (3)   2 and −6
    (4)   2 and 6
    (5) Not enough information is given.

3. Which of the following pairs satisfies the equation $p^2 + 9p + 20 = 0$?

    (1) −5 and 4
    (2)   5 and −4
    (3)   5 and 4
    (4) −5 and −4
    (5) Not enough information is given.

4. Which of the following pairs satisfies the equation $a^2 - 5a - 24 = 0$?

    (1)   3 and 8
    (2)   3 and −8
    (3) −3 and 8
    (4) −3 and −8
    (5) Not enough information is given.

Coordinates

A graph called a <u>coordinate system</u> can be used to describe algebraic relationships. Perpendicular lines *x* and *y* meet at an <u>origin</u>, (0,0). On this plane (a flat surface), the numbers to the right and above the origin are positive. The numbers to the left and below the origin are negative. The horizontal line is the *x*-axis and the vertical line is the *y*-axis. Each axis resembles a number line.

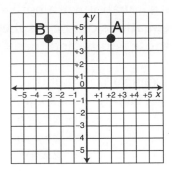

Each <u>point</u> on the plane is named by two numbers, an *x*-coordinate and a *y*-coordinate. The <u>coordinates</u> of point *A* are (2, 4), and the coordinates of point *B* are (−3, 4). The coordinates are called <u>ordered pairs</u> because the *x*-axis coordinate is always given first, and the *y*-axis coordinate is always given second (*x*, *y*).

Example 1: Plot the point (5, −4) on a coordinate grid.

Step 1 Start at the origin. Move the number of units of the *x*-coordinate in the appropriate direction, here 5 units to the right (the positive *x*-direction).

Step 2 From that point, move the number of units of the *y*-coordinate in the appropriate direction, here 4 units downward (the negative *y*-direction).

The location of point (5, −4) is shown by the dot on the grid.

You can use coordinates to draw a line segment or a figure on a coordinate system.

Example 2: Draw a line segment on the coordinate grid connecting points (4, 3) and (2, −5).

Step 1 Plot point (4, 3). Start at the origin. Move 4 units to the right on the *x*-axis, then 3 units up. Plot the point.

Step 2 Plot the point (2, −5). Start at the origin. Move 2 units to the right on the *x*-axis, then 5 units down. Plot the point.

Step 3 Connect the points by drawing a line segment.

The location of the points and segment are shown on the grid.

<u>Directions</u>: Plot the following points on the coordinate plane grid below.

1. (−1, 3)   3. (−3, 0)

2. (2, −2)   4. (−4, −4)

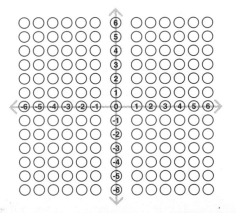

Graphing Linear Equations

An equation with both x and y variables with exponents of 1 is called a <u>linear equation</u>. Linear equations can be graphed on a coordinate system by finding two points on the line, plotting those points, and then drawing a line through the points.

Example 1: Graph the linear equation $x + 2y = 6$.

    Step 1: Pick a value for x, say $x = 0$. Substitute 0 into the equation for x. Solve for y.

$$x + 2y = 6$$
$$0 + 2y = 6$$
$$2y = 6$$
$$y = 3$$

When $x = 0$, $y = 3$.

Now we can plot the point (0, 3) on the graph. Notice that the point (0, 3) is on the y-axis. This point is called the <u>y-intercept</u>; the line intercepts or crosses the y-axis at this point.

Find the <u>x-intercept</u> by letting $y = 0$ and solving for x. (see Step 2) Although other points can be used, the x- and y- intercept are often the easiest points to find when graphing linear equations.

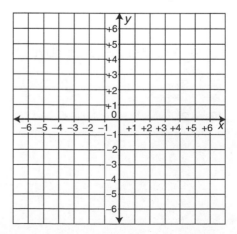

    Step 2: Substitute $y = 0$ to find the x-intercept.

$$x + 2y = 6$$
$$x + 2(0) = 6$$
$$x = 6$$

When $y = 0$, $x = 6$.

Now plot the point (6, 0) on the graph (remember that x is always given first) and draw a line through the points. Any point on this line is a solution to the linear equation $x + 2y = 6$. If you pick any point on the line, say (2, 2) and substitute into the equation, you will get a true statement.

$$x + 2y = 6$$
$$2 + 2(2) = 6$$
$$2 + 4 = 6$$

<u>Directions</u>: Graph the following equations on the same graph.

1. Line 1 $x + y = 4$

2. Line 2 $x - y = -4$

3. Line 3 $x - y = 4$

4. Line 4 $x + y = -4$

The <u>slope</u> of a line is the measure of the steepness of a line. Think of moving from point E to point F by first moving vertically ("rise"), then horizontally ("run"), as in Example 1. Slope is defined as "rise" divide by "run," or slope $(m) = \frac{\text{rise}}{\text{run}}$.

Example 1: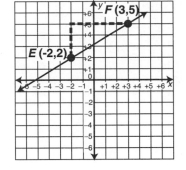

Example 2: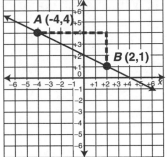

The slope of a line through points E and F is <u>positive</u>. Lines that slant upward toward the right have positive slopes. In Example 2, the slope of a line through points A and B is <u>negative</u>. Lines that point downward toward the right have negative slopes. Lines that are parallel to the x-axis (a horizontal line) have no slant and are said to have a <u>slope of 0</u>. Lines that are parallel to the y-axis (a vertical line) have no slant and are said to have an <u>undefined slope</u>.

When given a graph, you can determine the slope of a line by measuring both the rise and the run of the line. In Example 1, the vertical rise between points E and F is 3 and the horizontal run is 5. The slope (m) of line $\overline{EF}$ can be found by dividing the rise by the run.

$$m = \frac{\text{rise}}{\text{run}} = \frac{3}{5}$$

The slope of line $\overline{EF}$ is $\frac{3}{5}$.

Example 3: Find the slope of a line that passes through the points $(-2, 2)$ and $(4, 5)$.
Let $(-2, 2)$ = coordinate pair (x_1, y_1) and $(4, 5) = (x_2, y_2)$.

$$m = \frac{y_2 - y_1}{x_2 - x_1} = \frac{5 - 2}{4 - (-2)} = \frac{3}{6} = \frac{1}{2}$$

The graph shows the points and the line passing through them. Find the slope by substituting the x- and y- coordinates into the slope formula. The slope is $\frac{1}{2}$.

Finding the Equation of a Line

The equation $y = mx + b$ is in slope-intercept form for the equation of a line. When an equation is in this form, the slope of the line is given by m and the y-intercept is located at b. The graph of the equation $y = -3x + 2$ has a slope of -3 and a y-intercept at 2.

Example 1: What is the equation of the line shown on the graph?

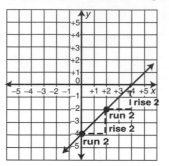

Step 1   Find the y-intercept of the line. The line crosses the y-axis at $(0, -4)$. Therefore, the y-intercept is -4.

Step 2   Find the slope of the line using the fraction rise over run: $\frac{2}{2} = 1$. As the line rises 2 units for every 2 units of run to the right (a positive direction), the slope is $+1$.

Step 3   Use the slope-intercept form to write the equation.
$y = 1x - 4$ or $y = x - 4$

You may need to rewrite an equation in slope-intercept form.

Example 2: Write the equation $2x - y = 3$ in slope-intercept form.

Step 2   Add or subtract to isolate the term with the y. In this situation, subtract $2x$.
$$2x - y - 2x = 3 - 2x$$

Step 2   Combine like terms. Use the commutative property to rearrange terms.
$$-y = -2x + 3$$

Step 3   Eliminate the negative variable.
$$\frac{-y}{-1} = \frac{-2x + 3}{-1}$$
$$y = \frac{-2x}{-1} + \frac{3}{-1}$$

Step 4   Simplify.
$$y = 2x - 3$$

In slope-intercept form, the equation $2x - y = 3$ is $y = 2x - 3$. The slope is 2 and the y-intercept is located at -3. The graph of the line is shown.

Directions: Choose the <u>one best answer</u> to each question.

1. Which ordered pair is a solution of $x + 2y = 7$?

    (1) $(3, -2)$

    (2) $(-3, 1)$

    (3) $(2, 3)$

    (4) $(3, 2)$

    (5) $(1, -3)$

2. Which of the following is the y-intercept for $2x - y = 9$?

    (1) $(9, -2)$

    (2) $(5, 1)$

    (3) $(0, -9)$

    (4) $(0, -5)$

    (5) $(-9, 0)$

3. Which of the following is the x-intercept for $3y - 4x = 8$?

    (1) $(-4, 0)$

    (2) $(3, 4)$

    (3) $(0, 0)$

    (4) $(2, -5)$

    (5) $(-2, 0)$

4. What is the slope of the line shown on the graph below.

    (1) $\dfrac{1}{2}$

    (2) 2

    (3) $\dfrac{2}{3}$

    (4) -3

    (5) $\dfrac{1}{3}$

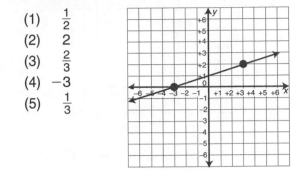

Directions: Mark your answers to questions 5 and 6 on the coordinate plane grids provided.

5. Show the location of the point whose coordinates are $(6, -5)$.

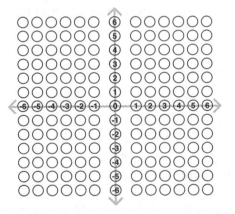

6. Show the location of the y-intercept for the line $y = 6x - 5$.

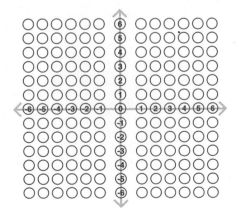

Questions 7 and 8 refer to the following graph.

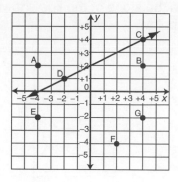

7. Which point lies at coordinates (2,–4)?

    (1) Point C
    (2) Point D
    (3) Point E
    (4) Point F
    (5) Point G

8. What is the slope of the line that passes through points D and C on the graph?

    (1) $-\dfrac{1}{2}$
    (2) $\dfrac{1}{3}$
    (3) $\dfrac{1}{2}$
    (4) $\dfrac{2}{3}$
    (5) 2

9. What is the y-intercept of the graph of the equation $2x + 3y = 6$?

    (1) 1
    (2) 2
    (3) 3
    (4) $\dfrac{2}{3}$
    (5) Not enough information is given.

10. What is the slope of the line that passes through points (0, 3) and (6, 1)?

    (1) $\dfrac{1}{3}$
    (2) $-\dfrac{1}{3}$
    (3) 2
    (4) 3
    (5) 6

11. Graph the equation $y = 5 - x$.

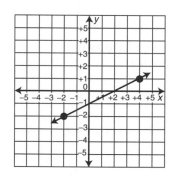

12. What is the equation of the line shown on the graph?

    (1) $y = \dfrac{1}{2}x + 1$
    (2) $y = \dfrac{1}{2}x - 1$
    (3) $y = x + 2$
    (4) $y = 2x + 1$
    (5) Not enough information is given.

Directions: Choose the <u>one best answer</u> to each question.

Directions: Mark your answers for questions 5 and 6 on the coordinate plane grids provided.

1. Find the slope of the line that passes through the points $(-2, 1)$ and $(3, -4)$.

   (1) -1
   (2) 1
   (3) 5
   (4) -5
   (5) 0

2. Where $m = 3$ and $n = 2$, evaluate $\frac{m - m^2 n}{3n}$.

   (1) $\frac{5}{2}$
   (2) 2
   (3) 1
   (4) $-\frac{3}{2}$
   (5) $-\frac{5}{2}$

3. If $x = -1$ and $y = 4$, evaluate the expression $\frac{5}{y-x} + \frac{4}{2} + 6x$.

   (1) $9\frac{1}{4}$
   (2) -9
   (3) 7
   (4) $5\frac{1}{2}$
   (5) -3

4. Sylvia is four times as old as Kim. If the difference between their ages is 24, how old is Sylvia?

   (1) 24
   (2) 28
   (3) 32
   (4) 36
   (5) 40

5. A point has an x-coordinate of -4 and a y-coordinate of 3. Show the location of the point on the coordinate grid.

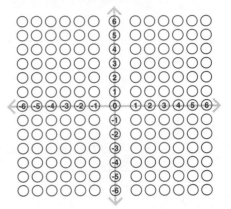

6. On the coordinate grid below, the three points show three corners of a rectangle. What point represents the fourth corner of the rectangle?

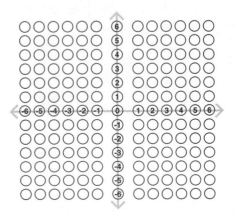

7. Which of the following are factors of $x^2 - 10x + 16$?

(1) $(x - 4)(x - 4)$
(2) $(x + 4)(x - 4)$
(3) $(x - 2)(x - 8)$
(4) $(x + 2)(x - 8)$
(5) $(x - 2)(x + 8)$

8. If $3q = 6$, what does $\frac{1}{2}q$ equal?

(1) 1
(2) 2
(3) 3
(4) 4
(5) 5

9. If $a = -1$ and $b = 2$, what is the value of the expression $2a^3 - 3ab$?

(1) 8
(2) 4
(3) −1
(4) −4
(5) −8

10. If $3(x - 1) = 2(x + 1)$, what does x equal?

(1) 5
(2) 4
(3) 3
(4) −4
(5) −5

11. Which of the following expressions describes all values for y as solutions for the inequality $4y + 14 > 18$?

(1) $y > 8$
(2) $y < 8$
(3) $y > 1$
(4) $y < -8$
(5) $y < -1$

12. What is the slope-intercept form of the equation $-4x + y = 8$?

(1) $-4x = 8 - y$
(2) $y = 4x + 8$
(3) $y = 4x - 8$
(4) $-y = -4x + 8$
(5) $4x = y + 8$

13. What is the slope of the line in the equation $x + 2y = 1$?

(1) 1
(2) −1
(3) $\frac{1}{2}$
(4) $-\frac{1}{2}$
(5) 2

14. Solve for c in the inequality $3c - 8 \le 7$.

(1) $c \le 15$
(2) $c \le 12$
(3) $c \le 8$
(4) $c \le 7$
(5) $c \le 5$

15. One number exceeds another number by 5. If the sum of the two numbers is 39, what is the smaller number?

(1) 16
(2) 17
(3) 18
(4) 19
(5) 20

16. Rhonda and Paul volunteered a total of 36 hours. If Rhonda volunteered 10 hours more than Paul, how many hours did Paul work?

(1) 10
(2) 13
(3) 16
(4) 18
(5) 23

17. Which of the following means the same as $a + a + a + a + a$?

   (1) $a + 5$
   (2) $3a^2$
   (3) $5a^2$
   (4) $5a$
   (5) $5 - a$

18. In $(p - 3)(3p + 8)(2p + 5) = 0$, which factor must be equal to zero?

   (1) $p - 3$
   (2) $3p + 8$
   (3) $2p + 5$
   (4) all of the three factors
   (5) any of the three factors

Question 19 refers to the following graph.

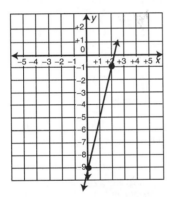

19. What is the equation of the line shown?

   (1) $y = 4x - 9$
   (2) $y = -4x - 9$
   (3) $y = -4x + 9$
   (4) $x = 4y - 9$
   (5) Not enough information is given.

Question 20 refers to the following graph.

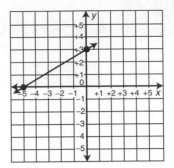

20. What is the slope of the line shown?

   (1) -5
   (2) $-\dfrac{3}{5}$
   (3) $\dfrac{3}{5}$
   (4) $\dfrac{5}{3}$
   (5) Not enough information is given.

21. What is the number 0.0007 written in scientific notation?

   (1) 70×10^3
   (2) 70×10^{-3}
   (3) 7×10^3
   (4) 7×10^{-3}
   (5) 7×10^{-4}

22. Which expression is the simplified form of $6x^2 - 3x + 2 - 4x^2 - x - 3$?

   (1) $10x^2 - 4x - 1$
   (2) $2x^2 - 4x - 1$
   (3) $2x^2 - 3x - 1$
   (4) $2x^2 - 2x + 5$
   (5) $10x^2 - 3x - 1$

23. What is the solution to the following equation?

   $$7x - 5 = 4x + 7$$

   (1) 1
   (2) 4
   (3) 5
   (4) 6
   (5) 7

Geometry

Angles and Lines

Naming Angles

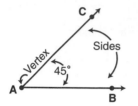

An <u>angle</u> consists of two <u>rays</u> with a common endpoint called a <u>vertex</u>. The rays form the sides of the angle. The angle at the left can be named ∠BAC, ∠CAB, or ∠A.

Angles are measured in degrees. For example, the measure of ∠A is 45°. You can write "the measure of ∠A" as m∠A.

Classifying Angles

Angles are classified by their measures.

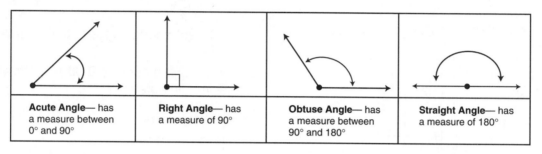

| Acute Angle— has a measure between 0° and 90° | Right Angle— has a measure of 90° | Obtuse Angle— has a measure between 90° and 180° | Straight Angle— has a measure of 180° |

Two angles are <u>complementary</u> if the sum of their measures is 90°. Two angles are <u>supplementary</u> if the sum of their measures is 180°. Two angles are <u>congruent</u> if they have the same measure.

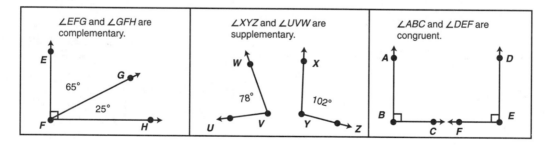

Types of Lines

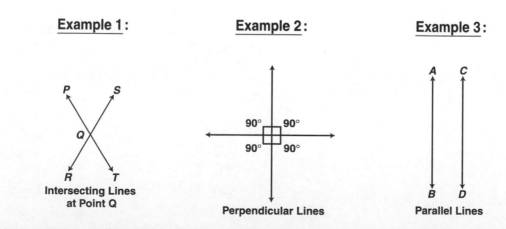

Example 1:
Intersecting Lines at Point Q

Example 2:
Perpendicular Lines

Example 3:
Parallel Lines

Lines and Angles

When two lines <u>intersect</u> (cross), four angles are formed. Each pair of nonadjacent angles are called <u>vertical angles</u>. Vertical angles are congruent.

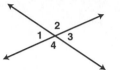

∠1 and ∠3 are vertical angles.
∠2 and ∠4 are vertical angles.

When a line called a <u>transversal</u> intersects two *parallel* lines (lines that are an equal distance apart at all points), pairs of angles called <u>corresponding angles</u> are formed. In the diagram, there are four pairs of corresponding angles. Because lines *p* and *q* are parallel, each pair of corresponding angles is congruent. The symbol ≅ means "is congruent to."

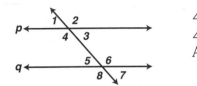

∠1 ≅ ∠5, ∠2 ≅ ∠6
∠3 ≅ ∠7, ∠4 ≅ ∠8
Also, ∠1 ≅ ∠3 ≅ ∠5 ≅ ∠7
∠2 ≅ ∠4 ≅ ∠6 ≅ ∠8

Triangles

A <u>triangle</u> is a three-sided polygon. A <u>polygon</u> is a closed figure in a plane that is made up of segments, called sides, that intersect only at their endpoints, called <u>vertices</u>.

Triangle *GED*, written △*GED*, has the following parts.

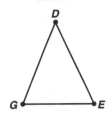

Sides: $\overline{GD}$, $\overline{DE}$, $\overline{EG}$
Vertices: *G, E, D*
Angles: ∠*GDE* or ∠*D*, ∠*GED* or ∠*E*, ∠*DGE* or ∠*G*

Classifying Triangles by Their Sides

Triangles can be classified according to the number of congruent sides they have.

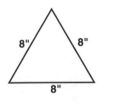

Equilateral: All Sides Equal

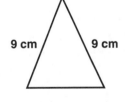

Isosceles: Two Equal Sides

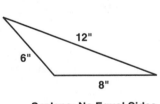

Scalene: No Equal Sides

Classifying Triangles by Their Angles

You can also classify triangles according to the measures of their angles. All triangles have at least two acute angles, but the third angle, which is used to classify the triangle, can be acute, right, or obtuse.

An **acute** triangle has three acute angles.
An **obtuse** triangle has one obtuse angle.

A **right** triangle has one right angle.
An **equiangular** triangle has three equal angles of 60°.

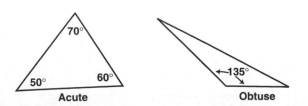

Acute   **Obtuse**   **Right**

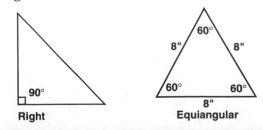

Equiangular

There are many basic principles or rules about triangles. The following rules will help you prepare for the GED Mathematics Test. If this is the first time you have studied basic geometry, your skills and knowledge will increase with practice.

Rule 1   The parts of an isosceles triangle have special names.

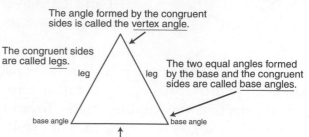

The angle formed by the congruent sides is called the vertex angle.

The congruent sides are called legs.

The two equal angles formed by the base and the congruent sides are called base angles.

base angle   base angle

The side opposite the vertex angle is called the base.

Rule 2   The sum of the lengths of any two sides of a triangle must always be greater than the third side.

Rule 3   The largest angle is opposite the longest side. In the right $\triangle ESL$, the right angle S is the largest angle. The side opposite the right angle is called the hypotenuse $(\overline{EL})$. In $\triangle XYZ$, $\angle Y$ is opposite the longest side $\overline{XZ}$.

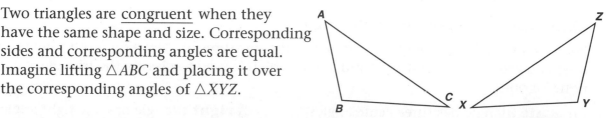

Rule 4   The sum of the three angles of a triangle is always 180°.

Rule 5   The sides that form the right angle in a right triangle are the legs of the triangle. The side opposite the right angle is the hypotenuse.

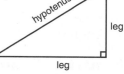

hypotenuse   leg

leg

Rule 6   The Pythagorean relationship is used to find the hypotenuse of a right triangle. The sum of the squares of the legs of a right triangle (a and b) equals the square of the hypotenuse (c).

$$c^2 = a^2 + b^2$$
$$c^2 = 6^2 + 8^2$$
$$c^2 = 36 + 64$$
$$c^2 = 100$$
$$\sqrt{c^2} = \sqrt{100}$$
$$c = 10$$

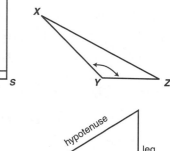

$a = 6$

$b = 8$

c

Rule 7   Two triangles are congruent when they have the same shape and size. Corresponding sides and corresponding angles are equal. Imagine lifting $\triangle ABC$ and placing it over the corresponding angles of $\triangle XYZ$.

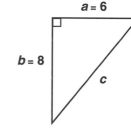

Rule 8   When two triangles have equal angles, the triangles are similar and have the same shape. A proportion can be made from corresponding sides of similar triangles.

$$\frac{4}{6} = \frac{8}{EG}$$
$$4\overline{EG} = 48$$
$$\frac{4\overline{EG}}{4} = \frac{48}{4}$$
$$\overline{EG} = 12$$

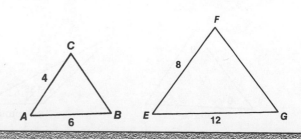

Directions: Use the information about angles, lines, and triangles to answer the following problems. Write the answers on the lines provided below the figures.

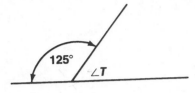

1. $m\angle T =$ _____

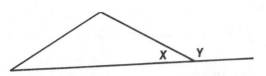

2. $m\angle X + m\angle Y =$ _____

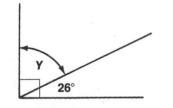

3. $m\angle Y =$ _____

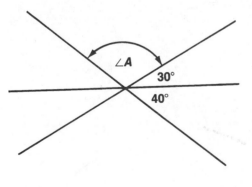

4. $m\angle A =$ _____

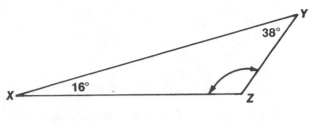

5. $m\angle Z =$ _____

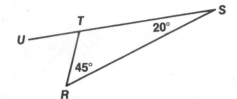

6. $m\angle RTU =$ _____

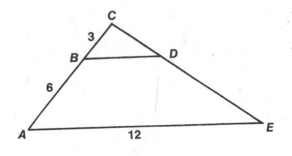

7. The value of x is _____

8. The length of $\overline{BD}$ is _____

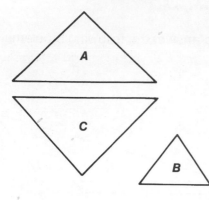

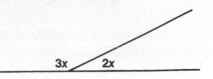

9. Which two of the above triangles appear to be congruent? _____

13. Find the value of *x*.

    x = _____

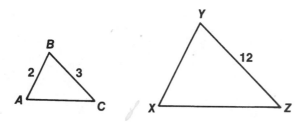

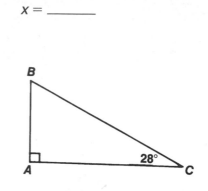

10. Find $\overline{XY}$ in △*XYZ* if △*ABC* and △*XYZ* are similar triangles.

    $\overline{XY}$ = _____

14. Find *m*∠*B*.

    m∠*B* = _____

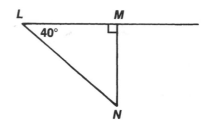

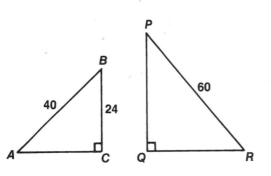

15. Find *m*∠*N*.

    m∠*N* = _____

11. Solve for $\overline{PQ}$ if △*ABC* and △*PQR* are similar.

    $\overline{PQ}$ = _____

12. The ratio of two complementary angles is 5:7. Find the measure of the larger angle.

    _____

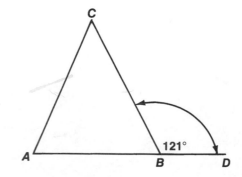

16. If $\overline{AC} = \overline{CB}$, find *m*∠*A*.

    m∠*A* = _____

By substituting the measurements of plane and solid geometric figures into formulas, you can solve a variety of problems. The measurements for the square and rectangle are referred to by the terms side, length, and width. When referring to the triangle, the terms base and height are used.

By adding the lengths and widths of the rectangle and square, you can find the distance around the objects, called the perimeter. The area of a figure is the surface that the figure covers. The volume of a three-dimensional figure is the space inside the figure. These formulas are given to you on the GED Mathematics Test.

Formulas for Perimeter, Circumference, Area, and Volume			
Rectangle $P = 2l + 2w$ $A = lw$	**Square** $P = 4s$ $A = s \times s = s^2$	**Triangle** $P = s + s + s$ $A = \frac{1}{2}bh$	**Circle** $C = \pi d$ or $2\pi r$ $A = \pi r^2$
Trapezoid $A = \frac{1}{2}h(b_1 + b_2)$	**Parallelogram** $A = bh$	**Cone** $V = \frac{1}{3}\pi r^2 h$	
Cylinder $V = \pi r^2 h$	**Rectangular solid** $V = lwh$	**Square Pyramid** $V = \frac{1}{3}bh$	**Cube** $V = s^3$

Rectangles, Squares, Triangles, Parallelograms, and Trapezoids

Example 1: Find the perimeter and area for each of the following.

Rectangle

8 in.

6 in.

Isosceles Triangle

5 in.   5 in.

4 in.

6 in.

$P = 2l + 2w$ $A = lw$
$= 2(8) + 2(6)$ $= 8 \cdot 6$
$= 16 + 12$ $= 48$ sq. in.
$= 28$ in.

$P = s + s + s$ $A = \frac{1}{2}bh$
$= 5 + 5 + 6$ $= \frac{1}{2}(6 \cdot 4) = \frac{24}{2}$
$= 16$ in. $= 12$ sq. in.

Parallelogram

10 mm

16 mm

20 mm

$P = 16 + 16 + 20 + 20$ $A = bh$
$= 72$ mm $= 20(10)$
                            $= 200$ sq. mm

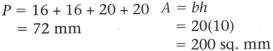

Example 2: Find the perimeter and area of this figure.

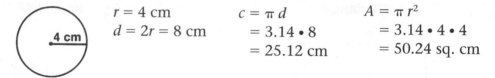

BCDE is a rectangle; therefore, $\overline{BC}$ is also 6 cm, and $\overline{AB}$ is $10 - 6$, or 4, cm. Since $\triangle ABE$ is a right triangle, you can use the Pythagorean relationship to find the length of $\overline{AE}$.

$$a^2 + b^2 = c^2$$
$$3^2 + 4^2 = c^2$$
$$9 + 16 = c^2$$
$$25 = c^2$$
$$c = \sqrt{25} = 5 \text{ cm}$$

Now find the perimeter and area.

$P = 10 + 3 + 6 + 5$
$P = 24$ cm

Area of rectangle *BCDE*:
$A = lw$
$= 6 \cdot 3$
$= 18$ sq. cm

Area of $\triangle ABE$
$A = \frac{1}{2}bh$
$= \frac{1}{2}(3)(4)$
$= 6$ sq. cm

Total area: $18 + 6 = 24$ sq. cm

Circles

<u>Circumference</u> is the distance around a circle. <u>Diameter</u> is the widest distance across a circle. The diameter always goes through the center of the circle. <u>Radius</u> is the distance from the center of the circle to the edge and always equals $\frac{1}{2}$ the diameter. The symbol π (pi) is a constant used in each of the formulas for the circle. The value of this constant is rounded to 3.14 or $\frac{22}{7}$.

Example 3: Find the circumference and area of the circle shown below.

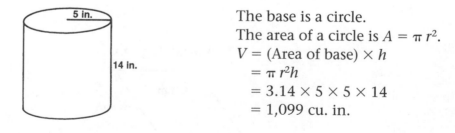

$r = 4$ cm
$d = 2r = 8$ cm

$c = \pi d$
$= 3.14 \cdot 8$
$= 25.12$ cm

$A = \pi r^2$
$= 3.14 \cdot 4 \cdot 4$
$= 50.24$ sq. cm

Volume of Geometric Solids

The <u>volume</u> of a three-dimensional figure is generally the area of the base of the figure times the height of the figure. (Cones and pyramids are exceptions.) When three like measurements are multiplied by each other, the answer is in <u>cubic</u> units.

Example 4: Find the volume of this cylinder.

The base is a circle.
The area of a circle is $A = \pi r^2$.
$V = (\text{Area of base}) \times h$
$= \pi r^2 h$
$= 3.14 \times 5 \times 5 \times 14$
$= 1,099$ cu. in.

Example 5: Find the volume of this rectangular solid if the length, width, and height are 7, 6, and 5 inches respectively.

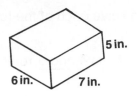

$V = lwh$
$= 7 \times 6 \times 5$
$= 210$ cu. in.

Example 6: Find the volume of this pyramid.

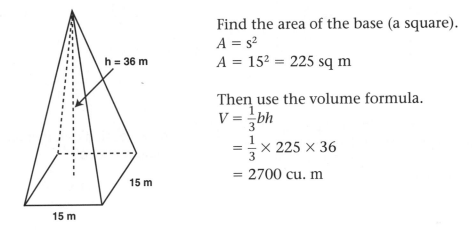

Find the area of the base (a square).
$A = s^2$
$A = 15^2 = 225$ sq m

Then use the volume formula.
$V = \frac{1}{3}bh$
$= \frac{1}{3} \times 225 \times 36$
$= 2700$ cu. m

Example 7: Find the volume of this cone to the nearest cubic inch.

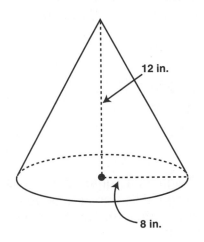

$V = \frac{1}{3}\pi r^2 h$
$= \frac{1}{3} \times 3.14 \times 8^2 \times 12$
$= \frac{1}{3} \times 3.14 \times 64 \times 12$
$= 803.84$, which rounds to 804 cu. in.

Directions: Select and then use the appropriate formula to solve each of the following problems. Choose the one best answer to each question.

Questions 1 and 2 refer to the following diagram.

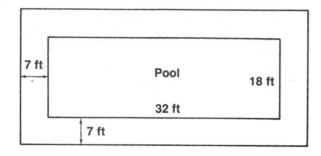

Questions 4 and 5 refer to the following figure.

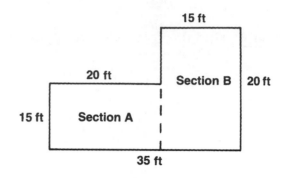

1. The measurements of a swimming pool are 32 feet by 18 feet. How much fencing is needed if the fence is to be built 7 feet from each side of the pool?

    (1) 100 ft.
    (2) 128 ft.
    (3) 134 ft.
    (4) 136 ft.
    (5) 156 ft.

2. Rectangular pool covers are sold in varying sizes. Which size cover would be the closest fit for the pool in the diagram above?

    (1) 400 sq. ft.
    (2) 500 sq. ft.
    (3) 600 sq. ft.
    (4) 700 sq. ft.
    (5) 800 sq. ft.

3. What is the area of a triangle whose base is 12 inches and height is 8 inches?

    (1) 100 sq. in.
    (2)   78 sq. in.
    (3)   50 sq. in.
    (4)   48 sq. in.
    (5)   15 sq. in.

4. Which expression determines the total area of the figure above?

    (1) $(15 \times 20) + (15 \times 20)$
    (2) $(15 \times 20)(15 \times 20)$
    (3) $(15 \times 20) - (15 \times 20)$
    (4) $(15 \times 20) \div (15 \times 20)$
    (5) $(15 \times 20 \times 20 \times 15)$

5. The diagram above is a driveway. How much will it cost to blacktop the driveway if blacktopping costs $2.50 per square foot?

    (1) $ 500
    (2) $ 750
    (3) $1,250
    (4) $1,500
    (5) $1,750

6. The height of a square pyramid is 12 cm. One edge of its base measures 7 cm. What is the volume of the pyramid in cubic centimeters?

    (1)   28 cu. cm
    (2)   49 cu. cm
    (3)   56 cu. cm
    (4) 196 cu. cm
    (5) Not enough information is given.

Questions 7 and 8 refer to the following diagram.

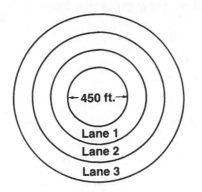

Question 10 refers to the following diagram.

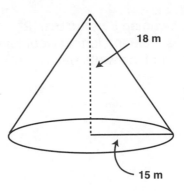

7. The diameter of the center of a circular three-lane auto racetrack is 450 feet. Each lane has a width of 40 feet. Which expression below determines the area of the racetrack?

(1) 3.14 × 370 × 370
(2) 3.14 × 345 × 345
(3) 3.14 × 120 × 120
(4) 3.14 × 570
(5) 3.14 × 450

8. What is the approximate outer circumference of the racetrack?

(1) 2,166.6 ft.
(2) 1,789.8 ft.
(3) 1,413.0 ft.
(4) 1,161.8 ft.
(5) 753.6 ft.

9. Jackie needed to buy a piece of glass to cover the top of a circular lamp table with a diameter of 24 inches. How much glass is needed for the job?

(1) 37.68 sq. in.
(2) 75.36 sq. in.
(3) 225.25 sq. in.
(4) 452.16 sq. in.
(5) 1,808.64 sq. in.

10. A pile of grain is shaped like a cone (as shown in the diagram). What is the volume of the pile of grain in cubic meters?

(1) 270
(2) 423
(3) 4,239
(4) 12,717
(5) 16,956

Question 11 refers to the following diagram.

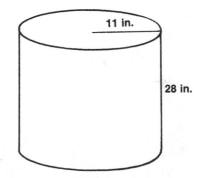

11. If one gallon contains 231 cubic inches, about how many gallons will the storage tank in the diagram hold?

(1) 11
(2) 46
(3) 90
(4) 121
(5) 10,638

Directions: Choose the one best answer to each question.

12. Vincent wanted to reduce a 12" × 16" picture so that the length would be 12". What would the width be?

    (1) 5 in.
    (2) 7 in.
    (3) 9 in.
    (4) 10 in.
    (5) 11 in.

Question 13 refers to the following diagram.

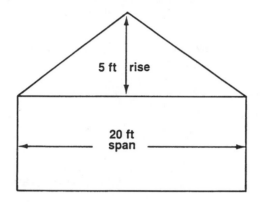

13. The pitch of a roof is the ratio of the vertical rise to the span. What is the pitch of a roof if the rise is 5 feet and the span is 20 feet?

    (1) 20:5
    (2) 5:1
    (3) 3:1
    (4) 1:4
    (5) 1:3

14. A 6-foot pole casts a 4-foot shadow. If the shadow of a tree is 25 feet, what is the height of the tree?

    (1) $25\frac{1}{2}$ ft.
    (2) $30\frac{1}{2}$ ft.
    (3) $37\frac{1}{2}$ ft.
    (4) $40\frac{1}{2}$ ft.
    (5) $45\frac{1}{2}$ ft.

15. A 3-foot seedling casts a 4-foot shadow at the same time a tree casts a 72-foot shadow. How tall is the tree?

    (1) 27 ft.
    (2) 54 ft.
    (3) 60 ft.
    (4) 72 ft.
    (5) 80 ft.

Question 16 refers to the following diagram.

16. The figure above shows a metal rod labeled AC in which AB:BC = 2:3. What is the length of the rod?

    (1) 20 ft.
    (2) 21 ft.
    (3) 24 ft.
    (4) 25 ft.
    (5) 30 ft.

Question 17 refers to the following diagram.

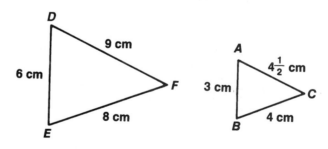

17. What kind of triangles are shown?

    (1) right
    (2) similar
    (3) congruent
    (4) equilateral
    (5) Not enough information is given.

Question 18 refers to the following diagram.

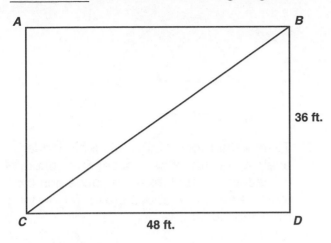

18. The rectangular flower bed in the center of a courtyard was planted with two colors of flowers. What is the length of $\overline{BC}$ in the diagram dividing the two colors of flowers?

(1) 50 ft.
(2) 60 ft.
(3) 65 ft.
(4) 70 ft.
(5) 75 ft.

Question 19 refers to the following diagram.

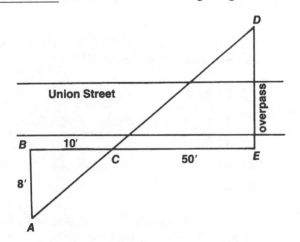

19. The engineers planned to build an overpass over Union Street. How long must the overpass $\overline{DE}$ be?

(1) 20 ft.
(2) 40 ft.
(3) 60 ft.
(4) 80 ft.
(5) 100 ft.

Question 20 refers to the following diagram.

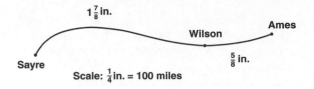

Scale: $\frac{1}{4}$ in. = 100 miles

20. How many miles does Alfred travel if he starts at Sayre and ends at Ames?

(1) 100 miles
(2) 150 miles
(3) 200 miles
(4) 250 miles
(5) 1,000 miles

Question 21 refers to the following diagram.

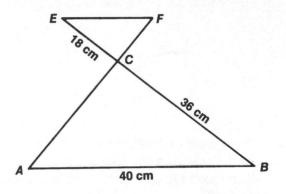

21. If triangles ACB and ECF are similar, what is the length of $\overline{EF}$ in the diagram above?

(1) 12 cm
(2) 18 cm
(3) 20 cm
(4) 24 cm
(5) 30 cm

22. Margaret is putting ribbon around a 12" × 18" bulletin board. How many feet of ribbon should she buy?

(1) 1
(2) $2\frac{1}{2}$
(3) 4
(4) 5
(5) 18

Question 23 refers to the following diagram.

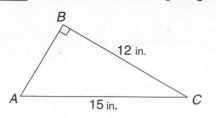

23. The triangle above is a right triangle. What is the length of $\overline{AB}$?

(1) 3 in.
(2) 4 in.
(3) 9 in.
(4) 12 in.
(5) 15 in.

Question 24 refers to the following diagram.

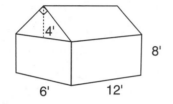

24. Stuart wants to put a new roof on his storage shed. He knows the roof is 12' long. Which expression should he use to find the width of the roof?

(1) 6×12
(2) $\frac{1}{2} \times 6 \times 4$
(3) $\sqrt{3^2 + 4^2}$
(4) $\sqrt{3^2 + 6^2}$
(5) $2(6) + 2(12)$

25. In a right triangle the short leg is 11 and the hypotenuse is 15. Which expression below will give the length of the other leg?

(1) $\sqrt{15 + 11}$
(2) $\sqrt{15 - 11}$
(3) $\sqrt{225 + 121}$
(4) $\sqrt{225 - 121}$
(5) Not enough information is given.

Question 26 refers to the following diagram.

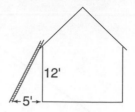

26. To repair her roof, Margie placed a ladder against the side of her house. The bottom of the ladder is 5 feet from the house and the top extends 2 feet above the roof. How long must the ladder be?

(1) 12 ft.
(2) 13 ft.
(3) 14 ft.
(4) 15 ft.
(5) 16 ft.

Question 27 refers to the following diagram.

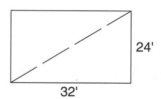

27. What is the length of the diagonal for the cement slab shown above?

(1) 27 ft.
(2) 30 ft.
(3) 40 ft.
(4) 45 ft.
(5) 56 ft.

28. In a right triangle, one acute angle is 30°. What is the measure of the other acute angle?

(1) 30°
(2) 45°
(3) 60°
(4) 90°
(5) 180°

Directions: Choose the one best answer to each question. You MAY use your calculator.

1. The length of a rectangle is 28 inches and the perimeter is 84 inches. What is the area of the rectangle?

   (1)   392 sq. in.
   (2)   784 sq. in.
   (3)   920 sq. in.
   (4) 1,000 sq. in.
   (5) 1,568 sq. in.

Question 2 refers to the following figure.

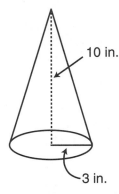

2. What is the volume of this cone in square inches?

   (1)   14.1 sq. in.
   (2)   18.8 sq. in.
   (3)   42.2 sq. in.
   (4)   94.2 sq. in.
   (5) 102.4 sq. in.

3. A rectangle and a triangle have equal areas. The length and width of the rectangle are 24 cm and 8 cm respectively. If the base of the triangle is 16 cm, what is the height of the triangle?

   (1) 24 cm
   (2) 20 cm
   (3) 16 cm
   (4) 12 cm
   (5)   8 cm

4. Al wants to build a concrete patio 9 inches thick. If the length of the patio is $14\frac{1}{2}$ feet and the width is $12\frac{3}{4}$ feet, about how many cubic feet of concrete will Al need?

   (1) 3,672 cu. ft.
   (2) 1,479 cu. ft.
   (3)   184 cu. ft.
   (4)   139 cu. ft.
   (5)   26 cu. ft.

5. Find the area of this parallelogram.

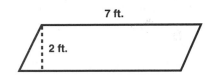

   (1)   7 sq. ft.
   (2)   9 sq. ft.
   (3) 14 sq. ft.
   (4) 18 sq. ft.
   (5) Not enough information is given.

6. A pyramid with a square base has one edge labeled 18 mm and a height of 36.5 mm. Which of the following expressions can be used to find the volume of the pyramid in cubic millimeters?

   (1) $18^3 (36.5)$
   (2) $\frac{1}{3} (18^2) (36.5)$
   (3) $18^2 (36.5)$
   (4) $\frac{1}{3} (18) (36.5)$
   (5) Not enough information is given.

7. In the figure below, if a ∥ b, b ∥ c, and a⊥d, which of the following statements must be true?

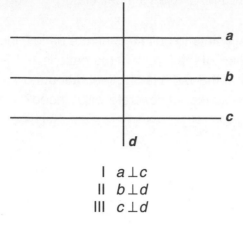

I $a \perp c$
II $b \perp d$
III $c \perp d$

(1) none
(2) I only
(3) I and II only
(4) II and III only
(5) I, II, and III

Question 8 refers to the following diagram.

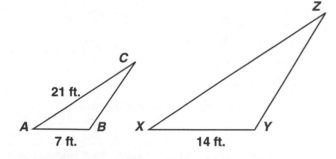

8. Triangular gardens ABC and XYZ are similar. If $\overline{A}$ = 21 feet, $\overline{AB}$ = 7 feet, and $\overline{XY}$ = 14 feet, what is the length of $\overline{XZ}$?

(1)   7 ft.
(2)   21 ft.
(3)   42 ft.
(4)   84 ft.
(5)   294 ft.

9. If the outer diameter of a cylindrical tube is 27.14 inches and the inner diameter is 24.36 inches, how thick is the wall?

(1) 3.14 in.
(2) 2.79 in.
(3) 2.42 in.
(4) 2.29 in.
(5) 1.39 in.

10. The dimensions of a rectangular solid are 2, 3, and 4 inches (l, w, h). If the dimensions are doubled, what is the ratio between the volume of the original and the volume of the new rectangular solid?

(1) 1:2
(2) 1:8
(3) 2:1
(4) 2:5
(5) 3:4

11. The legs of a right triangle measure 18 inches and 24 inches. How long is the hypotenuse?

(1) 18 in.
(2) 20 in.
(3) 24 in.
(4) 26 in.
(5) 30 in.

12. What is the area in square feet of the figure below?

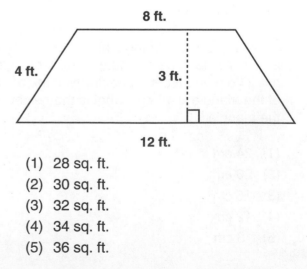

(1) 28 sq. ft.
(2) 30 sq. ft.
(3) 32 sq. ft.
(4) 34 sq. ft.
(5) 36 sq. ft.

Questions 13 and 14 refer to the following diagram.

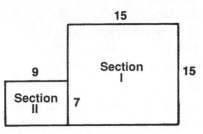

13. Which expression below shows the difference in area between Section I and Section II?

(1) $(7 \times 9) - (8 \times 9)$
(2) $(7 + 9) - (15 + 15)$
(3) $(15 \times 15) - (7 \times 9)$
(4) $(15 + 24) - 2(7 + 9)$
(5) $(15 \times 24) - (9 - 7)$

14. Which expression below shows the difference in perimeter between Section I and Section II?

(1) $2(7 + 9) - 2(15 + 24)$
(2) $2(7 \times 9) - 2(15 \times 24)$
(3) $2(15 + 15) - 2(7 + 9)$
(4) $2(15 + 24) - (7 + 9)$
(5) $2(15 + 24) - (7 \times 9)$

15. The perimeter of a rectangular garden is 84 feet. If the length is 24 feet, what is the width?

(1) 30 ft.
(2) 24 ft.
(3) 20 ft.
(4) 18 ft.
(5) 16 ft.

16. The perimeter of a rectangle is 80 feet. If its length is 20 feet 6 inches, what is the width of the rectangle?

(1) 29 ft.
(2) $19\frac{1}{2}$ ft.
(3) 18 ft. 6 in.
(4) 18 ft.
(5) 16 ft.

17. The area of one face of a cube is 25 sq. ft. What is the volume of the cube in cubic feet?

(1)   5 cu. ft.
(2)   25 cu. ft.
(3) 125 cu. ft.
(4) 225 cu. ft.
(5) 250 cu. ft.

Questions 18 and 19 refer to the following diagram.

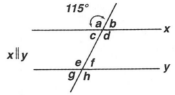

18. How many degrees are in $\angle b$?

(1) 115°
(2)   65°
(3) $57\frac{1}{2}°$
(4)   25°
(5) none of these

19. Which angle corresponds to $\angle c$?

(1) $\angle a$
(2) $\angle b$
(3) $\angle e$
(4) $\angle f$
(5) $\angle g$

Question 20 refers to the following diagram.

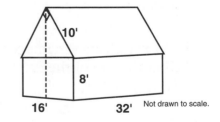

Not drawn to scale.

20. If the height of the barn walls is 8 feet, how high is the center of the roof from the ground?

(1)   6 ft.
(2)   8 ft.
(3)   11 ft.
(4)   14 ft.
(5)   32 ft.

Using the Calculator

When you take the GED Mathematics Test, you will be allowed to use a calculator on Part I of the test. This calculator, which will be provided by the testing center, is the CASIO *fx-260solar*. The information in this handbook is provided to help you use the calculator effectively.

The CASIO *fx-260solar* is a scientific calculator. Scientific calculators vary widely, some with a few functions and others with many functions. The CASIO *fx-260solar* has many more keys and functions than you need for the test. The keys that will be most helpful to you are labeled in the diagram below.

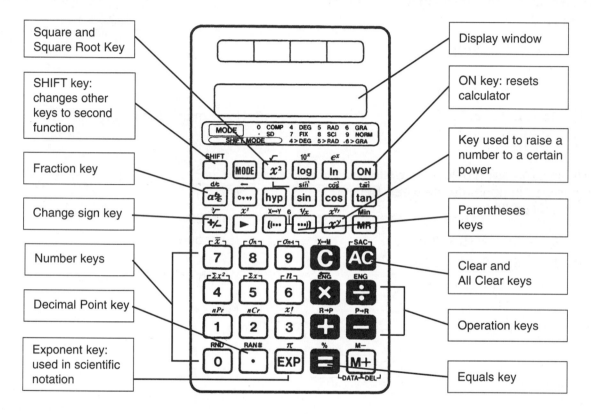

The display window is the calculator area that shows the numbers you have entered and results of calculations.

ON   The On key clears the memory and sets the display to 0. You will see the small letters "DEG" at the top of the display window, which shows that the calculator is in the proper format for your use.

AC   The All Clear key clears all the numbers and operations from the display. Always press AC or ON when you are ready to start a new problem.

C   The Clear key erases only the last number or operation that you entered. Use this key when you know that you have entered a number or sign incorrectly. Press C, then enter the correct number or operation.

(SHIFT)   The Shift key is used to get the second function for any key. The second functions are listed above each key. Press the Shift key to access any of these functions.

(=)   The Equals key shows the results of calculations you have entered.

(EXP)   The Exponent key is used to calculate a number to a power of ten.

(+) (−) (×) (÷) are the operations keys and permit you to perform basic arithmetic calculations: addition, subtraction, multiplication, and division. You may add or multiply in any order. But you must use correct order for division and subtraction. For division, enter the number being divided first. For subtraction, enter the number being taken away second.

(+/−)   Changes the sign of a number. To enter a negative number, enter the digits of the number first, then press (+/−).

Examples

Solve: 15 + (−25)   Enter: 15 (+) 25 (+/−) (=) −10

Solve: −12 × 20 ÷ (−2)   Enter: 12 (+/−) (×) 20 (÷) 2 (+/−) (=) 120

[(--) and (--)] are parentheses used to group symbols when an expression contains more than one operation. Put grouping symbols around the operation that must be performed first. Without parentheses, the calculator will always perform the multiplication and division steps first (following the order of operations).

Examples

Solve: $\dfrac{-12+8}{2}$ Enter: [(--) 12 (+/−) (+) 8 (--)] (÷) 2 (=) −2

Solve: 6(15 + 24)   Enter: 6 (×) [(--) 15 (+) 24 (--)] (=) 234

In the last example, the algebraic expression shows the number 6 next to an operation in parentheses. Remember that this means multiply. To evaluate the expression using a calculator, you must press (×) before entering the operation in parentheses.

(π)   Use the second function of (EXP) to evaluate an expression containing *pi* (π). Notice that the symbol π is printed above (EXP). Press (SHIFT) then (EXP) to access π.

Example

Solve: Find 12π.   Enter: 12 (×) (SHIFT) (EXP) (=) 37.69911184

    Enter: 12 (×) 3.14 (=) 37.68

%   The percent function is the second function of = . Using this function, you can enter a percent as written instead of converting it to a decimal.

Example

Solve: Find 65% of 150.   Enter: 150 ⊗ 65 (SHIFT) (=) 97.5

Order of Operations

Some calculators automatically follow the rules for order of operations. This is known as the algebraic ordering system. Other calculators carry out operations in the order that you enter them, even if that order is different from the rules. The CASIO *fx-260SOLAR* that you will use on the GED Mathematics Test is programmed with the order of operations.

Example

Nicky is buying 4 CDs that cost $12.99 each. If she gives the cashier a $100 bill, how much change should she receive?

To solve this problem using a CASIO *fx-260SOLAR* calculator, key in the expression to get an answer of 48.04.

$100 - (4 \times 12.99) = \$48.04$

Nicky should receive $48.04 in change.

Fractions and Decimals

Most calculators use only decimals and whole numbers, and many, like the CASIO *fx-260SOLAR*, will show a decimal to the right of the ones place. When using a calculator, you may change a fraction to a decimal, for example, $\frac{1}{4}$ to 0.25.

Example

Jason bought a DVD player for $495 and made a down payment of $\frac{1}{4}$ of the cost. How much was the down payment?

To solve this problem on a CASIO *fx-260SOLAR* calculator, you could change the $\frac{1}{4}$ to 0.25. Then enter the following:

$0.25 \times 495 =$

Since $\frac{1}{4}$ also means 1 divided by 4, you could use also use this sequence.

$1 \div 4 \times 495 =$

Or, you could use (a b/c). Use this sequence: 1 (a b/c) 4 ⊗ 495 (=). Then change your answer to a decimal by pressing (a b/c) again.

Either way, the down payment was $123.75.

If you are working with a mixed number like $1\frac{3}{4}$, you could keep the whole number as it is and change the fraction to a decimal. Thus you would use the form 1.75.

Or, you could use ⎡a b/c⎤. Press 1 ⎡a b/c⎤ 3 ⎡a b/c⎤ 4 to have the calculator read 1 ⌐3 ⌐4, meaning $1\frac{3}{4}$.

Percents

The percent key is one of the most useful keys on a calculator. When you use this key, you will not have to change a percent to a decimal or a decimal to a percent.

Example

Matilda paid 25% of her monthly salary of $2,455 for rent. How much did she pay for rent?

To solve this problem using the calculator, you do not have to change the percent to a decimal. Instead key in the following:

2,455 × 25 % =

The correct answer is $613.75.

Remember: You must press ⎡SHIFT⎤ and ⎡=⎤ to work with a percent.

Squares and Square Roots

⎡x²⎤ is the square key. Use it to square numbers or to perform operations using squares. This feature is useful when solving problems involving the Pythagorean Relationship.

Examples

Solve:	$9^2 = ?$	Enter: 9 ⎡x²⎤ 81
Solve:	$15^2 - 12^2 = ?$	Enter: 15 ⎡x²⎤ ⎡−⎤ 12 ⎡x²⎤ ⎡=⎤ 81
Solve:	$c = 9^2 + 4^2$	Enter: 9 ⎡x²⎤ ⎡+⎤ 4 ⎡x²⎤ ⎡=⎤ 97

The **square root function** is the second operation assigned to the ⎡x²⎤ key. To find the square root of a number, enter the number, then press SHIFT and the square key.

Examples

Solve:	Enter:
What is the square root of 385?	385 ⎡SHIFT⎤ ⎡x²⎤ (19.62141687 will be displayed)
Solve:	Enter:
$\sqrt{125} + \sqrt{36} = ?$	125 ⎡SHIFT⎤ ⎡x²⎤ ⎡+⎤ 36 ⎡SHIFT⎤ ⎡x²⎤ ⎡=⎤ 17.18033989

Exponents and Scientific Notation

To raise a number to a power other than 2, use $\boxed{x^y}$. Enter the base, press $\boxed{x^y}$, and enter the exponent.

Examples

Solve:	$6^4 = ?$	Enter: 6 $\boxed{x^y}$ 4 $\boxed{=}$ 1296
Solve:	$15^5 + 4^3 = ?$	Enter: 15 $\boxed{x^y}$ 5 $\boxed{+}$ 4 $\boxed{x^y}$ 3 $\boxed{=}$ 759439

In scientific notation, a number greater than or equal to one and less than ten is multiplied by a power of ten. Use the EXP key to enter a number given in scientific notation as standard notation.

Examples

Solve:	Express 4.2×10^7 in standard notation.	Enter: 4.2 $\boxed{EXP}$ 7 $\boxed{=}$ 42000000
Solve:	Express 5.78×10^6 in standard notation.	Enter: 5.78 $\boxed{EXP}$ 6 $\boxed{=}$ 5780000

Calculator instructions will be distributed at the time you take Part I of the GED Mathematics Test. Turn to page 100 or 118 to see these instructions.

Using Special Formats

What is the Standard Grid?

One type of special format question that appears on the GED Mathematics Test is the standard grid. Instead of choosing an answer in a multiple-choice question, you must find the answer yourself. Then you write and bubble in your answer on the grid.

Writing Whole Numbers in the Standard Grid

Example   Solve: Helen drove 195 miles on Monday and 228 miles on Tuesday.
How many miles did she drive in the two days?
The total number of miles for the two days is 195 + 228 = 423.

1. Write the answer 423 in the blank first row.

2. Darken in the corresponding circled numbers in the columns below. Note that the answer can start in one of several columns. Three correctly completed grids are shown below.

 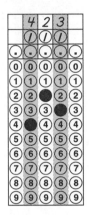 

Writing Fractions in the Standard Grid

Example   On Monday morning, 8 out of 29 customers at Bennie's Burrito paid cash.
What fraction paid cash?
The fraction is $\frac{8}{29}$. Two correctly completed grids are below.

Writing Decimals in the Standard Grid

Example Nathan studied for 2.35 hours on Monday, 4.25 hours on Tuesday, and 3.6 hours on Wednesday. How many hours did Nathan study in all during the three days? The problem asks you to find the total number of hours that Nathan spent studying. Add together the hours he studied: 2.35 + 4.25 + 3.6 = 10.2

Fill in your answer on the grid. Both grids shown below are filled in correctly.

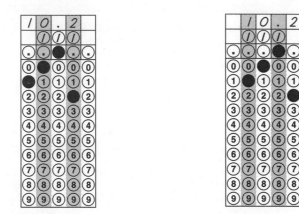

Converting Mixed Numbers for the Standard Grid

Example Maya worked $8\frac{1}{4}$ hours on Monday and $9\frac{1}{2}$ hours on Tuesday. How many hours did Maya work over the two days?

$$8\frac{1}{4} + 9\frac{1}{2} = 17\frac{3}{4}$$

The total number of hours that Maya worked is $17\frac{3}{4}$. Since you cannot enter mixed numbers on the standard grid, first change $17\frac{3}{4}$ to an improper fraction, $\frac{71}{4}$ or a decimal, 17.75. All grids shown below are correctly completed.

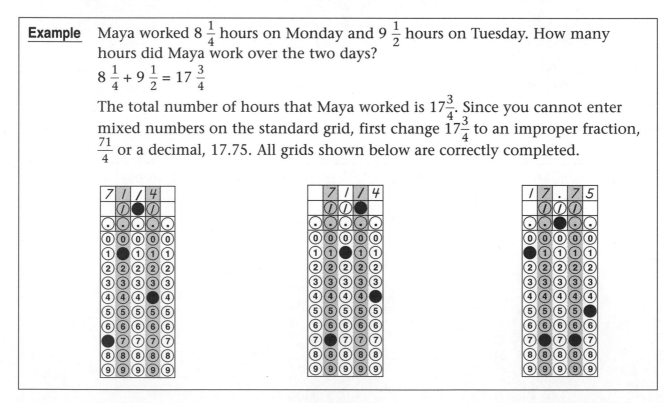

Note: Symbols such as $ and % cannot be entered into the grid. If the answer to a problem is in dollars or percent, grid the answer without the symbol.

Using the Coordinate Plane Grid

Questions on the GED Mathematics Test ask you to show the location of a point on a coordinate plane grid. To use the coordinate plane grid to record your answers, darken the bubbles to represent the ordered pair that shows that location.

Example   Three points are graphed on the coordinate plane grid shown below.

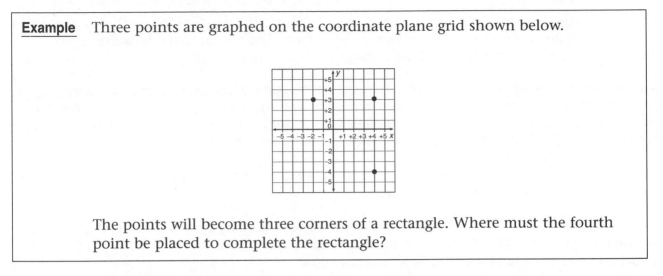

The points will become three corners of a rectangle. Where must the fourth point be placed to complete the rectangle?

Step 1   Complete the rectangle to find the location of the fourth point. A rectangle has four sides, and the opposite sides must be the same length. The remaining point must be at (−2,−4).

Step 2   Bubble in your answer on the coordinate plane grid. Start at the origin. Count 2 units left, then count 4 down. Fill in the circle neatly and completely.

The coordinate plane grid below shows the correct location of the fourth point.

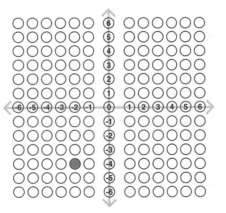

MATHEMATICS
Part I
Directions

The Mathematics Test consists of multiple-choice and alternate format questions intended to measure your general mathematical skills and problem-solving ability. The questions are based on short readings that often include a graph, chart, or diagram.

You will have 45 minutes to complete the 25 questions on Part I. Work carefully, but do not spend too much time on any one question. Be sure to answer every question. You will not be penalized for incorrect answers. When time is up, mark the last item you finished. This will tell you whether you can finish the real GED Test in the time allowed. Then complete the test.

Formulas you may need are given on page 101. Only some of the questions will require you to use a formula. Not all the formulas given will be needed.

Some questions contain more information than you will need to solve the problem; other questions do not give enough information. If the question does not give enough information to solve the problem, the correct answer choice is "Not enough information is given."

You may use a calculator on Part I. Calculator directions for the CASIO *fx-260SOLAR* scientific calculator can be found on page 100.

Record your answers on a copy of the separate answer sheet provided on page 171. Be sure all required information is properly recorded on the answer sheet.

To record your answers, mark the numbered space on the answer sheet that corresponds to the answer you select for each question on the test.

Example: If a grocery bill totaling $15.75 is paid with a $20.00 bill, how much change should be returned?

(1) $5.25
(2) $4.75
(3) $4.25
(4) $3.75
(5) $3.25

① ② ● ④ ⑤

The correct answer is $4.25; therefore, answer space 3 would be marked on the answer sheet.

Do not rest the point of your pencil on the answer sheet while you are considering your answer. Make no stray or unnecessary marks. If you change an answer, erase your first mark completely. Mark only one answer for each question; multiple answers will be scored as incorrect. Do not fold or crease your answer sheet.

When you finish the test, use the Performance Analysis Chart on page 115 to determine whether you are ready to take the real GED Test, and, if not, which skill areas need additional review.

Adapted with permission of the American Council on Education.

MATHEMATICS

Mixed numbers, such as $3\frac{1}{2}$, cannot be entered in the alternate format grid. Instead, represent them as decimal numbers (in this case, 3.5) or fractions $\left(\text{in this case, } \frac{7}{2}\right)$. No answer can be a negative number, such as -8.

To record your answer for an alternate format question

• begin in any column that will allow your answer to be entered;
• write your answer in the boxes on the top row;
• in the column beneath a fraction bar or decimal point (if any) and each number in your answer, fill in the bubble representing that character;
• leave blank any unused column.

Example:

The scale on a map indicates that $\frac{1}{2}$ inch represents an actual distance of 120 miles. In inches, how far apart on the map will two towns be if the actual distance between them is 180 miles?

The answer to the above example is $\frac{3}{4}$, or 0.75, inches. The answer could be gridded using any of the methods below.

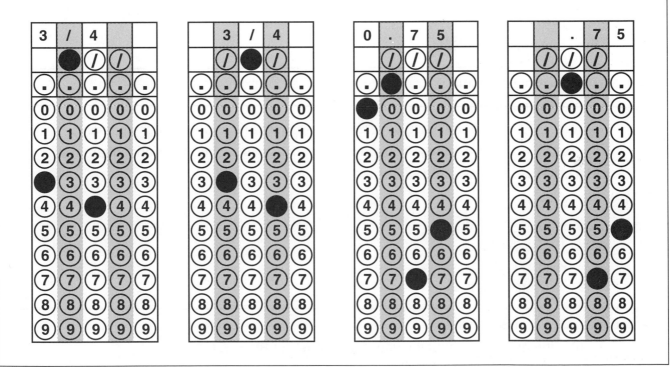

Points to remember:

• The answer sheet will be machine scored. **The circles must be filled in correctly.**
• Mark no more than one circle in any column.
• Grid only one answer even if there is more than one correct answer.
• A mixed number, such as $3\frac{1}{2}$, must be gridded as a decimal (3.5) or fraction $\left(\frac{7}{2}\right)$.
• No answer can be a negative number.

Adapted with permission of the American Council on Education.

CALCULATOR DIRECTIONS

To prepare the calculator for use the *first* time, press the (ON) (upper-rightmost) key. "DEG" will appear at the top-center of the screen and "0" at the right. This indicates the calculator is in the proper format for all your calculations.

To prepare the calculator for *another* question, press the (ON) or the red (AC) key. This clears any entries made previously.

To do any arithmetic, enter the expression as it is written. Press (=) (equals sign) when finished.

EXAMPLE A: $8 - 3 + 9$

> First press (ON) or (AC) .
> Enter the following:
>
> 8 (−) 3 (+) 9 (=)
>
> The correct answer is 14.

If an expression in parentheses is to be multiplied by a number, press (×) (multiplication sign) between the number and the parenthesis sign.

EXAMPLE B: $6(8 + 5)$

> First press (ON) or (AC) .
> Enter the following:
>
> 6 (×) ([(---) 8 (+) 5 (---)]) (=)
>
> The correct answer is 78.

To find the square root of a number

> • enter the number;
> • press (SHIFT) (upper-leftmost) key ("SHIFT" appears at the top-left of the screen);
> • press (x^2) (third from the left on top row) to access its second function: square root.
>   **DO NOT** press (SHIFT) and (x^2) at the same time.

EXAMPLE C: $\sqrt{64}$

> First press (ON) or (AC) .
> Enter the following:
>
> 64 (SHIFT) (x^2)
>
> The correct answer is 8.

To enter a negative number such as −8,

> • enter the number without the negative sign (enter 8);
> • press the "change sign" ((+/−)) key which is directly above the 7 key.

All arithmetic can be done with positive and/or negative numbers.

EXAMPLE D: $-8 - -5$

> First press (ON) or (AC) .
> Enter the following:
>
> 8 (+/−) (−) 5 (+/−) (=)
>
> The correct answer is −3.

Adapted with permission of the American Council on Education.

FORMULAS

AREA of a:

square	Area = side^2
rectangle	Area = length × width
parallelogram	Area = base × height
triangle	Area = $\frac{1}{2}$ × base × height
trapezoid	Area = $\frac{1}{2}$ × (base$_1$ + base$_2$) × height
circle	Area = π × radius^2; π is approximately equal to 3.14

PERIMETER of a:

square	Perimeter = 4 × side
rectangle	Perimeter = 2 × length + 2 × width
triangle	Perimeter = side$_1$ + side$_2$ + side$_3$
CIRCUMFERENCE of a circle	Circumference = π × diameter; π is approximately equal to 3.14

VOLUME of a:

cube	Volume = edge^3
rectangular container	Volume = length × width × height
square pyramid	Volume = $\frac{1}{3}$ × (base edge)^2 × height
cylinder	Volume = π × radius^2 × height; π is approximately equal to 3.14
cone	Volume = $\frac{1}{3}$ × π × radius^2 × height; π is approximately equal to 3.14

COORDINATE GEOMETRY	distance between points = $\sqrt{(x_2 - x_1)^2 + (y_2 - y_1)^2}$; (x_1, y_1) and (x_2, y_2) are two points in a plane.
	slope of a line = $\frac{y_2 - y_1}{x_2 - x_1}$; (x_1, y_1) and (x_2, y_2) are two points on a line.
PYTHAGOREAN RELATIONSHIP	$a^2 + b^2 = c^2$; a and b are legs and c the hypotenuse of a right triangle.
MEASURES OF CENTRAL TENDENCY	**mean** = $\frac{x_1 + x_2 + \ldots + x_n}{n}$; where the x's are the values for which a mean is desired, and n is the total number of values for x.
	median = the middle value of an odd number of *ordered* scores, and halfway between the two middle values of an even number of *ordered* scores.
SIMPLE INTEREST	interest = principal × rate × time
DISTANCE	distance = rate × time
TOTAL COST	total cost = (number of units) × (price per unit)

Adapted with permission of the American Council on Education.

Part I

Directions: You will have 45 minutes to complete questions 1–25. Choose the <u>one best answer</u> to each question. You MAY use your calculator.

1. Guido purchased a coat on sale from a menswear store for 40% off the original price of $144. If the sales tax was 5%, what amount of change did Guido receive from a $100 bill?

    (1) $ 9.28
    (2) $13.60
    (3) $44.00
    (4) $52.40
    (5) $57.60

2. Suppose you were applying for a job with a construction firm. They want to know if you can draw to scale. If you draw the lot shown below, with a scale of $\frac{1}{2}$ inch to equal 10 feet, what would be the dimensions of the lot in inches?

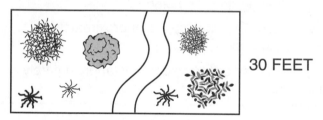

30 FEET

100 FEET

    (1) 1.0 × 0.3
    (2) 10 × 3
    (3) 3 × 1.5
    (4) 5 × 1.5
    (5) 6 × 20

3. What is the value of y if $y - 14 = 10 - y$?

    (1) −12
    (2) −2
    (3)   2
    (4) 12
    (5) 24

4. Tanya has three lengths of rope measuring $3\frac{1}{2}$ inches, $7\frac{3}{4}$ inches, and 4 inches. How many inches of rope does she have altogether?

    Mark your answer in the circles in the grid on your answer sheet.

5. The temperature at 12:00 noon is −12°F. At 2:00 P.M. the temperature is 6°F. If the temperature rises at a constant rate, what will be the temperature reading in degrees Fahrenheit at 4 P.M.?

    Mark your answer in the circles in the grid on your answer sheet.

Questions 6 and 7 refer to the following diagram.

SIGHT AND SOUND CD SALES

EACH O REPRESENTS 600 CDS	
COUNTRY AND WESTERN	o o o o o o o o o
RHYTHM AND BLUES	o o o o o o
CLASSICAL	o o o
JAZZ	o o o o

6. How many more rhythm-and-blues CDs were sold than jazz CDs?

(1) 1,200
(2) 1,800
(3) 2,400
(4) 3,600
(5) 5,400

7. Which of the following expressions determines how many times greater the country-and-western CD sales were than classical CD sales?

(1) $9(600) = 3(600)$

(2) $\frac{9(600)}{3(600)}$

(3) $\frac{3(600)}{9(600)}$

(4) $9(600) + 3(600)$

(5) $9(600) - 3(600)$

Question 8 refers to the following diagram.

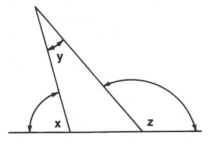

8. If $\angle z$ equals 120°, what is the measurement of $\angle y$?

(1) 80°
(2) 60°
(3) 40°
(4) 20°
(5) Not enough information is given.

Question 9 refers to the triangle below.

9. In the triangle, if $\overline{BF}$ bisects $\angle ABC$, $\overline{CD}$ bisects $\angle ACB$, the measurement of $\angle ABC$ = 68°, and the measurement of $\angle ACB$ = 72°, then the measurement of $\angle BEC$ =

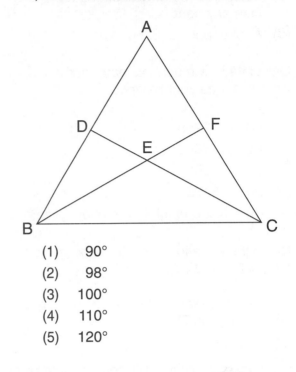

(1) 90°
(2) 98°
(3) 100°
(4) 110°
(5) 120°

10. Which of the following gives the correct answer to the question: "What is 5% of 380?"

(1) $\frac{380}{5}$

(2) $\frac{5}{380}$

(3) $5(380)$

(4) $0.5(380)$

(5) $0.05(380)$

11. Suppose there was the following activity one day in your checking account:

(a) deposited $630 check
(b) wrote a check for $125
(c) automatic withdrawal of $50 for loan payment
(d) ATM deposit of $250

Calculate how much this day's activity would change your balance.

(1) + $705
(2) + $805
(3) + $955
(4) +$1055
(5) Not enough information given.

12. Given the equation $x = 7(y - 2z)^2$, solve for x if $y = 9$ and $z = 2$.

Mark your answer in the circles in the grid on your answer sheet.

13. In a basketball game, Bill scored three times as many points as Jim. The sum of Bill and Jim's scores was 56 points. How many points did Bill score?

Mark your answer in the circles in the grid on your answer sheet.

Question 14 refers to the following chart.

Candidate	A	B	C	D	E
Number of Votes Received	40	90	204	?	10

14. In a town of 600 voters, 5 candidates ran for the office of mayor. If every voter voted for exactly one candidate, as illustrated in the chart above, what is the maximum number of votes Candidate D can receive?

(1) 120
(2) 256
(3) 334
(4) 466
(5) 500

Question 15 refers to the following diagram.

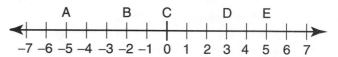

15. Which value on the number line above is equivalent to $-7.8 + 1.6 + 1.2$?

(1) A
(2) B
(3) C
(4) D
(5) E

Question 16 refers to the diagram below.

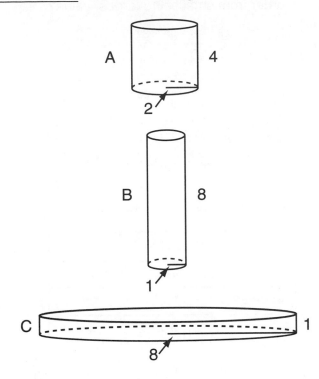

16. Which of the cylinders would hold the most water?

    (1) A
    (2) B
    (3) C
    (4) All cylinders hold the same amount of water.
    (5) Not enough information is given.

17. At what point does the graph of the line $y = 2x - 3$ cross the y-axis?

    Mark your answer in the circles on the coordinate plane grid on your answer sheet.

18. Which is the next value in the series $\sqrt{1}$, $\sqrt{4}$, $\sqrt{9}$, $\sqrt{16}$, $\sqrt{25}$?

    (1) $\sqrt{30}$
    (2) $\sqrt{36}$
    (3) $\sqrt{44}$
    (4) $\sqrt{49}$
    (5) $\sqrt{64}$

Question 19 refers to the following diagram.

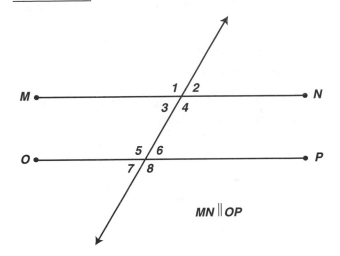

$MN \parallel OP$

19. Which statement is true about the diagram above?

    (1) $\angle 1$ is equal to $\angle 3$
    (2) $\angle 2$ and $\angle 8$ are alternate interior angles
    (3) $\angle 2$ and $\angle 6$ equal 180°
    (4) $\angle 2$ and $\angle 7$ equal 180°
    (5) $\angle 4$ and $\angle 5$ are alternate interior angles

20. Mountain Telephone Company charges $1.15 for the first three minutes and 12 cents for each additional minute for calls to Denver. What would be the cost of a 23-minute call?

    (1) $ 2.40
    (2) $ 2.76
    (3) $ 3.55
    (4) $ 3.91
    (5) $23.12

21. A hiker walks 12 miles due north. Then he turns and walks 16 miles due east. At this point, how many miles is the hiker from the starting point?

    Mark your answer in the circles in the grid on your answer sheet.

22. A carpet company runs the following ad in the newspaper:

    Free Carpet!
    For every 9 yards you buy, get 1 yard free!

    How much will 50 yards of carpet cost at $30.00 a yard if the customer takes advantage of this ad?

    Mark your answer in the circles in the grid on your answer sheet.

Question 23 refers to the following diagram.

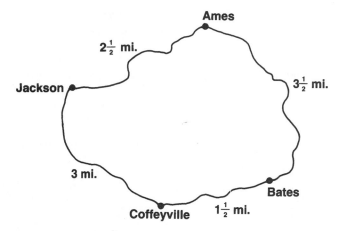

23. The Outfitters Backpacking Association planned its hiking outing to begin at Jackson and to end at Jackson. Which expression below states the average number of miles that the Outfitters planned to cover per hour if the hike was planned for 10 hours?

    (1) $\left(2\frac{1}{2} + 3 + 1\frac{1}{2} + 3\frac{1}{2}\right)$

    (2) $\left(2\frac{1}{2} + 3\frac{1}{2}\right)\left(3 + 1\frac{1}{2}\right) \div 4$

    (3) $\left(2\frac{1}{2} + 3\frac{1}{2}\right) - \left(3 + 1\frac{1}{2}\right) \div 10$

    (4) $\left(2\frac{1}{2} + 3\frac{1}{2} + 1\frac{1}{2} + 3\right) \div 10$

    (5) $\left(2\frac{1}{2} + 3\frac{1}{2}\right) \div \left(3 + 1\frac{1}{2}\right)$

24. Which of the following shows the correct order from smallest to largest value?

    (1) $\frac{2}{20}, \frac{28}{32}, \frac{15}{18}, \frac{32}{36}, \frac{32}{64}$

    (2) $\frac{28}{32}, \frac{15}{18}, \frac{32}{36}, \frac{32}{64}, \frac{2}{20}$

    (3) $\frac{15}{18}, \frac{32}{36}, \frac{32}{64}, \frac{2}{20}, \frac{28}{32}$

    (4) $\frac{2}{20}, \frac{32}{64}, \frac{15}{18}, \frac{28}{32}, \frac{32}{36}$

    (5) $\frac{32}{64}, \frac{15}{18}, \frac{28}{32}, \frac{2}{20}, \frac{32}{36}$

Question 25 refers to the chart below.

	WHOLE MILK	2% MILK
SERVING SIZE	8 oz	8 oz
CALORIES	150	120
FAT	8 g	4 g

25. After evaluating the nutrition information on the chart shown above, which of these is true for 2% milk?

    (1) It has 2% of the fat of whole milk.
    (2) It has one-half the fat of whole milk.
    (3) It has 2% of the nutritional value of whole milk.
    (4) It has 2% of the calories of whole milk.
    (5) It has one-half the calories of whole milk.

MATHEMATICS
Part II
Directions

The Mathematics Test consists of multiple-choice and alternate format questions intended to measure your general mathematical skills and problem-solving ability. The questions are based on short readings that often include a graph, chart, or diagram.

You will have 45 minutes to complete the 25 questions on Part II. Work carefully, but do not spend too much time on any one question. Be sure to answer every question. You will not be penalized for incorrect answers. When time is up, mark the last item you finished. This will tell you whether you can finish the real GED Test in the time allowed. Then complete the test.

Formulas you may need are given on page 109. Only some of the questions will require you to use a formula. Not all the formulas given will be needed.

Some questions contain more information than you will need to solve the problem; other questions do not give enough information. If the question does not give enough information to solve the problem, the correct answer choice is "Not enough information is given."

The use of calculators is not allowed on Part II.

Record your answers on a copy of the separate answer sheet provided on page 172. Be sure all required information is properly recorded on the answer sheet.

To record your answers, mark the numbered space on the answer sheet that corresponds to the answer you select for each question on the test.

Example: If a grocery bill totaling $15.75 is paid with a $20.00 bill, how much change should be returned?

(1) $5.25
(2) $4.75
(3) $4.25
(4) $3.75
(5) $3.25

① ② ● ④ ⑤

The correct answer is $4.25; therefore, answer space 3 would be marked on the answer sheet.

Do not rest the point of your pencil on the answer sheet while you are considering your answer. Make no stray or unnecessary marks. If you change an answer, erase your first mark completely. Mark only one answer for each question; multiple answers will be scored as incorrect. Do not fold or crease your answer sheet.

When you finish the test, use the Performance Analysis Chart on page 115 to determine whether you are ready to take the real GED Test, and, if not, which skill areas need additional review.

Adapted with permission of the American Council on Education.

MATHEMATICS

Mixed numbers, such as $3\frac{1}{2}$, cannot be entered in the alternate format grid. Instead, represent them as decimal numbers (in this case, 3.5) or fractions $\left(\text{in this case, } \frac{7}{2}\right)$. No answer can be a negative number, such as -8.

To record your answer for an alternate format question

- begin in any column that will allow your answer to be entered;
- write your answer in the boxes on the top row;
- in the column beneath a fraction bar or decimal point (if any) and each number in your answer, fill in the bubble representing that character;
- leave blank any unused column.

Example:

The scale on a map indicates that $\frac{1}{2}$ inch represents an actual distance of 120 miles. In inches, how far apart on the map will two towns be if the actual distance between them is 180 miles?

The answer to the above example is $\frac{3}{4}$, or 0.75, inches. The answer could be gridded using any of the methods below.

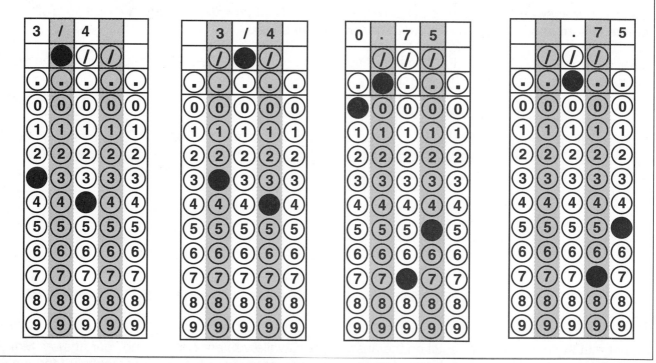

Points to remember:

- The answer sheet will be machine scored. **The circles must be filled in correctly.**
- Mark no more than one circle in any column.
- Grid only one answer even if there is more than one correct answer.
- A mixed number, such as $3\frac{1}{2}$, must be gridded as a decimal (3.5) or fraction $\left(\frac{7}{2}\right)$.
- No answer can be a negative number.

Adapted with permission of the American Council on Education.

FORMULAS

AREA of a:

square	Area = side^2
rectangle	Area = length × width
parallelogram	Area = base × height
triangle	Area = $\frac{1}{2}$ × base × height
trapezoid	Area = $\frac{1}{2}$ × (base$_1$ + base$_2$) × height
circle	Area = π × radius^2; π is approximately equal to 3.14

PERIMETER of a:

square	Perimeter = 4 × side
rectangle	Perimeter = 2 × length + 2 × width
triangle	Perimeter = side$_1$ + side$_2$ + side$_3$
CIRCUMFERENCE of a circle	Circumference = π × diameter; π is approximately equal to 3.14

VOLUME of a:

cube	Volume = edge^3
rectangular container	Volume = length × width × height
square pyramid	Volume = $\frac{1}{3}$ × (base edge)^2 × height
cylinder	Volume = π × radius^2 × height; π is approximately equal to 3.14
cone	Volume = $\frac{1}{3}$ × π × radius^2 × height; π is approximately equal to 3.14

COORDINATE GEOMETRY

distance between points = $\sqrt{(x_2 - x_1)^2 + (y_2 - y_1)^2}$; (x_1, y_1) and (x_2, y_2) are two points in a plane.

slope of a line = $\frac{y_2 - y_1}{x_2 - x_1}$; (x_1, y_1) and (x_2, y_2) are two points on a line.

PYTHAGOREAN RELATIONSHIP

$a^2 + b^2 = c^2$; a and b are legs and c the hypotenuse of a right triangle.

MEASURES OF CENTRAL TENDENCY

mean = $\frac{x_1 + x_2 + \ldots + x_n}{n}$; where the x's are the values for which a mean is desired, and n is the total number of values for x.

median = the middle value of an odd number of *ordered* scores, and halfway between the two middle values of an even number of *ordered* scores.

SIMPLE INTEREST

interest = principal × rate × time

DISTANCE

distance = rate × time

TOTAL COST

total cost = (number of units) × (price per unit)

Adapted with permission of the American Council on Education.

Part II

Directions: You will have 45 minutes to complete questions 26–50. Choose the <u>one best answer</u> to each question. You may NOT use your calculator.

<u>Question 26</u> refers to the diagram below.

26. If you were going to put a door in the wall under the stairs as shown below, which expression would you use to find the length of x?

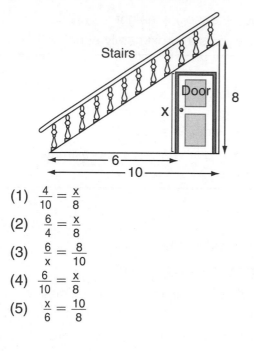

(1) $\frac{4}{10} = \frac{x}{8}$

(2) $\frac{6}{4} = \frac{x}{8}$

(3) $\frac{6}{x} = \frac{8}{10}$

(4) $\frac{6}{10} = \frac{x}{8}$

(5) $\frac{x}{6} = \frac{10}{8}$

<u>Questions 27 and 28</u> refer to the following chart.

Selected Public Libraries

Location	Number of Branches	Books
City A	4	383,000
City B	10	493,509
City C	5	548,244
City D	14	903,084
City E	35	3,164,632
City F	8	509,386

27. What is the median number of books for the selected libraries in the chart above?

(1) 383,000

(2) 493,507

(3) 509,386

(4) 528,815

(5) 548,244

28. How many more books do the City E libraries have than the City A libraries?

(1) 2,261,548

(2) 2,616,388

(3) 2,655,246

(4) 2,671,123

(5) 2,781,632

<u>Question 29</u> refers to the diagram below.

29. If you were laying out a baseball diamond, which of these statements would be true?

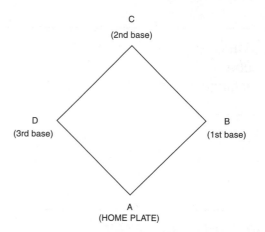

(1) Base path *AB* is parallel to base path *BC*.

(2) Base path *AB* is parallel to base path *CD*.

(3) Base path *AB* is parallel to base path *DA*.

(4) Base path *AB* is parallel to all other base paths.

(5) There are no parallel base paths, since all are at right angles.

30. Find the value of x in the equation $3x - 6 = x + 4$.

(1) 2

(2) 3

(3) 4

(4) 5

(5) 6

31. On 5 successive days a deliveryman listed his mileage as follows: 135, 172, 198, 127, and 203. If his truck averages 20 miles for each gallon of gas used, how many gallons of gas did he use during these 5 days?

Mark your answer in the circles in the grid on your answer sheet.

Question 32 refers to the following graph.

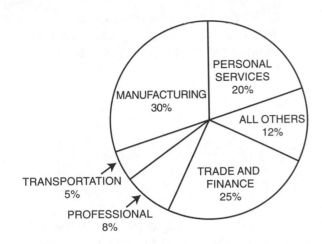

This circle graph shows how 180,000 wage earners in a certain city earned their living during a given period.

32. What was the number of persons engaged in transportation in the city during this period?

    (1) 3,600
    (2) 9,000
    (3) 10,000
    (4) 18,000
    (5) 36,000

33. For his new car, Henry will finance $10,000 for 2 years. What will be the difference between interest rates of 6.9% and 7.1%?

    (1) $ 20
    (2) $ 40
    (3) $ 200
    (4) $ 400
    (5) $2,000

Question 34 refers to the graph below.

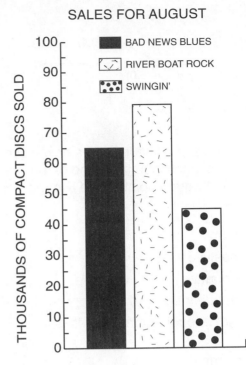

SALES FOR AUGUST

34. From the graph, which of these conclusions can be drawn?

    (1) Bad News Blues outsold Swingin' by 15,000 copies.
    (2) River Boat Rock outsold Swingin' by 3,300 copies.
    (3) Swingin' sold 4,000 copies in August.
    (4) Bad News Blues sold 65,000 copies in August.
    (5) After an upswing, CD sales declined in August.

35. Michael's retirement pay will be 2% of his average annual salary for the last 5 years multiplied by his years of experience. Which of the following will equal his retirement income if he worked 34 years and the average of his last 5 years' salary is $60,000?

    (1) $ 3,529
    (2) $ 6,000
    (3) $12,000
    (4) $40,800
    (5) Not enough information is given.

Question 36 refers to the following diagram.

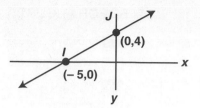

Question 39 refers to the following diagram.

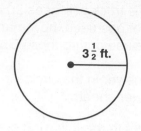

36. If the slope of a line indicates how much a line slants, describe the slope of the line passing through points *I* and *J* in the diagram above.

(1) zero
(2) positive
(3) negative
(4) not defined
(5) Not enough information is given.

37. Graph the point $(-3,4)$.

Mark your answer on the coordinate plane grid on your answer sheet.

38. How much is your annual breakfast cost if you spend an average of $2.25 each morning for 50 weeks a year, Monday through Friday?

(1) $112.50
(2) $250.00
(3) $562.50
(4) $787.50
(5) $821.25

39. The circular cover of a trampoline is pictured above. How many covers can be cut from a piece of fabric $2\frac{1}{3}$ yards by 7 yards?

(1) 2
(2) 3
(3) 4
(4) 5
(5) 6

40. If the angles of triangle *EFG* have the ratio of 2:3:4, what type of triangle is triangle *EFG*?

(1) acute
(2) equilateral
(3) right
(4) obtuse
(5) Not enough information is given.

41. Calculate John's net pay from the pay stub shown below. (FICA is the social security tax.)

Gross Pay	$2,185.60
Federal Income Tax	$434.99
State Income Tax	$199.89
FICA	$89.44

(1) $ 724.42
(2) $1,461.28
(3) $1,550.72
(4) $2,145.04
(5) $2,882.92

Question 42 refers to the diagram below.

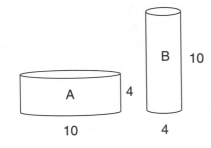

42. What is the relationship between the quantities the two containers will hold?

(1) A > B
(2) A < B
(3) A = B
(4) 2A = B
(5) 2B = A

43. A purse contains 6 nickels, 5 dimes, and 8 quarters. If one coin is drawn at random from the purse, what is the probability that the coin drawn will be a dime?

Mark your answer in the circles in the grid on your answer sheet.

Questions 44 and 45 refer to the following diagram.

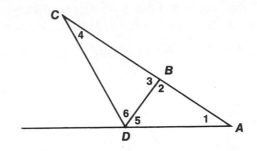

44. If ∠BCD is another name for ∠4, what is another name for ∠1?

(1) ∠ACD
(2) ∠BDA
(3) ∠DAB
(4) ∠CBC
(5) ∠CDB

45. Angles 2 and 3 are what type of angles?

(1) complementary
(2) supplementary
(3) vertical
(4) obtuse
(5) acute

Question 46 refers to the graph below.

46. Which of these statements accurately describes the rainfall in Moose Creek?

RAINFALL IN MOOSE CREEK

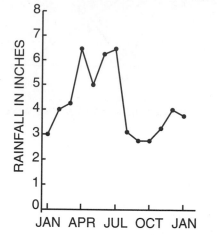

(1) April and July are equally rainy months.
(2) January is the driest month.
(3) There were 5 inches of rain in March.
(4) A flash flood occurs with $2\frac{1}{2}$ inches of rain in one hour.
(5) Less than 2 inches of rain in the summer months cause a drought.

Question 47 refers to the table below.

47. Sally, age 46, wishes to buy a $100,000 life insurance policy. From the table below, what will be the cost of this coverage for a year?

LIFE INSURANCE PREMIUM COSTS	
AGE	ANNUAL COST per $1000
44	29.50
45	30.15
46	31.50
47	32.85
48	33.50

(1) $ 31.50
(2) $ 32.36
(3) $ 315.00
(4) $ 323.60
(5) $3,150.00

Question 48 refers to the diagram below.

48. If you were setting up a trellis for growing green beans as shown below, how tall would the trellis (x) be, given the other dimensions shown?

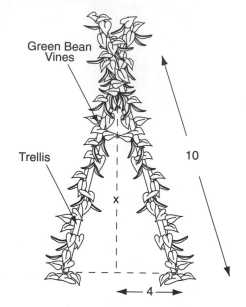

(1) Greater than 8 and less than 9
(2) Greater than 9 and less than 10
(3) Greater than 82 and less than 83
(4) Greater than 83 and less than 84
(5) Not enough information is given.

49. Amanda's shadow was 4 feet long when the shadow of a 16-foot statue was 12 feet long. How tall is Amanda?

(1) 5 ft.
(2) 5 ft. 1 in.
(3) 5 ft. 2 in.
(4) 5 ft. 3 in.
(5) 5 ft. 4 in.

50. It takes 15 minutes to drain a pool containing 45 gallons of water. If a similar pool takes 35 minutes to drain at the same rate, how many gallons of water are in the similar pool?

(1) 1,575
(2) 1,500
(3) 675
(4) 525
(5) 105

MATHEMATICS

Directions: The following charts can help you determine your strengths and weaknesses on the content and skill areas of the GED Mathematics Test. Use the Answer Key starting on page 162 to check your answers to the test. Then, on the charts for Part I and Part II, circle the numbers of the test questions you answered correctly. Put the total number of correct answers for each content area and skill area in each row and column. Look at the total items correct in each column to determine which areas are difficult for you. Use the page references to study those skills.

Part I

Cognitive Level/Content Area	Conceptual	Procedural	Application	Total Correct
Numbers and Operations (Pages 5–32)	**2**, 10, 11	18, 24	1, 4*, 5*, 20	_____/9
Measurement (Pages 33–50)			22*	_____/1
Data Analysis (Pages 33–50)	**23**	**14**	**6, 7, 25**	_____/5
Algebra (Pages 51–73)	3, 12*, **15**		13*	_____/4
Geometry (Pages 74–89)	**8, 9**, 17*, **19**		16, 21*	_____/6
Total Correct	_____/11	_____/3	_____/11	_____/25

Part II

Cognitive Level/Content Area	Conceptual	Procedural	Application	Total Correct
Numbers and Operations (Pages 5–32)		**26**, 31*, 41	35, 38	_____/5
Measurement (Pages 33–50)		**39**		_____/1
Data Analysis (Pages 33–50)		**27**, 43*, **47**	**28, 32**, 33, **34, 46**	_____/8
Algebra (Pages 51–73)		37*	30, **36**, 49, 50	_____/5
Geometry (Pages 74–89)	**29**	**44, 45**	**40, 42, 48**	_____/6
Total Correct	_____/1	_____/10	_____/14	_____/25

Items in **bold** are based on graphics. Items followed by an asterisk (*) involve alternate formats.

Numbers and Operations	(Pages 5–32)	_____/14
Measurement	(Pages 33–50)	_____/2
Data Analysis	(Pages 33–50)	_____/13
Algebra	(Pages 51–73)	_____/9
Geometry	(Pages 74–89)	_____/12
Total		_____/50

MATHEMATICS
Part I
Directions

The Mathematics Test consists of multiple-choice and alternate format questions intended to measure your general mathematical skills and problem-solving ability. The questions are based on short readings that often include a graph, chart, or diagram.

You will have 45 minutes to complete the 25 questions on Part I. Work carefully, but do not spend too much time on any one question. Be sure to answer every question. You will not be penalized for incorrect answers. When time is up, mark the last item you finished. This will tell you whether you can finish the real GED Test in the time allowed. Then complete the test.

Formulas you may need are given on page 119. Only some of the questions will require you to use a formula. Not all the formulas given will be needed.

Some questions contain more information than you will need to solve the problem; other questions do not give enough information. If the question does not give enough information to solve the problem, the correct answer choice is "Not enough information is given."

You may use a calculator on Part I. Calculator directions for the CASIO *fx-260SOLAR* scientific calculator can be found on page 118.

Record your answers on a copy of the answer sheet provided on page 171. Be sure all required information is properly recorded on the answer sheet.

To record your answers, mark the numbered space on the answer sheet that corresponds to the answer you select for each question on the test.

Example: If a grocery bill totaling $15.75 is paid with a $20.00 bill, how much change should be returned?

(1) $5.25
(2) $4.75
(3) $4.25
(4) $3.75
(5) $3.25

① ② ● ④ ⑤

The correct answer is $4.25; therefore, answer space 3 would be marked on the answer sheet.

Do not rest the point of your pencil on the answer sheet while you are considering your answer. Make no stray or unnecessary marks. If you change an answer, erase your first mark completely. Mark only one answer for each question; multiple answers will be scored as incorrect. Do not fold or crease your answer sheet.

When you finish the test, use the Performance Analysis Chart on page 133 to determine whether you are ready to take the real GED Test, and, if not, which skill areas need additional review.

Adapted with permission of the American Council on Education.

MATHEMATICS

Mixed numbers, such as $3\frac{1}{2}$, cannot be entered in the alternate format grid. Instead, represent them as decimal numbers (in this case, 3.5) or fractions $\left(\text{in this case, } \frac{7}{2}\right)$. No answer can be a negative number, such as -8.

To record your answer for an alternate format question

• begin in any column that will allow your answer to be entered;
• write your answer in the boxes on the top row;
• in the column beneath a fraction bar or decimal point (if any) and each number in your answer, fill in the bubble representing that character;
• leave blank any unused column.

Example:

The scale on a map indicates that $\frac{1}{2}$ inch represents an actual distance of 120 miles. In inches, how far apart on the map will two towns be if the actual distance between them is 180 miles?

The answer to the above example is $\frac{3}{4}$, or 0.75, inches. The answer could be gridded using any of the methods below.

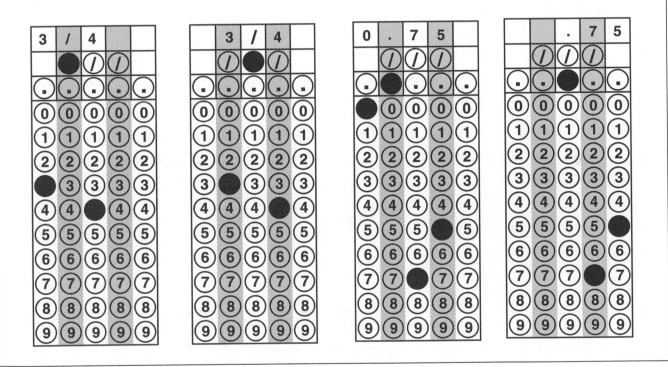

Points to remember:

• The answer sheet will be machine scored. **The circles must be filled in correctly.**
• Mark no more than one circle in any column.
• Grid only one answer even if there is more than one correct answer.
• A mixed number, such as $3\frac{1}{2}$, must be gridded as a decimal (3.5) or fraction $\left(\frac{7}{2}\right)$.
• No answer can be a negative number.

Adapted with permission of the American Council on Education.

CALCULATOR DIRECTIONS

To prepare the calculator for use the *first* time, press the (ON) (upper-rightmost) key. "DEG" will appear at the top-center of the screen and "0" at the right. This indicates that the calculator is in the proper format for all your calculations.

To prepare the calculator for *another* question, press the (ON) or the red (AC) key. This clears any entries made previously.

To do any arithmetic, enter the expression as it is written. Press (=) (equals sign) when finished.

EXAMPLE A: $8 - 3 + 9$

> First press (ON) or (AC).
> Enter the following:
>
> 8 (−) 3 (+) 9 (=)
>
> The correct answer is 14.

If an expression in parentheses is to be multiplied by a number, press (X) (multiplication sign) between the number and the parenthesis sign.

EXAMPLE B: $6(8 + 5)$

> First press (ON) or (AC).
> Enter the following:
>
> 6 (X) ([(--] 8 (+) 5 (--)]) (=)
>
> The correct answer is 78.

To find the square root of a number

- enter the number;
- press (SHIFT) (upper-leftmost) key ("SHIFT" appears at the top-left of the screen);
- press (x^2) (third from the left on top row) to access its second function: square root.
  DO NOT press (SHIFT) and (x^2) at the same time.

EXAMPLE C: $\sqrt{64}$

> First press (ON) or (AC).
> Enter the following:
>
> 64 (SHIFT) (x^2)
>
> The correct answer is 8.

To enter a negative number such as −8,

- enter the number without the negative sign (enter 8);
- press the "change sign" ((+/−)) key which is directly above the 7 key.

All arithmetic can be done with positive and/or negative numbers.

EXAMPLE D: $-8 - -5$

> First press (ON) or (AC).
> Enter the following:
>
> 8 (+/−) (−) 5 (+/−) (=)
>
> The correct answer is −3.

Adapted with permission of the American Council on Education.

FORMULAS

AREA of a:

square	Area = side^2
rectangle	Area = length × width
parallelogram	Area = base × height
triangle	Area = $\frac{1}{2}$ × base × height
trapezoid	Area = $\frac{1}{2}$ × (base$_1$ + base$_2$) × height
circle	Area = π × radius^2; π is approximately equal to 3.14

PERIMETER of a:

square	Perimeter = 4 × side
rectangle	Perimeter = 2 × length + 2 × width
triangle	Perimeter = side$_1$ + side$_2$ + side$_3$
CIRCUMFERENCE of a circle	Circumference = π × diameter; π is approximately equal to 3.14

VOLUME of a:

cube	Volume = edge^3
rectangular container	Volume = length × width × height
square pyramid	Volume = $\frac{1}{3}$ × (base edge)^2 × height
cylinder	Volume = π × radius^2 × height; π is approximately equal to 3.14
cone	Volume = $\frac{1}{3}$ × π × radius^2 × height; π is approximately equal to 3.14

COORDINATE GEOMETRY

distance between points = $\sqrt{(x_2 - x_1)^2 + (y_2 - y_1)^2}$; (x_1, y_1) and (x_2, y_2) are two points in a plane.

slope of a line = $\frac{y_2 - y_1}{x_2 - x_1}$; (x_1, y_1) and (x_2, y_2) are two points on a line.

PYTHAGOREAN RELATIONSHIP

$a^2 + b^2 = c^2$; a and b are legs and c the hypotenuse of a right triangle.

MEASURES OF CENTRAL TENDENCY

mean = $\frac{x_1 + x_2 + \ldots + x_n}{n}$; where the x's are the values for which a mean is desired, and n is the total number of values for x.

median = the middle value of an odd number of _ordered_ scores, and halfway between the two middle values of an even number of _ordered_ scores.

SIMPLE INTEREST interest = principal × rate × time

DISTANCE distance = rate × time

TOTAL COST total cost = (number of units) × (price per unit)

Adapted with permission of the American Council on Education.

Directions : You will have 45 minutes to complete questions 1–25. Choose the <u>one best answer</u> to each question. You MAY use your calculator.

1. The Smithson Building in the downtown area was resurfaced with 1,200 granite sections each 4' × 4'. Last year 30 sections needed to be repaired. What percent of the granite squares needed repair?

   (1) 2%

   (2) $2\frac{1}{2}$%

   (3) 20%

   (4) $20\frac{1}{2}$%

   (5) 25%

Question 2 refers to the following diagram.

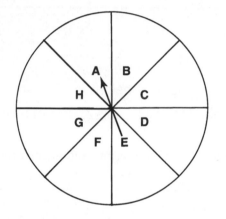

2. What is the probability of the spinner landing either on E or F on one spin?

   (1) $\frac{6}{8}$

   (2) $\frac{8}{6}$

   (3) $\frac{3}{4}$

   (4) $\frac{1}{4}$

   (5) $\frac{4}{1}$

3. Which of the following is a true proportion?

   (1) $\frac{1}{2} = \frac{5}{10}$

   (2) $\frac{15}{3} = \frac{30}{10}$

   (3) $\frac{4}{6} = \frac{8}{10}$

   (4) $\frac{5}{8} = \frac{15}{20}$

   (5) $\frac{3}{15} = \frac{6}{18}$

4. Calculate the average number of calories for the first four days of Eve's diet.

   Day one: 1,145 calories

   Day two: 1,395 calories

   Day three: 1,205 calories

   Day four: 1,715 calories

   Mark your answer in the circles in the grid on your answer sheet.

5. The gasoline gauge shows that the gasoline tank is $\frac{1}{3}$ full. In order to fill the tank, 16 gallons of gasoline are added. How many gallons of gasoline does the tank hold when full?

   Mark your answer in the circles in the grid on your answer sheet.

Question 6 refers to the following chart.

Cooling System Capacity (Quarts)	Quarts of Antifreeze Required for °F						
	4	5	6	7	8	9	10
8	-34°	-70°					
9		-50°	-82°				
10		-34°	-62°	-84°			
11			-47°	-76°			
12			-34°	-57°	-82°		
13				-45°	-66°	-84°	
14				-34°	-54°	-76°	
15					-43°	-62°	-82°
16					-34°	-52°	-70°

6. A 50% antifreeze solution is recommended for best protection for car radiators. According to the table below, if you were to create a 50% antifreeze solution by using 6 quarts of antifreeze for a 12-quart cooling system, to what temperature would your car be protected from winter's cold?

   (1) -34°
   (2) -50°
   (3) -70°
   (4) -82°
   (5) -84°

7. Which of the following statements is the smallest in value?

   (1) $6\frac{3}{4}$% of 50
   (2) 8% of 90
   (3) 50% of 100
   (4) $\frac{3}{10}$% of 70
   (5) $\frac{3}{4}$% of 240

Question 8 refers to the following diagram.

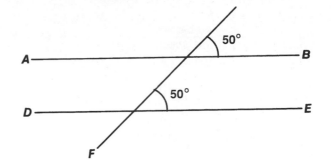

8. What type of line segments are $\overline{AB}$ and $\overline{DE}$ in the diagram above?

   (1) curved
   (2) perpendicular
   (3) vertical
   (4) intersecting
   (5) parallel

9. Center City Gazette can print 125 Sunday newspapers in $1\frac{1}{4}$ hours. How many hours will it take to print the circulation quota of 2,000 newspapers?

   (1) 6
   (2) 8
   (3) 12
   (4) 18
   (5) 20

10. A cardiac patient's blood-thinning medicine was changed from 2.5 milligrams to 2.0 milligrams. What percent change is this?

    (1) 0.5%
    (2) 2.5%
    (3) 5.0%
    (4) 10.0%
    (5) 20.0%

Question 11 refers to the following diagram.

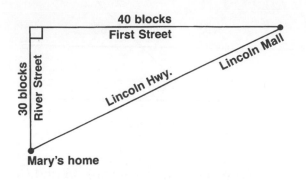

11. The diagram above shows two ways of going from Mary's home to Lincoln Mall. If First Street runs perpendicular to River Street, what is the distance in blocks if the trip is made on the Lincoln Highway?

(1) 20
(2) 30
(3) 40
(4) 50
(5) 60

12. The owner's manual for a string trimmer says that a 16:1 ratio of gasoline to 2-cycle oil must be used for its fuel. How many gallons of gasoline would be needed to go with an 8-ounce packet of the oil, if 1 gallon is equal to 128 ounces?

Mark your answer in the circles in the grid on your answer sheet.

13. Ben scored 7 more points than Jack in a basketball game. Paul scored 2 points less than Jack in the same game. If the three boys scored a total of 38 points, how many points did Jack score?

Mark your answer in the circles in the grid on your answer sheet.

14. Shandra combined the following juices to make fruit punch: 800 ml apple juice, 500 ml pineapple juice, 1,000 ml orange juice, and 200 ml grape juice. What was the total amount of fruit punch made in liters?

(1)   0.25 liters
(2)   2.5 liters
(3)   25 liters
(4)   250 liters
(5)   2500 liters

15. The graph below shows what happened to each $100 taken in by a small business firm. How many dollars out of each $100 received represented profit?

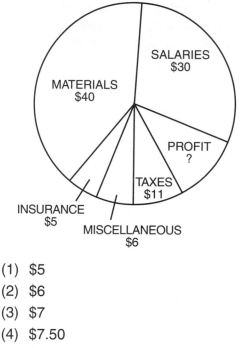

(1) $5
(2) $6
(3) $7
(4) $7.50
(5) $8

16. Five college students formed the Collegiate Cleaning Service to earn money during the summer months. The student leader was to receive $640 more than each of the other four students. If the students earned a total of $5,640 for the summer, what were the earnings of the student leader?

(1) $4,000
(2) $2,100
(3) $1,640
(4) $1,040
(5) $ 640

17. A point has an *x*-coordinate of 5 and a *y*-coordinate of −2. Show the location of the point.

Mark your answer on the coordinate plane grid on your answer sheet.

Question 18 refers to the following diagram.

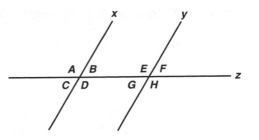

18. Which of the following solution sets is shown on the number line above?

(1) *x* > 7
(2) *x* < 7
(3) *x* < −7
(4) *x* > −7
(5) *x* = −7

Questions 19 and 20 refer to the following diagram.

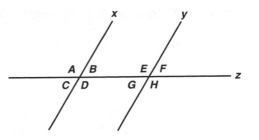

19. If lines *x* and *y* are parallel, which of the following angles is equal to ∠A?

(1) ∠B
(2) ∠F
(3) ∠G
(4) ∠C
(5) ∠H

20. If ∠E is 20° greater than ∠G, what is the measure of ∠E?

(1)   80°
(2)   90°
(3) 100°
(4) 110°
(5) 120°

21. The area of Sean's rectangular front lawn is $302\frac{3}{8}$ square feet. If the lawn has a length of $20\frac{1}{2}$ feet, what is its width in feet?

Mark your answer in the circles in the grid on your answer sheet.

22. Mr. Garza's annual income has gone from $32,000 to $48,000 in 6 years. By what percent has his annual income increased?

Mark your answer in the circles in the grid on your answer sheet.

Questions 23 and 24 refer to the following graph showing growth in population in Lincoln County between the years 1995 and 2003.

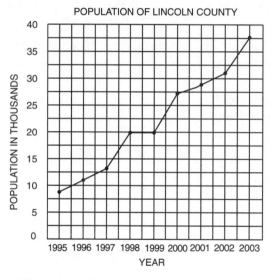

POPULATION OF LINCOLN COUNTY

23. What was the population of Lincoln County in the year 2000?

(1) 20,000
(2) 25,000
(3) 26,000
(4) 27,500
(5) 30,000

24. The population of Lincoln County did not change between which two years?

(1) 1996 and 1997
(2) 1997 and 1998
(3) 1998 and 1999
(4) 1999 and 2000
(5) 2000 and 2001

25. Lester measured the length of the street light's shadow to be 40 feet. Lester is 6 feet tall and his shadow's length was measured to be 4 feet long at the same time of day. How tall is the street light post?

(1) 40 ft.
(2) 60 ft.
(3) 80 ft.
(4) 100 ft.
(5) 120 ft.

MATHEMATICS
Part II
Directions

The Mathematics Test consists of multiple-choice and alternate format questions intended to measure your general mathematical skills and problem-solving ability. The questions are based on short readings that often include a graph, chart, or diagram.

You will have 45 minutes to complete the 25 questions on Part II. Work carefully, but do not spend too much time on any one question. Be sure to answer every question. You will not be penalized for incorrect answers. When time is up, mark the last item you finished. This will tell you whether you can finish the real GED Test in the time allowed. Then complete the test.

Formulas you may need are given on page 127. Only some of the questions will require you to use a formula. Not all the formulas given will be needed.

Some questions contain more information than you will need to solve the problem; other questions do not give enough information. If the question does not give enough information to solve the problem, the correct answer choice is "Not enough information is given."

The use of calculators is not allowed on Part II.

Record your answers on a copy of the answer sheet provided on page 172. Be sure all required information is properly recorded on the answer sheet.

To record your answers, mark the numbered space on the answer sheet that corresponds to the answer you select for each question on the test.

Example: If a grocery bill totaling $15.75 is paid with a $20.00 bill, how much change should be returned?

(1) $5.25
(2) $4.75
(3) $4.25
(4) $3.75
(5) $3.25

① ② ● ④ ⑤

The correct answer is $4.25; therefore, answer space 3 would be marked on the answer sheet.

Do not rest the point of your pencil on the answer sheet while you are considering your answer. Make no stray or unnecessary marks. If you change an answer, erase your first mark completely. Mark only one answer for each question; multiple answers will be scored as incorrect. Do not fold or crease your answer sheet.

When you finish the test, use the Performance Analysis Chart on page 133 to determine whether you are ready to take the real GED Test, and, if not, which skill areas need additional review.

Adapted with permission of the American Council on Education.

MATHEMATICS

Mixed numbers, such as $3\frac{1}{2}$, cannot be entered in the alternate format grid. Instead, represent them as decimal numbers (in this case, 3.5) or fractions $\left(\text{in this case, } \frac{7}{2}\right)$. No answer can be a negative number, such as -8.

To record your answer for an alternate format question

- begin in any column that will allow your answer to be entered;
- write your answer in the boxes on the top row;
- in the column beneath a fraction bar or decimal point (if any) and each number in your answer, fill in the bubble representing that character;
- leave blank any unused column.

Example:

The scale on a map indicates that $\frac{1}{2}$ inch represents an actual distance of 120 miles. In inches, how far apart on the map will two towns be if the actual distance between them is 180 miles?

The answer to the above example is $\frac{3}{4}$, or 0.75, inches. The answer could be gridded using any of the methods below.

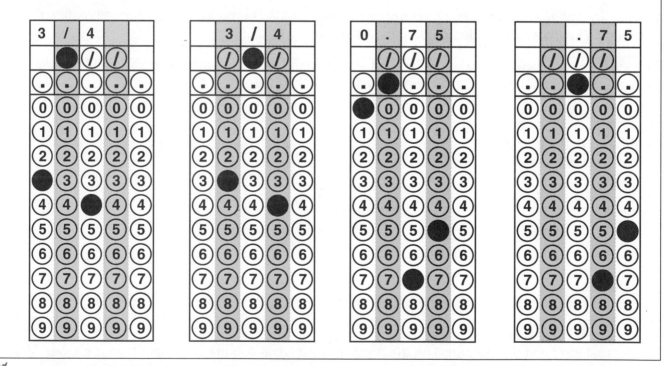

Points to remember:

- The answer sheet will be machine scored. **The circles must be filled in correctly.**
- Mark no more than one circle in any column.
- Grid only one answer even if there is more than one correct answer.
- A mixed number, such as $3\frac{1}{2}$, must be gridded as a decimal (3.5) or fraction $\left(\frac{7}{2}\right)$.
- No answer can be a negative number.

Adapted with permission of the American Council on Education.

FORMULAS

AREA of a:

square	Area = side^2
rectangle	Area = length $\times$ width
parallelogram	Area = base $\times$ height
triangle	Area = $\frac{1}{2}$ $\times$ base $\times$ height
trapezoid	Area = $\frac{1}{2}$ $\times$ (base$_1$ + base$_2$) $\times$ height
circle	Area = π $\times$ radius^2; π is approximately equal to 3.14

PERIMETER of a:

square	Perimeter = 4 $\times$ side
rectangle	Perimeter = 2 $\times$ length + 2 $\times$ width
triangle	Perimeter = side$_1$ + side$_2$ + side$_3$
CIRCUMFERENCE of a circle	Circumference = π $\times$ diameter; π is approximately equal to 3.14

VOLUME of a:

cube	Volume = edge^3
rectangular container	Volume = length $\times$ width $\times$ height
square pyramid	Volume = $\frac{1}{3}$ $\times$ (base edge)^2 $\times$ height
cylinder	Volume = π $\times$ radius^2 $\times$ height; π is approximately equal to 3.14
cone	Volume = $\frac{1}{3}$ $\times$ π $\times$ radius^2 $\times$ height; π is approximately equal to 3.14

COORDINATE GEOMETRY

distance between points = $\sqrt{(x_2 - x_1)^2 + (y_2 - y_1)^2}$; (x_1, y_1) and (x_2, y_2) are two points in a plane.

slope of a line = $\frac{y_2 - y_1}{x_2 - x_1}$; (x_1, y_1) and (x_2, y_2) are two points on a line.

PYTHAGOREAN RELATIONSHIP

$a^2 + b^2 = c^2$; a and b are legs and c the hypotenuse of a right triangle.

MEASURES OF CENTRAL TENDENCY

mean = $\frac{x_1 + x_2 + \ldots + x_n}{n}$; where the x's are the values for which a mean is desired, and n is the total number of values for x.

median = the middle value of an odd number of *ordered* scores, and halfway between the two middle values of an even number of *ordered* scores.

SIMPLE INTEREST

interest = principal $\times$ rate $\times$ time

DISTANCE

distance = rate $\times$ time

TOTAL COST

total cost = (number of units) $\times$ (price per unit)

Adapted with permission of the American Council on Education.

Part II

Question 26 refers to the following graph.

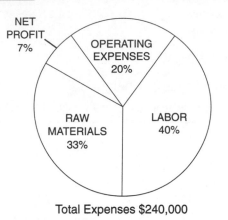

Total Expenses $240,000

26. According to the graph, how many dollars were spent for labor?

    (1) $ 4,000
    (2) $ 9,600
    (3) $ 48,000
    (4) $ 96,000
    (5) $960,000

27. Some health insurance plans are designed so that once the deductible has been met, the patient pays 20% of all doctors' bills. Once the deductible is met, how much would the patient pay on a bill of $120?

    (1) $20
    (2) $24
    (3) $48
    (4) $60
    (5) $90

28. The Regal Book Store has 100 overstocked books to sell. The manager is going to mark some of the books $2 each and the remaining books $3 each. How many books must be priced at each price to receive $245?

    (1) 25 $2 books and 75 $3 books
    (2) 35 $2 books and 65 $3 books
    (3) 50 $2 books and 50 $3 books
    (4) 55 $2 books and 45 $3 books
    (5) 65 $2 books and 35 $3 books

Question 29 refers to the following diagram.

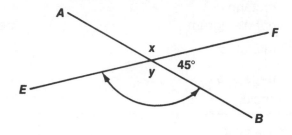

29. What is the value of $\angle y$ in the diagram above?

    (1)   35°
    (2)   45°
    (3)   95°
    (4) 115°
    (5) 135°

Question 30 refers to the following graph.

30. According to the graph, by how many dollars do the sales in the meat department exceed the sales in the dairy department?

    (1) $ 100
    (2) $ 1,000
    (3) $ 1,500
    (4) $ 1,800
    (5) $10,000

31. In a large class, 80 students took a test. When the test papers were graded, it was found that 10% of the students had A papers, 25% of the students had B papers, 30% of the students had C papers, 15% of students had D papers, and the rest failed the test. How many students failed the test?

Mark your answer in the circles in the grid on your answer sheet.

Questions 32 and 33 refer to the following diagram.

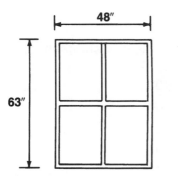

32. Weather stripping is sold by the yard. Regina has six windows, as shown above, that need to be weather stripped. Which expression below determines the number of yards of weather stripping that will be needed?

(1) $6 \times 2(63 + 48) \div 12$
(2) $6 \times 2(63 + 48) \div 6$
(3) $6 \times 2(63 + 48) \div 36$
(4) $6 \times 2(63 + 48) \div 4$
(5) $6 \times 2(63 + 48) \div 16$

33. If one yard of weather stripping costs $.69, what is the total cost for the number of yards needed?

(1) $76.59
(2) $52.53
(3) $35.25
(4) $25.53
(5) $24.84

34. The difference between $\frac{1}{4}$ of a number and $\frac{1}{6}$ of the same number is 18. Which equation shows the correct relationship?

(1) $\frac{1}{4}x - \frac{1}{6}x = 18$
(2) $\frac{1}{4}x + \frac{1}{6}x = 18$
(3) $\frac{1}{4} + 18 = \frac{1}{6}x$
(4) $\frac{1}{6}x - \frac{1}{4}x = 18$
(5) $\frac{1}{6}x - 18 = \frac{1}{4}x$

35. Airplane pilots must consider the fact that they will need more feet of runway for landing when the outside temperature is hot than when it is cold. This is because hot air is less dense than cold air and so does not provide as much resistance to the plane's movement. Which of the following graphs best represents this idea?

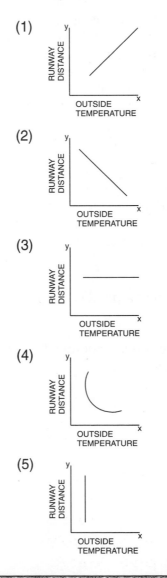

Question 36 refers to the following diagram.

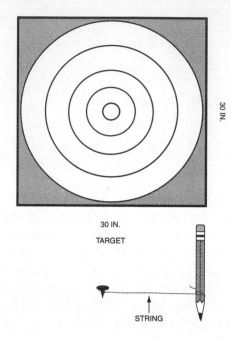

30 IN.

TARGET

STRING

36. A target can be made by using a piece of string tied to a pencil. To make a target such as the one in the diagram, where the bull's eye is 6 inches across and every ring is the same width, how many inches long should the string be for drawing each circle, starting with the bull's eye?

(1) 0, 3, 6, 9, 12
(2) 0, 6, 14, 22, 30
(3) 3, 6, 9, 12, 15
(4) 6, 8, 10, 12, 14
(5) 6, 12, 18, 24, 30

37. Show the location of a point with the coordinates (-2, -5).

Mark your answer on the coordinate plane grid on your answer sheet.

Questions 38 and 39 refer to the following diagram.

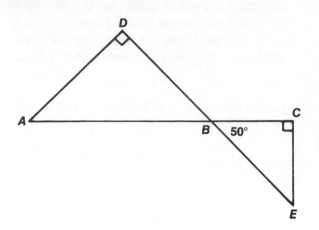

38. What is the measurement of $\angle DAB$?

(1) 40°
(2) 60°
(3) 90°
(4) 100°
(5) 110°

39. What is the measurement of $\angle DBC$?

(1) 100°
(2) 110°
(3) 120°
(4) 130°
(5) 140°

40. If $3x - 1 = 11$, what is the value of $x^2 + x$?

(1) 12
(2) 15
(3) 16
(4) 18
(5) 20

Question 41 refers to the figure below.

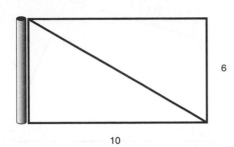

41. In order to keep a chain link gate from sagging, a rod can be installed on the diagonal as shown in the diagram. Which of the following calculations will give the correct length of the rod?

(1) $\sqrt{6^2 + 10^2}$

(2) $36 + 100$

(3) $6(10)(\frac{1}{2})$

(4) $\frac{1}{2}(6 + 10)$

(5) Not enough information is given.

Question 42 refers to the diagram below.

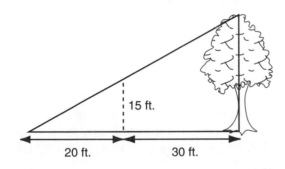

42. A notice in the newspaper states that home owners with trees taller than 50 feet will pay an assessment. In order to determine the height of your tree, you make a diagram. Which is the correct expression for finding the height of your tree?

(1) $\frac{x}{15} = \frac{50}{20}$

(2) $\frac{15}{x} = \frac{50}{20}$

(3) $\frac{15(20)}{50}$

(4) $\frac{50(20)}{15}$

(5) Not enough information is given.

43. If $a = -1$ and $y = 2$, what is the value of the expression $2a^3 - 3ay$?

Mark your answer in the circles on the grid on your answer sheet.

Question 44 refers to the following graph.

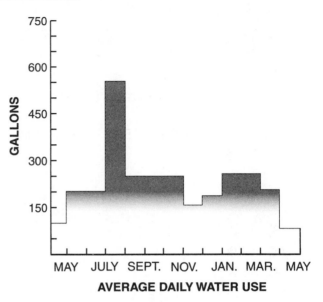

AVERAGE DAILY WATER USE

44. Based on the graph, which of the following conclusions can you draw?

(1) Water use increases as outside temperature increases.

(2) The daily average use in March was 250 gallons.

(3) Heavy August use was caused by a drought.

(4) May is the month with the heaviest rainfall.

(5) Water use increases steadily after the first of the year.

`45. An English class has an enrollment of 14 boys and 12 girls. On a rainy day 4 boys and 3 girls are absent. If a student is called on at random to recite a poem, what is the probability that the student is a girl?

(1) $\frac{9}{19}$

(2) $\frac{10}{19}$

(3) $\frac{12}{26}$

(4) $\frac{9}{14}$

(5) Not enough information is given.

46. If $n = -3$ and $x = (n + 5)(n - 5)$, what is the value of x?

(1)   64
(2)   16
(3)   9
(4)   −9
(5) −16

47. In the figure below, $\triangle ABC$ is a right triangle and CD ⊥ AB. If the measure of $\angle CAD = 40°$, what is the measure of $\angle DCB$?

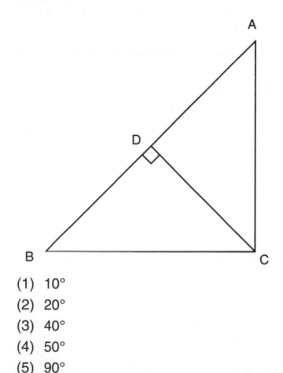

(1) 10°
(2) 20°
(3) 40°
(4) 50°
(5) 90°

48. What is the perimeter of the figure below?

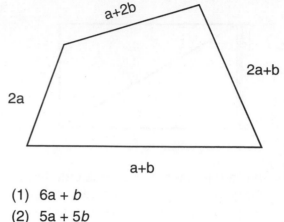

(1) $6a + b$
(2) $5a + 5b$
(3) $6a + 4b$
(4) $4a + 4b$
(5) $3a + 5b$

49. If the square of a number is added to the same number increased by 4, the result is 60. If n represents the number, which equation can be used to find n?

(1) $n^2 + 4 = 60$
(2) $n^2 + 4n = 60$
(3) $n^2 + n + 4 = 60$
(4) $n^2 + 60 = 4n + 4$
(5) $n^2 + n = 60$

50. A dealer sells books at 40% above cost. How much does a dealer pay for a shipment of 6 dozen books that he sells for $7 per book?

(1) $360
(2) $380
(3) $450
(4) $504
(5) $520

MATHEMATICS

Directions: The following charts can help you determine your strengths and weaknesses on the content and skill areas of the GED Mathematics Test. Use the Answer Key starting on page 166 to check your answers to the test. Then, on the charts for Part I and Part II, circle the numbers of the test questions you answered correctly. Put the total number of correct answers for each content area and skill area in each row and column. Look at the total items correct in each column to determine which areas are difficult for you. Use the page references to study those skills.

Part I

Cognitive Level/Content Area	Conceptual	Procedural	Application	Total Correct
Numbers and Operations (Pages 5–32)	3	22*	1, 5*, 7, 9, 10	____/7
Measurement (Pages 33–50)			12*, 14	____/2
Data Analysis (Pages 33–50)		2, 4*	**6, 15, 23, 24**	____/6
Algebra (Pages 51–73)	17*, **18**		13*, 16, 25	____/5
Geometry (Pages 74–89)	**8, 11, 19, 20**		21*	____/5
Total Correct	____/7	____/3	____/15	____/25

Part II

Cognitive Level/Content Area	Conceptual	Procedural	Application	Total Correct
Numbers and Operations (Pages 5–32)			27, 31*, 50	____/3
Measurement (Pages 33–50)	**32, 33**			____/2
Data Analysis (Pages 33–50)			**26, 30, 35, 44**, 45	____/5
Algebra (Pages 51–73)	37*	34, 40, 43*, 46, 49	28	____/7
Geometry (Pages 74–89)	**29, 38, 39, 47, 48**		**36, 41, 42**	____/8
Total Correct	____/8	____/5	____/12	____/25

Items in **bold** are based on graphics. Items followed by an asterisk (*) involve alternate formats.

Numbers and Operations	(Pages 5–32)	____/10
Measurement	(Pages 33–50)	____/4
Data Analysis	(Pages 33–50)	____/11
Algebra	(Pages 51–73)	____/12
Geometry	(Pages 74–89)	____/13
Total		____/50

UNIT 1: NUMBERS AND OPERATIONS

Whole Number Concepts (page 5)

1. $324 < 432$

2. $1,036 > 1,008$

3. $12,992 > 12,991$

4. $85,063 < 85,630$

5. 293; 329; 392; 923; 932

6. 5,316; 5,631; 6,153; 6,315; 6,531

7. 8,914; 9,842; 18,429; 19,482; 98,421

8. 9,775 rounds to 9,800

9. 6,998,546 rounds to 7,000,000

10. 56,701 rounds to 60,000

11. 11,324 rounds to 11,000

12. Thursday

13. Friday

14. Saturday

15. The sales in order from lowest to highest are: Friday, Sunday, Thursday, Tuesday, Monday, Wednesday, Saturday.

Estimating with Whole Numbers (page 6)

1. **(3) $3,552** 592 rounds to 600
   $600 \times \$6 = \$3,600$
   $3,552 is closest to $3,600.

2. **(4) 2,046,000** Round 11 to 10 and 186,282 to 186,300.
   $186,300 \times 10 = 1,863,000$
   2,046,000 is the next larger answer. Note that option (3) 1,860,000 is not correct because 11 is greater than 10 and 186,282 is greater than 186,000, the numbers used to obtain this estimate.

3. **(2) 60** Round. 29,000 to 30,000
   $\frac{30,000}{500} = 60$

4. **(5) 645** Round each number to the nearest hundred:
   $3,500 - 2,800 = 700$.
   In this problem estimating does not help. You must find the exact answer:
   $3,452 - 2,807 = 645$

Whole Numbers: Computation Practice (page 7)

1.
$$\begin{array}{r} 144 \\ \times\ 23 \\ \hline 432 \\ 2\,88\ \\ \hline 3,312 \end{array}$$

2.
$$\begin{array}{r} 24,593 \\ -10,638 \\ \hline 13,955 \end{array}$$

3.
$$\begin{array}{r} 37,454 \\ 41,345 \\ 49,496 \\ +22,738 \\ \hline 151,033 \end{array}$$

4.
$$\begin{array}{r} 28 \\ 32\overline{)896} \\ 64 \\ \hline 256 \\ 256 \end{array}$$

5.
$$\begin{array}{r} 9,675 \\ \times\ 326 \\ \hline 58\,050 \\ 193\,50\ \\ 2\,902\,5\ \ \\ \hline 3,154,050 \end{array}$$

6.
$$\begin{array}{r} 90,000 \\ -82,575 \\ \hline 7,425 \end{array}$$

7.
$$\begin{array}{r} 6,400 \\ 36\overline{)230,400} \\ 216 \\ \hline 14\ 4 \\ 14\ 4 \end{array}$$

8.
$$\begin{array}{r} 861 \\ 495 \\ +827 \\ \hline 2,183 \end{array}$$

9.
$$\begin{array}{r} 8,622 \\ \times\ 393 \\ \hline 25\,866 \\ 775\,98\ \\ 2\,586\,6\ \ \\ \hline 3,388,446 \end{array}$$

10. $16,774 \times 19 = 318,706$

11. $\$2,284 \times 65 = \$148,460$

12. $608,439 \div 123 = 4,947$

13. $184,000 \div 35 = 5,257$

14. $50,566 \times 66 = 3,337,356$

15. $325,666 \div 156 = 2,088$

16.
$$\begin{array}{r} 658{,}235 \\ -621{,}791 \\ \hline 36{,}444 \end{array}$$

18.
$$\begin{array}{r} 8{,}311 \\ -7{,}059 \\ \hline 1{,}252 \end{array}$$

17.
$$\begin{array}{r} 7{,}478 \\ +\,9{,}757 \\ \hline 17{,}235 \end{array}$$

GED Practice: Whole Numbers (page 8)

1. **(3) 59**
$$\begin{array}{r} 753 \\ -694 \\ \hline 59 \end{array}$$

2. **(4) $1,125**

225 groups of 3
3)675 videos
$$\begin{array}{r} \underline{6} \\ 7 \\ \underline{6} \\ 15 \\ 15 \end{array}$$

$$\begin{array}{r} 225 \\ \times\ \$5 \\ \hline \$1{,}125 \end{array}$$

3. **(4) 5,462**
$$\begin{array}{r} 356 \\ \times\ 8 \\ \hline 2{,}848 \end{array} \qquad \begin{array}{r} 1{,}307 \\ \times\ 2 \\ \hline 2{,}614 \end{array}$$

$$\begin{array}{r} 2{,}848 \\ +2{,}614 \\ \hline 5{,}462 \end{array}$$

4. **(4) 5,241,799**
$$\begin{array}{r} 4{,}600{,}602 \\ +\ 641{,}197 \\ \hline 5{,}241{,}799 \end{array}$$

5. **(4) 747**
$$\begin{array}{r} 3{,}121 \\ -2{,}374 \\ \hline 747 \end{array}$$

6. **65,658**
$$\begin{array}{r} 2{,}118 \\ \times\ 31 \\ \hline 2\ 118 \\ 63\ 54 \\ \hline 65{,}658 \end{array}$$

GED Practice: Whole Numbers II (pages 9–10)

1. **(3) 2,000**

Monday	531
Tuesday	116
Wednesday	285
Thursday	432
Friday	157
Saturday	+480
	2,001

2,001 rounds to 2,000

2. **(4) 258**
$$\begin{array}{r} 116 \\ +157 \\ \hline 273 \end{array} \qquad \begin{array}{r} 531 \\ -273 \\ \hline 258 \end{array}$$

3. **(3) $33.50**
$134 \div 4 = 33.5$

4. **(3) 308**
174 sq. ft. + 134 sq. ft. = 308 sq. ft.

5. **(1) 12 in.**
$$\begin{array}{r} 36 \\ +24 \\ \hline 60 \end{array} \qquad \begin{array}{r} 72 \\ -60 \\ \hline 12 \end{array}$$

6. **(4) August**

Month	Deposit	End-of-Month Balance
April	$75	$ 75
May	50	125
June	55	180
July	45	225
August	40	265
September	75	340

7. **(1) $265**
$50 + $55 + $45 + $40 + $75 = $265
or $340 − $75 = $265

8. **(5) September**

9. **(4) $265**
$340 − $135 = $205
$205 + $60 = $265

10. **(4) $504**
84 × 6 = 504

11. **(3) 150 miles**
3 × 50 = 150

12. **(4) $59,580**
12 × 3 = 36
1,655 × 36 = 59,580

13. **$980**
$455 + $156 + $344 + $25 = $980

GED Practice: Solving Word Problems (page 12)

1. (2) 18,881
$$9,204 + 9,677 = 18,881$$

2. (3) 1,753
$$7,432 - 5,679 = 1,753$$

3. (5) $39

$$\begin{array}{r} \$259 \\ -\ 25 \\ \hline \$234 \end{array} \qquad \begin{array}{r} \$\ 39 \\ 6)\overline{\$234} \\ \underline{18} \\ 54 \\ 54 \end{array}$$

4. (3) $6,834

$$\begin{array}{r} \$169 \\ \times\ 36 \\ \hline 1\ 014 \\ 5\ 07 \\ \hline \$6,084 \end{array} \qquad \begin{array}{r} \$6,084 \\ +\ 750 \\ \hline \$6,834 \end{array}$$

5. (3) 1,230
$$390 + 94 + 355 + 18 + 184 + 189 = 1,230$$

6. $759
$$\$289 + \$195 = \$484$$
$$\$1,243 - \$484 = \$759$$

GED Practice: Solving Word Problems II (page 13)

1. (3) $10,000

$$\begin{array}{r} \$\ 10,000 \\ 15)\overline{\$150,000} \\ 15 \end{array}$$

2. (4) 448

$$\begin{array}{r} 14 \\ \times\ 4 \\ \hline 56 \end{array} \qquad \begin{array}{r} 56 \\ \times\ 8 \\ \hline 448 \end{array}$$

3. 160

$$\begin{array}{r} 105 \\ \times\ 3 \\ \hline 315 \end{array} \qquad \begin{array}{r} 475 \\ -315 \\ \hline 160 \end{array}$$

4. (3) $384,734
$$78,598 + 89,345 + 46,969 + 56,812 + 64,001$$
$$+\ 49,009 = 384,734$$

5. (3) $15,501
$$56,812 + 64,001 = 120,813$$
$$89,345 + 46,969 = 136,314$$
$$136,314 - 120,813 = 15,501$$

Missing and Extraneous (Too Much) Information Practice (page 15)

1. the number of Republicans

2. the number of people in the Marble family

3. the number of bicycles sold

4. Extra information: union dues of $325. The answer is $18,750 − $15,750 = $3,000.

5. Extra information: the 1,574 papers sold by the Tribune and the daily amounts for all three papers. The answer is 2,631 − 587 = 2,044.

Order of Operations (page 16)

1. $3(7 + 4) - 18 \div 9 = 3(11) - 18 \div 9 = 33 - 2 = 31$

2. $\dfrac{5 \times 4 + 2}{17 - 2 \times 3} = \dfrac{20 + 2}{17 - 6} = \dfrac{22}{11} = 2$

3. $6(7 - 5) + 4 = 6(2) + 4 = 12 + 4 = 16$

4. $14 + 28 \div 7 = 14 + 4 = 18$

5. $\dfrac{5 \times 6 + 2}{12 - 4} = \dfrac{30 + 2}{8} = \dfrac{32}{8} = 4$

6. $8 + 4 \times 2 = 8 + 8 = 16$

7. $\frac{(6-2)}{(3+1)} = \frac{4}{4} = 1$

8. $5 + 2 \times 4 = 5 + 8 = 13$

9. $\frac{8}{2} + \frac{18}{6} = 4 + 3 = 7$

10. $6(3+7) - 4(4-2) = 6(10) - 4(2) = 60 - 8 = 52$

11. $\frac{21}{(5-2)} = \frac{21}{3} = 7$

12. $36 + \frac{12}{6} = 36 + 2 = 38$

13. $(5 \times 24) \div (14 \times 16) = 0.536$

14. $100 - 35 \times 24 = -740$

15. $(28 \div 4) + (45 \div 9) = 12$

16. $(80 \times \$24) \div (80 \times \$12) = \$2$

17. $\$250 - (3 \times \$88) + (4 \times \$22) = \$74$

18. $(74 \times \$29) \times (44 \div 4) = \$23,606$

19. $9 \times 18 \times 6 + 6 \div 12 = 972.5$

20. $(8+9) \times (4+16) = 340$

21. $(\$156 + \$345) \times \$335 = \$167,835$

22. $(\$195 + \$185) \div 44 = \$8.64$

23. $(\$1,900 - \$450) \div \$280 = \$5.18$

24. $\$280 - \$45 - \$33 = \$202$

Set-Up Problems Practice (page 17)

1. $\$19,500 - 12 \times \$1,100$

2. $60 - 5 \times 2$

3. $(27 \times \$3) + (30 - 27) \times \$1$ OR
$27(\$3) + (30 - 27)(\$1)$

GED Practice: Set-Up Problems (page 18)

1. **(5) Not enough information is given.**
You need to know the number of items
Ernesto sold. (28 days is extraneous
information.)

2. **(5) 52($110 − $100) ÷ 4** You must change
average cost per week for the family of four to
average cost per year per family member.

3. **(3) 2(36 ÷ 2)**

4. **(4)** $\frac{\$6,096}{24}$

5. **(1) (40 + 31 + 51) ÷ 3**

6. **(1) 3(657)**

Fractions: Computation Practice (page 19)

1. $\frac{1}{3} \div \frac{3}{4} = \frac{1}{3} \times \frac{4}{3} = \frac{4}{9}$

2. $\frac{3}{5} \times \frac{22}{1} = \frac{66}{5} = 13\frac{1}{5}$

3. $32 \times \frac{13}{16} = \frac{32}{1} \times \frac{13}{16} = \frac{416}{16} = 26$

4. $\begin{array}{r} 22\frac{5}{9} = 22\frac{25}{45} \\ -14\frac{1}{5} = 14\frac{9}{45} \\ \hline 8\frac{16}{45} \end{array}$

5. $\begin{array}{r} \frac{7}{10} = \frac{21}{30} \\ +\frac{11}{30} = \frac{11}{30} \\ \hline \frac{32}{30} = 1\frac{2}{30} = 1\frac{1}{15} \end{array}$

6. $\begin{array}{r} 6\frac{3}{5} = 6\frac{6}{10} \\ 12\frac{1}{2} = 12\frac{5}{10} \\ +7\frac{3}{5} = 7\frac{6}{10} \\ \hline 25\frac{17}{10} = 26\frac{7}{10} \end{array}$

7. $6 \div 1\frac{1}{2} = \frac{6}{1} \div \frac{3}{2} = \frac{6}{1} \times \frac{2}{3} = \frac{12}{3} = 4$

8. $5\frac{1}{4} \div 12\frac{1}{5} = \frac{21}{4} \div \frac{61}{5} = \frac{21}{4} \times \frac{5}{61} = \frac{105}{244}$

9. $2\frac{1}{3} \times 1\frac{1}{5} = \frac{7}{3} \times \frac{6}{5} = \frac{42}{15} = 2\frac{12}{15} = 2\frac{4}{5}$

10. $\begin{array}{r} 8 = 7\frac{8}{8} \\ -7\frac{7}{8} \\ \hline \frac{1}{8} \end{array}$

11. $\begin{array}{r} 12\frac{1}{4} = 12\frac{4}{16} \\ 5\frac{13}{16} = 5\frac{13}{16} \\ 4\frac{5}{8} = 4\frac{10}{16} \\ +3\frac{1}{2} = 3\frac{8}{16} \\ \hline 24\frac{35}{16} = 26\frac{3}{16} \end{array}$

12.

$$15\frac{3}{7} = 15\frac{27}{63} = 14\frac{90}{63}$$
$$-14\frac{5}{9} = 14\frac{35}{63} = 14\frac{35}{63}$$
$$\overline{\hspace{5em}\frac{55}{63}}$$

13. $1\frac{3}{4} \times 3 = \frac{7}{4} \times \frac{3}{1} = \frac{21}{4} = 5\frac{1}{4}$

14. $3\frac{1}{2} \div 4 = \frac{7}{2} \div \frac{4}{1} = \frac{7}{2} \times \frac{1}{4} = \frac{7}{8}$

15. $\frac{3}{5} \div 8 = \frac{3}{5} \div \frac{8}{1} = \frac{3}{5} \times \frac{1}{8} = \frac{3}{40}$

16.

$$8\frac{9}{10} = 8\frac{54}{60}$$
$$12\frac{1}{2} = 12\frac{30}{60}$$
$$+4\frac{5}{12} = 4\frac{25}{60}$$
$$\overline{\hspace{5em}24\frac{109}{60} = 25\frac{49}{60}}$$

17.

$$9\frac{3}{8} = 9\frac{6}{16} = 8\frac{22}{16}$$
$$-5\frac{9}{16} = 5\frac{9}{16} = 5\frac{9}{16}$$
$$\overline{\hspace{5em}3\frac{13}{16}}$$

18.

$$18\frac{3}{4}$$
$$+ 8$$
$$\overline{26\frac{3}{4}}$$

19. $6 \times 1\frac{1}{2} \times 3\frac{3}{4} = \frac{6}{1} \times \frac{3}{2} \times \frac{15}{4} = \frac{270}{8} = 33\frac{3}{4}$

20.

$$10\frac{2}{3} = 10\frac{8}{12} = 9\frac{20}{12}$$
$$- 3\frac{3}{4} = 3\frac{9}{12} = 3\frac{9}{12}$$
$$\overline{\hspace{5em}6\frac{11}{12}}$$

21.

$$25\frac{3}{4} = 25\frac{6}{8}$$
$$+ 21\frac{5}{8} = 21\frac{5}{8}$$
$$\overline{\hspace{5em}46\frac{11}{8} = 47\frac{3}{8}}$$

22.

$$24 = 23\frac{2}{2}$$
$$- 18\frac{1}{2} = 18\frac{1}{2}$$
$$\overline{\hspace{5em}5\frac{1}{2}}$$

23. $3\frac{2}{5} \times 3\frac{1}{3} = \frac{17}{5} \times \frac{10}{3} = \frac{170}{15} = 11\frac{1}{3}$

24. $4\frac{2}{3} \div 2\frac{1}{3} = \frac{14}{3} \div \frac{7}{3} = \frac{14}{3} \times \frac{3}{7} = \frac{42}{21} = 2$

25.

$$2\frac{1}{2} = 2\frac{30}{60}$$
$$3\frac{1}{3} = 3\frac{20}{30}$$
$$4\frac{1}{4} = 4\frac{15}{60}$$
$$+ 5\frac{2}{5} = 5\frac{24}{60}$$
$$\overline{\hspace{5em}14\frac{89}{60} = 15\frac{29}{60}}$$

GED Practice: Fractions (page 20)

1. $8\frac{1}{4} = \frac{33}{4}$ **or 8.25**

$3\frac{1}{2} \times 3 = \frac{7}{2} \times \frac{3}{1} = \frac{21}{2} = 10\frac{1}{2}$ yd.

$1\frac{1}{4} \times 5 = \frac{5}{4} \times \frac{5}{1} = \frac{25}{4} = 6\frac{1}{4}$ yd.

$$10\frac{1}{2} = 10\frac{2}{4} \qquad\qquad 25 = 24\frac{4}{4}$$
$$+ 6\frac{1}{4} = 6\frac{1}{4} \qquad\qquad - 16\frac{3}{4} = 16\frac{3}{4}$$
$$\overline{\hspace{4em}16\frac{3}{4}} \qquad\qquad \overline{\hspace{4em}8\frac{1}{4}}$$

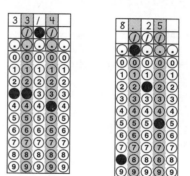

2. (1) 35

$21\frac{7}{8} \div \frac{5}{8} = \frac{175}{8} \times \frac{8}{5} = \frac{1,400}{40} = 35$

3. (5) 54 ft.

$4\frac{1}{2} \div \frac{1}{2} = \frac{9}{2} \times \frac{2}{1} = \frac{18}{2} = 9$

9×6 feet $= 54$ feet

4. (4) $23\frac{3}{4}$

$4\frac{3}{4} \times 5 = \frac{19}{4} \times \frac{5}{1} = \frac{95}{4} = 23\frac{3}{4}$

5. (1) rent

$$\frac{1}{3} = \frac{10}{30}$$
$$\frac{1}{5} = \frac{6}{30}$$
$$\frac{1}{6} = \frac{5}{30}$$
$$\frac{1}{5} = \frac{6}{30}$$
$$\frac{1}{10} = \frac{3}{30}$$

6. (4) $\frac{1}{6}$

$$\frac{1}{3} = \frac{2}{6}$$
$$- \frac{1}{6} = \frac{1}{6}$$
$$\overline{\hspace{3em}\frac{1}{6}}$$

7. (4) $475

$$\frac{\$2375}{1} \times \frac{1}{5} =$$
$$\frac{2375}{5} = \$475$$

GED Practice: Fractions II (page 21)

1. **(4)** $28 - (12\frac{1}{2} + 13\frac{3}{4})$

2. **(3) 60**

$75 \times \frac{1}{5} = \frac{75}{1} \times \frac{1}{5} = \frac{75}{5} = 15$

$75 - 15 = 60$

3. **(5)** $51\frac{3}{4}$ **ft.**

$2 \times 1\frac{3}{4} = \frac{2}{1} \times \frac{7}{4} = \frac{14}{4} = 3\frac{2}{4} = 3\frac{1}{2}$

$15 = 14\frac{2}{2}$

$\underline{- 3\frac{1}{2} = 3\frac{1}{2}}$

$11\frac{1}{2}$

$11\frac{1}{2} \times 4\frac{1}{2} = \frac{23}{2} \times \frac{9}{2} = \frac{207}{4} = 51\frac{3}{4}$ ft.

4. **(5) 150**

$1\frac{1}{5} \times 125 = \frac{6}{5} \times \frac{125}{1} = \frac{750}{5} = 150$

5. **(4)** $7\frac{1}{3}$

$55 \times \frac{2}{15} = 7\frac{1}{3}$

6. **(4) 821**

$6{,}775 \div 8\frac{1}{4} = 821\frac{7}{33}$

7. $269\frac{1}{2}$ **or** $\frac{539}{2}$ **or 269.5**

$44 \times 6\frac{1}{8} = \frac{44}{1} \times \frac{49}{8} = \frac{2156}{8} = \frac{539}{2} = 269.5$

Decimals: Computation Practice (page 22)

1.
$$\begin{array}{r} .04 \\ \times\ .09 \\ \hline 0.0036 \end{array}$$

2.
$$\begin{array}{r} .368 \\ \times\ .62 \\ \hline 736 \\ 2208 \\ \hline 0.22816 \end{array}$$

3.
$$\begin{array}{r} .7\ =\ .70 \\ \underline{-.35\ =\ .35} \\ 0.35 \end{array}$$

4.
$$\begin{array}{r} 0.2234 \\ 4)\overline{0.8936} \\ \underline{8} \\ 9 \\ \underline{8} \\ 13 \\ \underline{12} \\ 16 \\ 16 \end{array}$$

5.
$$\begin{array}{r} \$50.00 \\ \underline{-\$25.25} \\ \$24.75 \end{array}$$

6.
$$\begin{array}{r} \$700.00 \\ \underline{-\$446.58} \\ \$253.42 \end{array}$$

7.
$$\begin{array}{r} \$14.59 \\ \underline{-\ \ 7.00} \\ \$\ 7.59 \end{array}$$

8.
$$\begin{array}{r} \$14.25 \\ \underline{\times\ \ \ \ 11} \\ 14\ 25 \\ 142\ 5 \\ \hline \$156.75 \end{array}$$

9.
$$\begin{array}{r} .8 \\ \underline{\times\ .007} \\ 0.0056 \end{array}$$

10.
$$\begin{array}{r} 0.461 \\ 15)\overline{6.915} \\ \underline{60} \\ 91 \\ \underline{90} \\ 15 \\ 15 \end{array}$$

11. $2.33385 + 14.5323 = 16.86615$

12. $14.566 \div 4.9 = 2.972653$

13. $2223.44 + 19.665 = 2{,}243.105$

14. $0.6877 + 0.4 + 13.4 = 14.4877$

15. $59.67 \times 0.089 = 5.31063$

16. $389.532 \div 0.459 = 848.6535948$ rounds to 848.7

17. $0.999999 + 5 + 9.89999 = 15.899989$

18. $0.9 - 0.009 = 0.891$

19. $\$664.59 + \$.49 = \$665.08$

20. $32.224 \div 22.3 = 1.445022422$ rounds to 1.4

GED Practice: Decimals (page 23)

1. **(1) 0.6**

$1.3 + 1.8 + 2.1 + 1.6 + 1.5 + 1.1 = 9.4$

$10 - 9.4 = 0.6$

2. (2) $450.00

$150 \times (\$10.95 - \$7.95) = 150 \times \$3 = \$450$

3. (3) $579

$$\begin{array}{r} \$57.75 \\ \times\ \ \ \ 36 \\ \hline 346\ 50 \\ 1\ 732\ 5 \\ \hline \$2,079.00 \end{array} \qquad \begin{array}{r} \$2,079.00 \\ -\$1,500.00 \\ \hline \$579.00 \end{array}$$

4. (3) $1,785

$150 \times (\$37.75 - \$25.85) =$
$150 \times \$11.90 = \$1,785.00$

5. (4) $482.80

$\$12.07 \times 40 = \$482.80$

6. (2) $253.60

$18.41 \times 40 - 12.07 \times 40 = 253.60$

GED Practice Decimals II (page 24)

1. (4) $919.63

$\$121.53 + \$48.77 + \$25.41 + \$84.66 = \$280.37$
$\$1,200 - \$280.37 = \$919.63$

2. (4) 50

$$\begin{array}{r} 50. \\ 2.98\overline{)149.00} \\ 149\ 0 \end{array}$$

3. (1) $.47

$$\begin{array}{r} \$.471 \text{ rounds to } \$.47 \\ 52\overline{)\$24.500} \\ \underline{20\ 8} \\ 3\ 70 \\ \underline{3\ 64} \\ 60 \\ \underline{52} \\ 8 \end{array}$$

4. (1) $1.00 (15)

5. (5) $141.36

$$\begin{array}{r} \$\ 19.98 \\ \times\ \ \ \ \ \ 6 \\ \hline \$119.88 \text{ for screwdrivers} \end{array}$$

$24 \div 2 = 12$ sets of two batteries
$12 \times \$1.79 = \$21.48$ for batteries
$\$119.88 + \$21.48 = \$141.36$

6. 222.7

$$\begin{array}{r} 26.2 \\ \times\ \ \ 8.5 \\ \hline 1310 \\ 2096 \\ \hline 222.70 \end{array}$$

Percents: Computation Practice (page 25)

Example for $\frac{1}{8}$:

To find the decimal:

$$\begin{array}{r} 0.125 \\ 8\overline{)1.000} \\ \underline{8} \\ 20 \\ \underline{16} \\ 40 \\ 40 \end{array}$$

To find the percent:

$$\begin{array}{r} 0.125 \\ \times\ \ 100 \\ \hline 12.500 = 12.5\% \end{array}$$

	FRACTION	DECIMAL	PERCENT
1.	$\frac{1}{8}$	0.125	12.5% or $12\frac{1}{2}$%
2.	$\frac{1}{4}$	0.25	25%
3.	$\frac{1}{3}$	0.333	33.3% or $33\frac{1}{3}$%
4.	$\frac{3}{8}$	0.375	37.5% or $37\frac{1}{2}$%
5.	$\frac{1}{2}$	0.5	50%
6.	$\frac{3}{5}$	0.6	60%
7.	$\frac{5}{8}$	0.625	62.5% or $62\frac{1}{2}$%
8.	$\frac{2}{3}$	0.667	66.7% or $66\frac{2}{3}$%
9.	$\frac{3}{4}$	0.75	75%
10.	$\frac{4}{5}$	0.8	80%
11.	$\frac{7}{8}$	0.875	87.5% or $87\frac{2}{3}$%
12.	$\frac{9}{10}$	0.9	90%

13. $125\% \times 90 = 1.25 \times 90 = 112.5$

14. To find the percent, divide the part by the whole.

$$0.6 = 60\%$$
$$5\overline{)3.0}$$
$$3\,0$$

15. $\frac{1}{8}\% = 0.125\%$

$$\frac{1}{8}\% \text{ of } 561 = \frac{1}{8} \times \frac{1}{100} \times 561 = 0.70125$$

OR 0.125% of $561 = 0.00125 \times 561 = 0.70125$

16. To find the percent, divide the part by the whole.

$$0.52 = 52\%$$
$$25\overline{)13.00}$$
$$12\,5$$
$$50$$
$$50$$

17. To find the number, divide 306 by 0.34. (0.34 = 34%)

$$9\,00$$
$$.34\overline{)306.00}$$
$$306$$

18. To find the percent, divide the part by the whole.

$$0.50 = 50\%$$
$$90\overline{)45.00}$$
$$45\,0$$

19. 3% of $391 = 0.03 \times 391 = 11.73$

20. To find the number, divide 81 by 0.09 (0.09 = 9%)

$$9\,00$$
$$.09\overline{)81.00}$$
$$81$$

21. To find the number, divide 22 by 1.10. (1.10 = 110%)

$$20$$
$$1.10\overline{)22.00}$$

22. **25%**
To find the percent, divide the part by the whole.

$$0.25 = 25\%$$
$$396\overline{)99.00}$$
$$792$$
$$1980$$
$$1980$$

GED Practice: Percents (page 26)

1. **(3) $34.50**

$$\begin{array}{r} \$46 \\ \times.25 \\ \hline 2\,30 \\ 9\,2 \\ \hline \$11.50 \end{array} \qquad \begin{array}{r} \$46.00 \\ -11.50 \\ \hline \$34.50 \end{array}$$

2. **(4) 52%**

$$\frac{\text{New} - \text{Old}}{\text{Old}} = \frac{\$11.75 - \$7.75}{\$7.75} = \frac{4.00}{7.75}$$

$$0.516 \text{ rounds to } 52\%$$
$$7.75\overline{)\$4.00\,000}$$
$$3\,87\,5$$
$$12\,50$$
$$7\,75$$
$$4\,750$$
$$4\,650$$
$$100$$

3. **(4) 33,125 miles** To find the number of miles, change the percent to a decimal and divide.

$$33,12\,5$$
$$.8\overline{)26,500.0}$$
$$24$$
$$2\,5$$
$$2\,4$$
$$10$$
$$8$$
$$20$$
$$16$$
$$4\,0$$
$$4\,0$$

4. (3) $304.20

$$
\begin{array}{r}
\$1\,95 \\
\times\ \ .03 \\
\hline
\$5.85
\end{array}
$$

52 weeks = 1 year

$$
\begin{array}{r}
\$5.85 \\
\times\ 52 \\
\hline
11\ 70 \\
292\ 5 \\
\hline
\$304.20
\end{array}
$$

5. (3) $38.64
$28 \times 138\% = 38.64$

6. (2) $260
$\$195 \div 0.75 = \$260$

7. (2) $128.12
$\$156.25 \times 18\% = 28.125 = \$28.13$
$\$156.25 - \$28.13 = \$128.12$

GED Practice: Percents II (page 27)

1. (2) $100 Change $6\frac{1}{4}\% = 6.25\% = 0.0625$

$$
\begin{array}{r}
\$1,600 \\
\times\ .0625 \\
\hline
8000 \\
3\ 200 \\
96\ 00 \\
\hline
\$100.0000
\end{array}
$$

2. (4) $425

$$
\begin{array}{r}
\$2,500 \\
-\ 1,000 \\
\hline
\$1,500
\end{array}
\qquad
\begin{array}{r}
\$1,500 \\
\times\ .15 \\
\hline
75\ 00 \\
150\ 0 \\
\hline
\$225.00
\end{array}
\qquad
\begin{array}{r}
\$200 \\
+\ 225 \\
\hline
\$425
\end{array}
$$

3. (3) $1,980

$$
\begin{array}{r}
\$2,750 \\
-\ \ 275 \\
\hline
\$2,475
\end{array}
\qquad
\begin{array}{r}
\$2,475 \\
\times\ \ .80 \\
\hline
\$1,980.00
\end{array}
$$

4. (4) $22.49
$\$29.95 \times 70\% = 20.965$
$\$20.97 \times 7.25\% = 1.52$
$\$20.97 + \$1.52 = \$22.49$

5. (5) Not enough information is given.

6. (3) $30,965.90
$\$28,540 \times 8.5\% = 2,425.9$
$\$28,540 + 2,425.90 = 30,965.90$

7. (2) $13,100
$\$180,000 \times 4.5\% + \$5,000 = \$13,100$

GED Practice: Ratio and Proportion (page 29)

1. (3) 28

$$\frac{\text{margarine}}{\text{flour}} = \frac{\text{margarine}}{\text{flour}}$$

$\dfrac{3}{3\frac{1}{2}} \diagup\!\!\!\!\diagup \dfrac{24}{x}$ Cross multiply.

$3x = 24\left(3\frac{1}{2}\right)$
$3x = 84$
$x = 28$ cups

2. (2) $539.25

$\dfrac{\$35.95}{2} \diagup\!\!\!\!\diagup \dfrac{x}{30}$ Cross multiply.

$2x = 30(\$35.95)$
$2x = \$1078.50$
$x = \$539.25$

3. (5) $1,500

$\dfrac{\$375}{3} \diagup\!\!\!\!\diagup \dfrac{x}{12}$

$3x = 12(\$375)$
$3x = \$4,500$
$x = \$1,500$

4. (5) $22.50

$$\frac{\text{cost}}{\text{value of policy}}$$

$\dfrac{\$.75}{\$1,000} \diagup\!\!\!\!\diagup \dfrac{x}{\$30,000}$

$\$1,000x = \$22,500$
$x = \$22.50$

5. (3) 45

$\dfrac{12}{x} = \dfrac{20}{75}$

$20x = 900$
$x = 45$

6. (4) $210

$\dfrac{90}{600} = \dfrac{x}{1400}$

$600x = \$126,000$
$x = \$210$

7. 40 minutes

$\dfrac{26}{1} \times \dfrac{1040}{x}$

$26x = 1040$
$x = 40$

GED Review: Numbers and Operations (pages 30-32)

1. **(3)** $7 \times (9 - 3)$ (order of operations)

2. **(5)** $\frac{3}{10}$ **0.3 30%** (fractions, decimals, and percents)

3. **(5) 89%** (percents)

$$\begin{array}{r} 225 \\ -\ 25 \\ \hline 200 \end{array}$$

$$225 \overline{)200.000} = 0.888 = 89\%$$
$$\begin{array}{r} 1800 \\ \hline 2000 \\ 1800 \\ \hline 200 \end{array}$$

4. **(4) $100.20** (percents)

$$\begin{array}{r} \$\ 125.25 \\ \times \quad\ .20 \\ \hline \$25.0500 \end{array} \qquad \begin{array}{r} \$125.25 \\ -\ 25.05 \\ \hline \$100.20 \end{array}$$

5. **227** (whole numbers)

$$\begin{array}{r} 229 \\ -18 \\ \hline 211 \end{array} \qquad \begin{array}{r} 211 \\ +\ 16 \\ \hline 227 \end{array}$$

6. **105** (Percents)
   $84 \times 0.25 = 21$
   $84 + 21 = 105$

7. **(1) $22** (decimals)

$$\begin{array}{r} \$\ 6 \\ \times\ 3 \\ \hline \$18 \end{array} \qquad \begin{array}{r} \$18 \\ +\ 5 \\ \hline \$23 \end{array} \qquad \begin{array}{r} \$45 \\ -\ 23 \\ \hline \$22 \end{array}$$

8. **(3) $37.63** (fractions, decimals, and percents)
   $\$56 \times 0.16 = \$8.96$
   $\$56 - \$8.96 = \$47.04$
   $\frac{1}{5} \times \$47.04 = \$9.41$
   $\$47.04 - \$9.41 = \$37.63$

9. **(4) 62** (fractions)
   35 minutes = $\frac{7}{12}$ hr. Ship travels 24 miles per hr. By 8:35, ship traveled $2\frac{7}{12}$ hrs.
   $2\frac{7}{12} \times 24 = 62$

10. **(2) $22.26** (percents)
    $\$6.95 \times 2 + \$8.95 \times 2 = \$31.80$
    $\$31.80 \times 0.30 = \$9.54$
    $\$31.80 - \$9.54 = \$22.26$

11. **(4) $739.20** (order of operations)
    $12 \times 5 + 8 + 4 = 72$ hours
    40 hrs. at $8.40 = \$336.00$
    32 hrs. at $12.60 = \underline{\$403.20}$
    $\qquad\qquad\qquad \$739.20$

12. **(1) $5.40** (decimals and percent)
    $0.48\ (1) + (0.34 \times 44) = 15.44 \times 0.35 = \$5.40$

13. **(2) 123** (fractions)
    $15\frac{1}{2} \div \frac{1}{8} = \frac{31}{2} \div \frac{1}{8} = \frac{31}{2} \times \frac{8}{1} = \frac{248}{2} = 124$
    However, the 124th hole would be drilled in the end of the plate, therefore, only 123 holes can be drilled.

14. **(4) $1\frac{1}{7}$ and $\frac{8}{7}$** (fractions)

15. **(5) a loss of 25 pounds** (positive and negative numbers)

16. **(5) 0.20×325** (percents)
    Change 20% to 0.20. "Of" means multiply.

17. **(1) 57 in.** (ratio and proportion)
    $\frac{3 \text{ mi.}}{1 \text{ in.}} = \frac{171 \text{ mi.}}{x} \qquad 3x = 171x \qquad x = 57 \text{ in.}$

18. **$13\frac{1}{2}$ or $\frac{27}{2}$ or 13.5** (fractions)
    $1\frac{1}{2} + 3 + 4\frac{1}{2} + 4\frac{1}{2} = 12 + \frac{3}{2} = 12 + 1\frac{1}{2} = 13\frac{1}{2} = \frac{27}{2} = 13.5$

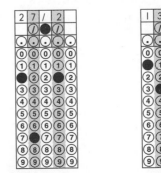

19. 0.289 (decimals)

$0.220 + 0.242 + 0.204 + 0.333 + 0.514 +$
$0.187 + 0.442 + 0.208 + 0.318 + 0.301 +$
$0.212 = \frac{3.181}{11} = 0.289$

UNIT 2: MEASUREMENT AND DATA ANALYSIS

Data Analysis: Mean, Median, and Number Series Practice (page 33)

1. 87.5
Add the test scores.
$97 + 72 + 89 + 90 + 90 + 87 = 525$
Divide by the number of test scores.

$$
\begin{array}{r}
87.5 \\
6\overline{)525.0} \\
48 \\
\hline
45 \\
42 \\
\hline
30 \\
30 \\
\end{array}
$$

2. 58°
Arrange numbers in order from smallest to largest.
53°
56°
57°
58° ← middle value = median
59°
61°
62°

3. 3
Each term is divided in half: $6 \div 2 = 3$

4. $49,420
$
\begin{array}{r}
\$\ 65,500 \\
56,000 \\
49,250 \\
32,750 \\
+\ 43,600 \\
\hline
\$247,100 \\
\end{array}
$

$\frac{\$247,100}{5} = \$49,420$

GED Practice: Probability (page 35)

1. (2) $\frac{1}{5}$ $\quad \frac{white}{total} = \frac{3}{3+4+2+6} = \frac{3}{15} = \frac{1}{5}$

2. (2) $\frac{1}{4}$ $\quad \frac{mixed}{total} = \frac{3}{4+3+5} = \frac{3}{12} = \frac{1}{4}$

3. (5) $\frac{1}{4}$ $\quad \frac{creme}{total} = \frac{6}{6 \times 4} = \frac{6}{24} = \frac{1}{4}$

4. (1) $\frac{1}{9}$ $\quad \frac{dimes}{total} = \frac{5}{15+5+25} = \frac{5}{45} = \frac{1}{9}$

5. (3) $\frac{1}{4}$ $\quad \frac{1\ card\ drawn}{4\ total\ cards} = \frac{1}{4}$

6. (1) $\frac{1}{2}$ $\quad \frac{red}{total} = \frac{50}{50+50} = \frac{50}{100} = \frac{1}{2}$

Measurement: Computation Practice (page 36)

1. 1 minute
2. 1 year
3. 24 hours
4. 12 inches
5. 5,280 feet
6. 0.09 kg
7. 0.00788 L
8. 5300 mm
9. 0.18 m
10. 131 mm

11. 9 pounds 2 ounces
$
\begin{array}{r}
8\ pounds \quad 1\ ounce \\
+\ \qquad 17\ ounces \\
\hline
8\ pounds\ 18\ ounces = 9\ pounds\ 2\ ounces \\
\end{array}
$

12. 1,800 pounds
2 tons = 4,000 pounds
$
\begin{array}{r}
4,000 \\
-2,200 \\
\hline
1,800 \\
\end{array}
$

13. $.50
1 gallon = 4 quarts
$\frac{\$2.00}{4} = \$.50$

14. 14 pieces, 4 in. piece left
12 feet $\times$ 12 = 144 inches
$\frac{144}{10} = 14$ R 4

15. 64.4 km
64,400 m $\div$ 1000 = 64.4 km

16. 0.108 kg
$108 \div 1000 = 0.108$ kg

GED Practice: Measurement (page 37)

1. (5) 300,000
50 2-liter bottles $\times$ 3 = 150 2-liter bottles
= 300 liters
300 L $\times$ 1000 = 300,000 milliliters

2. (2) 192

Change 288 ounces to 18 pounds
(16 ounces = 1 pound).

```
       18                    192
   16)288               18)3,456
       16                    1 8
      128                    1 65
      128                    1 62
                               36
                               36
```

3. (4) 0.3642 km/min

$(6.07 \times 60) \div 1000 = 0.3642$

4. 120 minutes

```
2 hr.   15 min.
3 hr.
        45 min.
1 hr.   40 min.
+2 hr.  20 min.
8 hr. 120 min. = 10 hr.
```

$\dfrac{10 \text{ hours}}{5 \text{ days}} = 2 \text{ hours}$

2 hours = 120 minutes

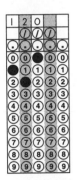

5. (2) $85.44

8 dozen = $8 \times 12 = 96$ tires
21 lb. 8 oz. = 21.5 lb.

```
        × 96
        129 0
        1935
      2,064.0 lb.
```

Find 2,064 lb. on the chart (1,500–2,999).
The shipping charge is $.89 per tire.

```
      $  .89
      ×    96
        5 34
        80 1
      $85.44
```

GED Practice: Tables (page 38)

1. (3) United States

2. (3) 9

Gold 16
Silver 25
$25 - 16 = 9$

3. (4) 46

$28 + 16 + 15 = 59$
$4 + 6 + 3 = 13$
$59 - 13 = 46$

4. 14

$39 - 25 = 14$

5. 3

$11 + 28 + 15 = 54$
$33 + 1 + 17 = 51$
$54 - 51 = 3$

GED Practice: Circle Graphs (page 39)

1. (2) 2.4

Find 10% of 24 hrs.

```
      24
     ×.10
     2.40
```

2. (2) commercials, sports, and weather

$20\% + 20\% + 10\% = 50\%$

3. (1) $\dfrac{1}{20}$

$\dfrac{\text{editorials}}{100} = \dfrac{5}{100} = \dfrac{1}{20}$

4. (3) North America, Asia, and Africa
Since the continent land masses are given in percents, convert 9,000,000 to a percent: 9,000,000 ÷ 58,000,000 = 0.155 = 15.5%. Then choose the continents with land masses greater than 15.5%

5. (4) 8,700,000
Add the percents:
Antarctica + Australia = 9% + 6% = 15%. Convert the total percentage to square miles: 58,000,000 × .15 = 8,700,000

6. (2) (0.3 − 0.06) × 58,000,000
Change each percent to a decimal. Subtract. Multiply the result by the total land mass.

GED Practice: Charts (pages 40–41)

1. (3) 97,602
7,420,166 − 7,322,564 = 97,602

2. (5) 5,736,987
7,322,564 − 1,585,577 = 5,736,987

3. (5) Philadelphia

4. (4) Houston
increase of 148,832

5. (4) 12,000
7,420,166 − 7,322,564 = 97,602
97,602 ÷ 8 = 12,200.25
rounded to nearest thousand 12,000

6. (4) 5,983,879
7,420,166 − 1,436,287 = 5,983,879

7. (2) 6–17

8. (2) 0–5 and 18–44

9. (4) 65+
$4,840 > (2 × $2,402)

10. (3) $1822.00
$1,242
+ 2,402
$3,644 ÷ 2 = $1,822

11. (1) 1999
2.46 to 1

12. (1) 1995
1995   546 ÷ 928 = 0.588 = 59%
1996   508 ÷ 1,002 = 0.507 = 51%
1997   535 ÷ 994 = 0.538 = 54%
1998   567 ÷ 1,118 = 0.507 = 51%
1999   421 ÷ 1,035 = 0.407 = 41%

13. 515.4
546 + 508 + 535 + 567 + 421 = 2,577
2,577 ÷ 5 = 515.4

GED Practice: Line Graphs (page 42)

1. (3) $650 million

2. (2) 1998 – 1999

3. (4) $\frac{5}{13}$
$\frac{250}{650} = \frac{5}{13}$

4. 225%
650 − 200 = 450
$\frac{450}{200} = 2.25 = 225\%$

5. 25%
$\frac{50}{200} = \frac{1}{4} = 25\%$

GED Practice: Bar Graphs (pages 43–44)

1. **(4) Australia and China**

2. **(1) Australia**

3. **(5) 110,000,000**
   120,000,000 − 10,000,000 =110,000,000

4. **(1) Australia and China**

5. **(2) Russia**

6. **(5) 100,000,000**

7. **(5) 250,000**

   $$
   \begin{aligned}
   &250 \text{ January}\\
   &300 \text{ June}\\
   &250 \text{ August}\\
   +\,&200 \text{ September}\\
   \hline
   &1,000 \text{ (thousands)}
   \end{aligned}
   $$
   1,000,000 ÷ 4 = 250,000

8. **(3) the price of tickets for admission**

9. **(1) (200 + 325 + 275 + 350) ÷ 4**

10. **(4) $1,500,000**
    300,000 people × $5 = $1,500,000

11. **(5) 100,000**
    $\frac{1}{3} \times 300,000 = \frac{300,000}{3} = 100,000$

12. **(3) 11%**
    Add the monthly totals.

    $$
    \begin{array}{r}
    0.108\\
    3225\overline{)350.000}\\
    322\ 5\\
    \hline
    27\ 500\\
    25\ 800\\
    \hline
    1\ 700
    \end{array}
    $$
    0.108 rounds to 0.11 or 11%

GED Practice: Mixed Practice (pages 45–47)

1. **(1) $1.1 billion**
   $4.4 billion − $3.3 billion = $1.1 billion

2. **(1) $1.0 billion**
   $9.5 billion − $8.5 billion = $1.0 billion

3. **(1) 14,000,000**
   63,000,000 − 49,000,000 = 14,000,000

4. **(3) Cable TV subscribers steadily increased.**

5. **(5) 2000**

6. **(4) $3.0 million**
   $3.25 million − $0.25 million = $3.0 million

7. **(2) (0.25 + 0.3 + 0.5) ÷ 3**

8. **(3) 8,470**
   121,000 × 0.07 = 8,470

9. **(5) Type G**

10. **(5) $\frac{1}{25}$**
    Type F = 4%; 4% = $\frac{4}{100} = \frac{1}{25}$

11. **(2) 145,821**
    281,113 − 135,292 = 145,821

12. **(2) 304,932**

    $$
    \begin{aligned}
    &53,542\\
    +\,&251,390\\
    \hline
    &304,932
    \end{aligned}
    $$

13. **(3) 53,542 ÷ (53,542 + 251,390)**

14. **(1) Air Force**
    Air Force $\frac{53,542}{304,932} = 18\%$

    Army $\frac{60,787}{374,433} = 16\%$

    Navy $\frac{42,261}{323,374} = 13\%$

    Marines $\frac{8,928}{144,220} = 6\%$

15. **7,245**
    60,787 − 53,542 = 7,245

16. 52,200 (rounded to the nearest hundred)

```
    53,542              52,196
    60,787           3)156,590
  + 42,261             15
  ─────────            ──
   156,590              6
                        6
                       ──
                        5
                        3
                       ──
                       29
                       27
                       ──
                       20
                       18
                       ──
                        2
```

17. 29,723

```
   281,113
 − 251,390
 ─────────
    29,723
```

GED Review: Measurement and Data Analysis (pages 48–50)

1. (2) 45 and 53 (number series)
Each term is increased by 8.

2. (1) $\frac{1}{4}$ (probability)
$\frac{13 \text{ diamonds}}{52 \text{ cards}} = \frac{1}{4}$

3. (1) $\frac{1}{10}$ (probability)
There is only one 8 on the spinner. Therefore, the probability of landing on an 8 is $\frac{1}{10}$.

4. (2) 16, 8, 4, 2, 1 (number series)
The number series takes a given number and divides it by 1, then 2, then 4, and so on. Only option 2 shows this pattern.

5. (2) $3,242.50 (median)
Order the numbers from smallest to largest.
$2,675
$2,683
$2,751 ⎫
$3,734 ⎭ ── middle values
$4,270
$4,671
Add the middle values

```
   $ 2,751
 +   3,734
 ─────────
   $ 6,485
```
median: $6,485 ÷ 2 = $3,242.50

6. $3,464 (mean)

```
   $ 4,270        $20,784 ÷ 6 = $3,464
     2,675
     2,751
     3,734
     2,683
 +   4,671
 ─────────
   $20,784
```

7. $250 (tables, decimals)
Mid-size:
$\frac{20,000 \text{ miles}}{20 \text{ mpg}} = 1,000 \times \$1.25 = \$1,250.00$
Subcompact:
$\frac{20,000 \text{ miles}}{25 \text{ mpg}} = 800 \times \$1.25 = \$1,000.00$

```
   $1,250
 −  1,000
 ────────
   $  250
```

8. **20°** (positive and negative numbers)
$(5°) - (-15°)$
$5° + 15° = +20°$

9. **(2) 13.5** (measurement)
Find the number of cans in $1\frac{1}{2}$ cases.
1 case = 24 cans, $\frac{1}{2}$ case = 12 cans
$1\frac{1}{2}$ cases = 36 cans
Find the total ounces of tuna. $36 \times 6 = 216$
Divide to find pounds. $216 \div 16 = 13.5$

10. **(2) 29.25** (mean, median, and number series practice)
$29.86 + 28.32 + 25.21 + 27.36 = 110.75$
$28 \times 5 = 140; 140 - 110.75 = 29.25$

11. **(5) 53,850** (mean, median, and number series practice)

```
  $125,000        $53,850
    85,000     8)430,800
    56,000        40
    46,400        30
    46,400        24
    24,000        68
    24,000        64
 +  24,000        40
 ─────────        40
  $430,800         0
```

12. **59.4** (charts, decimals, and fractions)
The dog falls into the "up to 90 lbs" category, and therefore should be fed a maximum of $4\frac{1}{2}$ cans daily.
$4.5 \times 13.2 = 59.4$

13. **(5) 8** (charts, decimals, and fractions)
The dog is 32 pounds over the 90-pound mark. These 32 pounds allow the dog to have 2 cans over the 6 cans allowed for 90-pound dogs.
$6 + 2 = 8$

14. **(3) $1,267.50** (charts, percents)
At $28,000, the taxpayer would owe $787.50 plus 6% of $8,000 (the excess over $20,000).
$\$8,000 \times 6\% = \$8,000 \times .06 = \$480$
$\$787.50 + \$480 = \$1,267.50$

15. **(2) $\frac{1}{5}$** (probability)
5 of the 25 cards will have numbers greater than 45.
$\frac{5}{25} = \frac{1}{5}$

16. **(4) 63** (measurement)
14 yds. = 504 inches
$504 \div 8 = 63$

UNIT 3: ALGEBRA

Introduction (page 51)

1. $x - 3$

2. $4x$

3. $b + h$

4. $36y$

5. $\frac{50}{x}$

6. $15 + x$

7. $2x + 1$

8. $\frac{d}{7}$

Powers and Roots of Numbers (page 52)

1. $8 \times 8 = 64$

2. $1 \times 1 \times 1 \times 1 \times 1 = 1$

3. $2 \times 2 \times 2 = 8$

4. $5 \times 5 \times 5 = 125$

5. $\sqrt{16} = 4$ because $4 \times 4 = 16$

6. $\sqrt{25} = 5$ because $5 \times 5 = 25$

7. $\sqrt{100} = 10$ because $10 \times 10 = 100$

8. $\sqrt{121} = 11$ because $11 \times 11 = 121$

9. $3 \times 3 \times 3 \times 3 = 81$

10. $12 \times 12 = 144$

11. $\sqrt{169} = 13$ because $13 \times 13 = 169$

12. $\sqrt{225} = 15$ because $15 \times 15 = 225$

13. $3{,}500 = 3.5 \times 10^3$

14. $29{,}000 = 2.9 \times 10^4$

15. $85{,}700 = 8.57 \times 10^4$

16. $26{,}410 = 2.641 \times 10^4$

17. $2{,}100 = 2.1 \times 10^3$

18. $0.005 = 5.0 \times 10^{-3}$

19. $0.0024 = 2.4 \times 10^{-3}$

20. $0.012 = 1.2 \times 10^{-2}$

21. $0.035 = 3.5 \times 10^{-2}$

22. $0.221 = 2.21 \times 10^{-1}$

Simplifying Algebraic Expressions (page 53)

1. $2x^2 - 1$

2. $-2y + 6$

3. $9p + 6$

4. $-5z^2 + 5$

5. $-4r - 3$

6. $2x^2 + 27$

7. $3y - 29$

8. $-9y$

9. $10st$

10. $1 - 4a$

11. $35x - 14$

12. $10p^2$

13. $2p^2 + 3pq - 10q^2$

Evaluating Algebraic Expressions Using Substitutions (page 54)

1. $bc - ad = (5)(6) - 3(1) = 30 - 3 = 27$

2. $\dfrac{xy - yz}{xyz} = \dfrac{-1(2) - 2(-4)}{-1(2)(-4)} = \dfrac{-2 + 8}{8} = \dfrac{6}{8} = \dfrac{3}{4}$

3. $\dfrac{b^3}{b^2} = \dfrac{5^3}{5^2} = \dfrac{125}{25} = 5$

4. $x^3 + (y - 2z) = (-1)^3 + [2 - 2(-4)] = -1 + 2 + 8 = -1 + 10 = 9$

5. $\dfrac{10cd}{abc} = \dfrac{10(6)(1)}{3(5)(6)} = \dfrac{60}{90} = \dfrac{2}{3}$

6. $\dfrac{3(x + z)}{x} = \dfrac{3(-1 + -4)}{-1} = \dfrac{3(-5)}{-1} = \dfrac{-15}{-1} = 15$

7. $a^3 - b^3 = (3)^3 - (5)^3 = 27 - 125 = -98$

8. $ay + by = 3(2) + 5(2) = 6 + 10 = 16$

9. $(5x - 5z) + ab = [5(-1) - 5(-4)] + (3)(5) = (-5 + 20) + 15 = 15 + 15 = 30$

10. $3a^2b - 6 = 3(3)^2(5) - 6 = 3(9)(5) - 6 = 135 - 6 = 129$

11. $3x(xy - b) = 3(-1)[(-1)(2) - 5] = 3(-1)(-7) = 21$

12. $\dfrac{y}{x} + yz = \dfrac{2}{-1} + 2(-4) = -2 + (-8) = -10$

13. $a(7 - a)^2 = 3(7 - 3)^2 = 3(4)^2 = 3(16) = 48$

14. $\dfrac{bc - 5a}{b} = \dfrac{(5)(6) - 5(3)}{5} = \dfrac{30 - 15}{5} = \dfrac{15}{5} = 3$

15. $\dfrac{3(y + z)}{x} = \dfrac{3(2 + -4)}{-1} = \dfrac{3(2 - 4)}{-1} = \dfrac{3(-2)}{-1} = \dfrac{-6}{-1} = 6$

16. $\dfrac{a}{b} + \dfrac{b}{c} = \dfrac{3}{5} + \dfrac{5}{6} = \dfrac{18}{30} + \dfrac{25}{30} = \dfrac{43}{30} = 1\dfrac{13}{30}$

Solving One-Step Equations (page 55)

1. $x = 9$

2. $y = -24$

3. $x = 12$

4. $r = 33$

5. $m = 65$

6. $x = -24$

7. $x = 3$

8. $n = -8$

9. $12n = 36$
$\dfrac{12n}{12} = \dfrac{36}{12}$
$n = 3$

10. $n + 10 = 80$
$n + 10 - 10 = 80 - 10$
$n = 70$

11. $n - 6 = 2$
$n - 6 + 6 = 2 + 6$
$n = 8$

12. $n - 13 = 39$
$n - 13 + 13 = 39 + 13$
$n = 52$

Solving Two-Step Equations (page 56)

1.
$$4x + 7 = 11$$
$$4x + 7 - 7 = 11 - 7$$
$$4x = 4$$
$$\frac{4x}{4} = \frac{4}{4}$$
$$x = 1$$

2.
$$6x - 13 = 17$$
$$6x - 13 + 13 = 17 + 13$$
$$6x = 30$$
$$\frac{6x}{6} = \frac{30}{6}$$
$$x = 5$$

3.
$$\frac{x}{8} + 9 = 10$$
$$\frac{x}{8} + 9 - 9 = 10 - 9$$
$$\frac{x}{8} = 1$$
$$8\left(\frac{x}{8}\right) = 1(8)$$
$$x = 8$$

4.
$$\frac{x}{2} - 6 = 2$$
$$\frac{x}{2} - 6 + 6 = 2 + 6$$
$$\frac{x}{2} = 8$$
$$2\left(\frac{x}{2}\right) = 8(2)$$
$$x = 16$$

5.
$$-8x + 12 = 36$$
$$-8x + 12 - 12 = 36 - 12$$
$$-8x = 24$$
$$\frac{-8x}{-8} = -\frac{24}{8}$$
$$x = -3$$

6.
$$\frac{-x}{9} - 7 = 3$$
$$\frac{-x}{9} - 7 + 7 = 3 + 7$$
$$\frac{-x}{9} = 10$$
$$-9\left(\frac{-x}{9}\right) = 10(-9)$$
$$x = -90$$

7.
$$3x - 4 = 10$$
$$3x + 4 - 4 = 10 - 4$$
$$3x = 6$$
$$\frac{3x}{3} = \frac{6}{3}$$
$$x = 2$$

8.
$$-2x + 7 = -25$$
$$-2x + 7 - 7 = -25 - 7$$
$$-2x = -32$$
$$\frac{-2x}{-2} = \frac{-32}{-2}$$
$$x = 16$$

9.
$$5 - 5x = -10$$
$$5 - 5 - 5x = -10 - 5$$
$$-5x = -15$$
$$\frac{-5x}{-5} = \frac{-15}{-5}$$
$$x = 3$$

10.
$$14 + \frac{x}{4} = -2$$
$$14 - 14 + \frac{x}{4} = -2 - 14$$
$$\frac{x}{4} = -16$$
$$4\left(\frac{x}{4}\right) = -16(4)$$
$$x = -64$$

11.
$$25 + 10x = 75$$
$$25 - 25 + 10x = 75 - 25$$
$$10x = 50$$
$$\frac{10x}{10} = \frac{50}{10}$$
$$x = 5$$

12.
$$-8 - 2x = -4$$
$$-8 + 8 - 2x = -4 + 8$$
$$-2x = 4$$
$$\frac{-2x}{-2} = -\frac{4}{2}$$
$$x = -2$$

13.
$$-1 + \frac{x}{3} = 2$$
$$-1 + 1 + \frac{x}{3} = 2 + 1$$
$$\frac{x}{3} = 3$$
$$3\left(\frac{x}{3}\right) = 3(3)$$
$$x = 9$$

14.
$$17 - \frac{x}{10} = 5$$
$$17 - 17 - \frac{x}{10} = 5 - 17$$
$$-\frac{x}{10} = -12$$
$$-10\left(-\frac{x}{10}\right) = -12(-10)$$
$$x = 120$$

15.
$$8 - 3x = 17$$
$$8 - 8 - 3x = 17 - 8$$
$$-3x = 9$$
$$\frac{-3x}{-3} = -\frac{9}{3}$$
$$x = -3$$

16.

$$\frac{x}{4} - 3 = 7$$
$$\frac{x}{4} - 3 + 3 = 7 + 3$$
$$\frac{x}{4} = 10$$
$$4\left(\frac{x}{4}\right) = (10)4$$
$$x = 40$$

Solving Multi-Step Equations (page 57)

1.
$$100 + 7x = 250 - 18x$$
$$100 - 250 + 7x - 7x = 250 - 250 - 18x - 7x$$
$$-150 = -25x$$
$$6 = x$$

2.
$$5n - 6 = 4n + 2$$
$$5n - 4n - 6 + 6 = 4n - 4n + 2 + 6$$
$$n = 8$$

3. Multiply and remove the parentheses before solving the equation.
$$3(x - 4) - 2(x - 8) = 1$$
$$3x - 12 - 2x + 16 = 1$$
$$x + 4 = 1$$
$$x + 4 - 4 = 1 - 4$$
$$x = -3$$

4.
$$14x - x + 1 = 14$$
$$13x + 1 = 14$$
$$13x + 1 - 1 = 14 - 1$$
$$13x = 13$$
$$x = 1$$

5.
$$5x + 8 = 4x - 12$$
$$5x - 4x + 8 - 8 = 4x - 4x - 12 - 8$$
$$x = -20$$

6.
$$5x - 75 = 3x + 7$$
$$5x - 3x - 75 + 75 = 3x - 3x + 7 + 75$$
$$2x = 82$$
$$x = 41$$

7.
$$10(x - 3) - 7x = 0$$
$$10x - 30 - 7x = 0$$
$$3x - 30 = 0$$
$$3x - 30 + 30 = 0 + 30$$
$$3x = 30$$
$$x = 10$$

8.
$$16 + 3x = x + 32$$
$$16 - 16 + 3x - x = x - x + 32 - 16$$
$$2x = 16$$
$$x = 8$$

9.
$$3x + 1 = 25 - x$$
$$3x + x + 1 - 1 = 25 - 1 - x + x$$
$$4x = 24$$
$$x = 6$$

10.
$$36 = 18x - 12x + 6$$
$$36 = 6x + 6$$
$$36 - 6 = 6x + 6 - 6$$
$$30 = 6x$$
$$5 = x$$

11.
$$4x + 4 = 20$$
$$4x + 4 - 4 = 20 - 4$$
$$4x = 16$$
$$x = 4$$

12.
$$9x - 6 = 48$$
$$9x - 6 + 6 = 48 + 6$$
$$9x = 54$$
$$x = 6$$

13.
$$2x + 10 = 3x + 14$$
$$2x - 2x + 10 = 3x - 2x + 14$$
$$10 - 14 = x + 14 - 14$$
$$-4 = x$$

14.
$$5x - 4 = 3x + 4$$
$$5x - 3x - 4 = 3x - 3x + 4$$
$$2x - 4 = 4$$
$$2x - 4 + 4 = 4 + 4$$
$$2x = 8$$
$$x = 4$$

15.
$$5(x + 3) = x + 15$$
$$5x + 15 = x + 15$$
$$5x - x + 15 = x - x + 15$$
$$4x + 15 = 15$$
$$4x + 15 - 15 = 15 - 15$$
$$4x = 0$$
$$\frac{4x}{4} = \frac{0}{4}$$
$$x = 0$$

Solving Word Problems (page 58)

1.
Let n = 1st consecutive number
Let $n + 1$ = 2nd consecutive number
$$n + (n + 1) = 111$$
$$2n + 1 = 111$$
$$2n + 1 - 1 = 111 - 1$$
$$2n = 110$$
$$n = 55$$
$$n + 1 = 56$$
check: $55 + 56 = 111$

2.
Let n = Pam's age
Let $n + 4$ = Marion's age
$$n + (n + 4) = 32$$
$$2n + 4 = 32$$
$$2n + 4 - 4 = 32 - 4$$
$$2n = 28$$
$$n = 14$$
$$n + 4 = 14 + 4 = 18$$
check: $14 + 18 = 32$

3.

Let n = smaller number
Let $3n$ = larger number
$$3n + n = 180$$
$$4n = 180$$
$$n = 45$$
$$3n = 3(45) = 135$$
check: $45 + 135 = 180$

4.

Let n = amount Jessica spent
Let $2n$ = amount Riley spent
$$n + 2n = \$300$$
$$3n = \$300$$
$$n = \$100$$
$$2n = \$200$$
check: $\$100 + \$200 = \$300$

5.

Let n = smaller number
Let $6n$ = larger number
$$6n + n = \$98$$
$$7n = \$98$$
$$n = \$14$$
$$6n = \$84$$
check: $84 + 14 = 98$

6. Let n = number of hours Eleanor worked
Let $n + 10$ = number of hours Evelyn worked
$$n + (n + 10) = 36$$
$$2n + 10 = 36$$
$$2n + 10 - 10 = 36 - 10$$
$$2n = 26$$
$$n = 13$$
$$n + 10 = 13 + 10 = 23$$
check: $13 + 23 = 36$

Solving Word Problems (page 59)

1. (4) 1
Let x = the number
$$12(x + 2) = 36$$
$$12x + 24 = 36$$
$$12x = 12$$
$$x = 1$$

2. (2) 40 You are asked for Jerry's laps.
Let x = Bill's laps
$2x$ = Jerry's laps
$$2x + x = 60$$
$$3x = 60$$
$$x = 20$$
$$2x = 2(20) = 40$$

3. (4) 9

Let x = 1st number
$x + 1$ = 2nd number
$x + 2$ = 3rd number
$$x + x + 1 + x + 2 = 24$$
$$3x + 3 = 24$$
$$3x = 21$$
$$x = 7$$
$$x + 2 = 7 + 2 = 9$$

4. (3) 18
Let x = the number
$$2(3x) - 10 = x + 80$$
$$6x - 10 = x + 80$$
$$6x - 10 + 10 = x + 80 + 10$$
$$6x = x + 90$$
$$6x - x = 90$$
$$5x = 90$$
$$x = 18$$

5. (2) 5
Let x = the number
$$3(20 - x) = 45$$
$$60 - 3x = 45$$
$$-3x = -15$$
$$x = 5$$

6. (3) 6

Let x = the first number
$x + 2$ = the second number
$x + 4$ = the third number
$$x + (x + 2) + (x + 4) = 2(x + 4)$$
$$3x + 6 = 2x + 8$$
$$x = 2$$
The largest number is $x + 4$. Substitute.
$$x + 4 = 2 + 4 = 6$$

7. (4) 8

Let x = the number of quarters
x = the number of nickels also
$2x$ = the number of dimes
$$x + x + 2x = 16$$
$$4x = 16$$
$$x = 4 \text{ and } 2x = 8$$

8. (3) $41.25

Let x = the number of nickels
$(43)(2) = 86$ = the number of nickels
$(3 \times 86) + 4 = 262$ = the number of dimes
43 quarters = $10.75
86 nickels = $ 4.30
262 dimes = $ 26.20
$41.25

Formula Problems: Interest, Distance and Cost (pages 60–61)

1. **(4) 7%**
   $i = \$56$
   $p = \$800$
   $t = 1$ year
   $$r = \frac{i}{pt} = \frac{\$56}{\$800 \times 1 \text{ yr.}} = 0.07 = 7\%$$

2. **(4) \$1,276.50**
   $p = \$1,200$
   $r = 8\frac{1}{2}\% = .085$
   $t = 9 \text{ mos.} = \frac{3}{4}$ year
   $i = prt$
   $$= \$1,200 \times 0.085 \times \frac{3}{4} = \frac{306}{4} = \$76.50$$
   $p = \$1,200.00$
   $i = \quad +76.50$
   $\overline{\quad\quad \$1,276.50}$

3. **(4) \$1,622.50**
   $n = $ number of books $= 550$
   $r = $ cost per book $= \$2.95$
   $c = nr$
   $\quad = 550(\$2.95)$
   $\quad = \$1,622.50$

4. **(3) 217 miles**
   $r = 124$ miles per hour
   $t = 1\frac{3}{4}$ hours
   $d = rt$
   $\quad = 124 \times 1\frac{3}{4}$
   $\quad = \frac{124}{1} \times \frac{7}{4} = \frac{868}{4}$
   $\quad = 217$

5. **(2) \$255**
   $p = \$3,000$
   $r = 8\frac{1}{2}\%$
   $t = 1$ year
   $\quad i = prt$
   $\quad\quad = \$3,000 \times 0.085 \times 1$
   $\quad\quad = \$255$

6. **(4) 65 mph**
   $d = 390$ miles
   $t = 6$ hours
   $\quad r = \frac{d}{t}$
   $\quad\quad = \frac{390}{6}$
   $\quad\quad = 65$

7. **(3) 51 mph**
   $d = 160 + 146$
   $t = 4 + 2$
   $\quad r = \frac{d}{t}$
   $\quad\quad = \frac{160 + 146}{4 + 2}$
   $\quad\quad = \frac{306}{6}$
   $\quad\quad = 51$

8. **(5) \$4,625**
   $i = \$370$
   $r = 8\%$
   $t = 1$ year
   $\quad p = \frac{i}{rt}$
   $\quad\quad = \frac{\$370}{0.08 \times 1}$
   $\quad\quad = \frac{\$370}{0.08}$
   $\quad\quad = \$4,625$

9. **(3) 316.5**

Car:	Truck:
$r = 55$ mph	$r = 50.5$ mph
$t = 3$ hours	$t = 3$ hours
$d = rt$	$d = rt$
$\quad = 55 \times 3$	$\quad = 50.5 \times 3$
$\quad = 165$	$\quad = 151.5$

   $165 + 151.5 = 316.5$

10. **(4) \$1.65**
    First find the rate or price per unit.
    $$r = \frac{c}{n} = \frac{\$10.80}{12} = \$.90$$
    Then add the profit to the price to find the actual selling price.
    $\$.90 + \$.75 = \$1.65$

11. **(2) 10**
    $c = \$25$
    $r = \$2.50$
    $\quad n = \frac{c}{r}$
    $\quad\quad = \frac{\$25}{\$2.50}$
    $\quad\quad = 10$

12. **(1) 5%**
    $i = \$120$
    $t = 1$ year
    $p = \$2,400$
    $\quad r = \frac{i}{pt}$
    $\quad\quad = \frac{120}{(\$2,400)(1 \text{ yr.})} = \frac{120}{\$2,400} = 0.05 = 5\%$

13. **(3) $1\frac{1}{2}$ hours**
    $$\frac{25}{50} + \frac{65}{65} = \frac{1}{2} + 1 = 1\frac{1}{2}$$

14. (5) $1,737.50

$n = 250$
$r = \$6.95$
$c = nr$
$\quad = 250 \times \$6.95$
$\quad = \$1,737.50$

Solving Inequalities (page 62)

1. $x > 1$

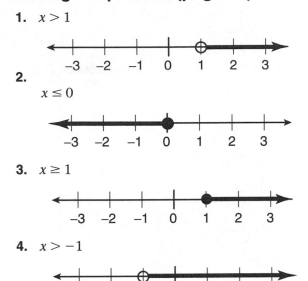

2.
$x \le 0$

3. $x \ge 1$

4. $x > -1$

Factoring (page 63)

1. $10x + 60 = 10(x + 6)$

2. $16x - 4 = 4(4x - 1)$

3. $4x^2 + 12x = 4x(x + 3)$

4. $6x^2 + 12x = 6x(x + 2)$

5. $8x^2 + 16x = 8x(x + 2)$

6. $10x^2 + 20x = 10x(x + 2)$

7. $x^2 - 5x + 4 = (x - 4)(x - 1)$

8. $x^2 - 8x + 7 = (x - 7)(x - 1)$

9. $x^2 - 3x - 10 = (x - 5)(x + 2)$

10. $x^2 - x - 6 = (x - 3)(x + 2)$

11. $x^2 + 8x - 20 = (x + 10)(x - 2)$

12. $x^2 + 3x - 10 = (x + 5)(x - 2)$

Solving Quadratic Equations by Substitution (page 64)

1. (2) 7 and 2

Substitute 7	Substitute 2
$x^2 - 9x + 14 = 0$	$x^2 - 9x + 14 = 0$
$7^2 - 9(7) + 14 = 0$	$2^2 - 9(2) + 14 = 0$
$49 - 63 + 14 = 0$	$4 - 18 + 14 = 0$
$0 = 0$	$0 = 0$

2. (4) 2 and 6

Substitute 2	Substitute 6
$x^2 - 8x + 12 = 0$	$x^2 - 8x + 12 = 0$
$2^2 - 8(2) + 12 = 0$	$6^2 - 8(6) + 12 = 0$
$4 - 16 + 12 = 0$	$36 - 48 + 12 = 0$
$0 = 0$	$0 = 0$

3. (4) −5 and −4

Substitute -5
$p^2 + 9p + 20 = 0$
$(-5)^2 + 9(-5) + 20 = 0$
$25 - 45 + 20 = 0$
$0 = 0$

Substitute -4
$p^2 + 9p + 20 = 0$
$(-4)^2 + 9(-4) + 20 = 0$
$16 - 36 + 20 = 0$
$0 = 0$

4. (3) −3 and 8

Substitute -3	Substitute 8
$a^2 - 5a - 24 = 0$	$a^2 - 5a - 24 = 0$
$(-3)^2 - 5(-3) - 24 = 0$	$(8)^2 - 5(8) - 24 = 0$
$9 + 15 - 24 = 0$	$64 - 40 - 24 = 0$
$0 = 0$	$0 = 0$

Coordinates (page 65)

1 – 4.

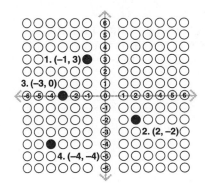

Graphing Linear Equations (page 66)

1–4.

Line 1: $x + y = 4$
if $x = 0$, $y = 4$ (0, 4)
if $y = 0$, $x = 4$ (4, 0)

Line 2: $x - y = -4$
if $x = 0$, $-y = -4$
$y = 4$ (0, 4)
if $y = 0$, $x = -4$ (−4, 0)

Line 3: $x - y = 4$
if $x = 0$, $-y = 4$
$y = -4$ (0, −4)
if $y = 0$, $x = 4$ (4, 0)

Line 4: $x + y = -4$
if $x = 0$, $y = -4$ (0, −4)
if $y = 0$, $x = -4$ (−4, 0)

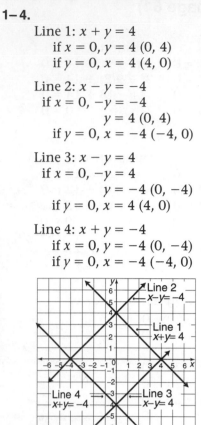

Graphing Problems (pages 69–70)

1. (4) (3, 2)
Substitute each pair.
$x + 2y = 7$
$3 + 2(2) = 7$
$3 + 4 = 7$
$7 = 7$

2. (3) (0, −9)
The y-intercept always has 0 for the x-coordinate. Choice (3) is the only choice with a zero for the x-coordinate that satisfies the equation.
Check: $2x - y = 9$
$2(0) - (-9) = 9$
$0 + 9 = 9$

3. (5) (–2, 0)
The x-intercept always has 0 for the y-coordinate. Since choices (1), (3), and (5) have zeros for the y coordinate, we must find the x-intercept by letting $y = 0$ in the equation and solving for x.
$3y - 4x = 8$
$3(0) - 4x = 8$
$-4x = 8$
$\dfrac{-4x}{-4} = \dfrac{8}{-2}$
$x = -2$
Choice (5) has the correct coordinates, (−2, 0).

4. (5) $\dfrac{1}{3}$
$m = \dfrac{y_2 - y_1}{x_2 - x_1}$
$m = \dfrac{2 - 0}{3 - (-3)}$
$m = \dfrac{2}{6} = \dfrac{1}{3}$

5.

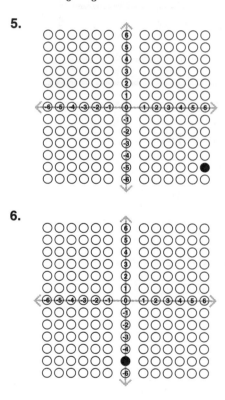

6.

7. (4) Point F

8. (3) $\dfrac{1}{2}$

9. (2) 2
$2x + 3y = 6$
$2x + 3y - 2x = 6 - 2x$
$3y = 6 - 2x$
$3y = -2x + 6$
$\dfrac{3y}{3} = \dfrac{-2x + 6}{3}$
$y = \dfrac{-2x}{3} + \dfrac{6}{3}$
$y = \dfrac{-2x}{3} + 2$

10. **(2)** $-\frac{1}{3}$

$$m = \frac{y_2 - y_1}{x_2 - x_2}$$

$$m = \frac{1 - 3}{6 - 0} = \frac{-2}{6} = -\frac{1}{3}$$

11.

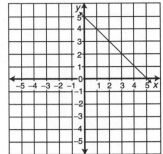

12. **(2)** $y = \frac{1}{2}x - 1$

GED Review: Algebra (pages 71–73)

1. **(1) –1** (slope of a line)

$$m = \frac{y_2 - y_1}{x_2 - x_1} = \frac{-4 - 1}{3 - (-2)} = \frac{-5}{5} = -1$$

2. **(5)** $-\frac{5}{2}$ (algebraic expressions)

$$\frac{m - m^2 n}{3n} = \frac{3 - (3^2)(2)}{3(2)} =$$

$$\frac{3 - 9(2)}{6} = \frac{3 - 18}{6} = \frac{-15}{6} = -\frac{5}{2}$$

3. **(5) –3** (algebraic expressions)

$$\frac{5}{y - x} + \frac{4}{2} + 6x$$

$$\frac{5}{4 - (-1)} + \frac{4}{2} + 6(-1) =$$

$$\frac{5}{5} + \frac{4}{2} - 6 =$$

$$1 + 2 - 6 = -3$$

4. **(3) 32** (word problems)

Let x = Kim's age
Let $4x$ = Sylvia's age
$4x - x = 24$
$3x = 24$
$x = 8$
Sylvia = $4x = 4(8) = 32$ years old

5. (coordinates)

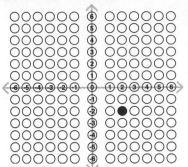

6. **The fourth point of the rectangle is at (2, –2).** (coordinates)

7. **(3)** $(x - 2)(x - 8)$ (factoring)

$(x - 2)(x - 8)$
$x^2 - 10x + 16$

8. **(1) 1** (one-step equations, algebraic expressions)

$3q = 6$
$\frac{3q}{3} = \frac{6}{3}$
$q = 2$
$\frac{1}{2}q = \frac{1}{2} \cdot \frac{2}{1} = \frac{2}{2} = 1$

9. **(2) 4** (algebraic expressions)

$2a^3 - 3ab$
$2(-1)^3 - 3(-1)(2) =$
$2(-1) - 3(-2) =$
$-2 + 6 = 4$

10. **(1) 5** (multi-step equations)

$3(x - 1) = 2(x + 1)$
$3x - 3 = 2x + 2$
$3x - 2x - 3 + 3 = 2x - 2x + 2 + 3$
$x = 5$

11. **(3)** $y > 1$ (inequalities)

$4y + 14 > 18$
$4y + 14 - 14 > 18 - 14$
$4y > 4$
$y > 1$

12. **(2)** $y = 4x + 8$ (equation of a line)

$-4x + y = 8$
$-4x + 4x + y = 8 + 4x$
$y = 8 + 4x$
$y = 4x + 8$

13. **(4)** $-\frac{1}{2}$ (equation of a line)

$x + 2y = 1$
$x + 2y - x = 1 - x$
$2y = 1 - x$
$\frac{2y}{2} = \frac{1 - x}{2}$
$y = \frac{1}{2} - \frac{1}{2}x$
$y = -\frac{1}{2}x + \frac{1}{2}$

14. **(5) $c \leq 5$** (inequalities)
$$3c - 8 \leq 7$$
$$3c - 8 + 8 \leq 7 + 8$$
$$3c \leq 15$$
$$c \leq 5$$

15. **(2) 17** (word problems)
Let a = 1st number
Let $a + 5$ = 2nd number
$$a + (a + 5) = 39$$
$$2a + 5 = 39$$
$$2a + 5 - 5 = 39 - 5$$
$$2a = 34$$
$$a = 17$$

16. **(2) 13** (word problems)
Let n = Paul's hours
Let $n + 10$ = Rhonda's hours
$$n + (n + 10) = 36$$
$$2n + 10 = 36$$
$$2n + 10 - 10 = 36 - 10$$
$$2n = 26$$
$$n = 13$$

17. **(4) $5a$** (simplifying algebraic expressions)
$$a + a + a + a + a = 5a$$

18. **(5) any of the three factors** (algebraic expressions)
Any number times zero equals zero.

19. **(1) $y = 4x - 9$** (equation of a line)
y-intercept = –9
slope = $\frac{4}{1} = 4$
$$y = mx + b$$
$$y = 4x - 9$$

20. **(3) $\frac{3}{5}$** (slope of a line)

21. **(5) 7×10^{-4}** (powers and roots)

22. **(2) $2x^2 - 4x - 1$** (simplifying algebraic expressions)

23. **(2) 4** (multi-step equations)
$$7x - 5 = 4x + 7$$
$$7x - 4x - 5 + 5 = 4x - 4x + 7 + 5$$
$$3x = 12$$
$$\frac{3x}{3} = \frac{12}{3}$$
$$x = 4$$

UNIT 4: GEOMETRY

Solving Geometric Figure Problems (pages 77–78)

1. $$125° + \angle T = 180°$$
$$125° - 125° + \angle T = 180° - 125°$$
$$\angle T = 55°$$

2. $\angle X + \angle Y = 180°$

$\angle X + \angle Y$ form a straight line, 180°

3. $$\angle Y + 26° = 90°$$
$$\angle Y + 26° - 26° = 90° - 26°$$
$$\angle Y = 64°$$

4. $$\angle A + 30° + 40° = 180°$$
$$\angle A + 70° = 180°$$
$$\angle A + 70° - 70° = 180° - 70°$$
$$\angle A = 110°$$

5. $$\angle Z + 38° + 16° = 180°$$
$$\angle Z + 54° = 180°$$
$$\angle Z + 54° - 54° = 180° - 54°$$
$$\angle Z = 126°$$

6. First find $\angle RTS$.
$$180° = 45° + 20° + \angle RTS$$
$$180° = 65° + \angle RTS$$
$$180° - 65° = 65° - 65° + \angle RTS$$
$$115° = \angle RTS$$
Then find $\angle RTU$.
$$\angle RTS + \angle RTU = 180°$$
$$115° + \angle RTU = 180°$$
$$115° - 115° + \angle RTU = 180° - 115°$$
$$\angle RTU = 65°$$

7. $$2x = 70°$$
$$x = 35°$$

8. Larger Triangle is similar to Smaller Triangle
$$\frac{AC}{AE} = \frac{BC}{BD}$$
$$\frac{9}{12} = \frac{3}{BD}$$
$$9\,BD = 36$$
$$\frac{9\,BD}{9} = \frac{36}{9}$$
$$\overline{BD} = 4$$

9. Triangles A and C may be congruent because they seem to have the same size and shape.

10. $$\frac{AB}{BC} = \frac{XY}{YZ}$$
$$\frac{2}{3} = \frac{XY}{12}$$
$$3XY = 24$$
$$\overline{XY} = 8$$

11.

$$\frac{AB}{BC} = \frac{PR}{PQ}$$

$$\frac{40}{24} = \frac{60}{PQ}$$

$$40PQ = 1{,}440$$

$$\overline{PQ} = 36$$

12.
Let $5x$ = one angle
Let $7x$ = other angle
$$5x + 7x = 90°$$
$$12x = 90°$$
$$x = 7\tfrac{1}{2}°$$
Larger angle = $7x = 7(7\tfrac{1}{2}°) = 52\tfrac{1}{2}°$

13.
$$2x + 3x = 180°$$
$$5x = 180°$$
$$x = 36°$$

14.
$$\angle A + \angle B + \angle C = 180°$$
$$90° + \angle B + 28° = 180°$$
$$\angle B + 118° = 180°$$
$$\angle B + 118° - 118° = 180° - 118°$$
$$\angle B = 62°$$

15.
$$\angle L + \angle M + \angle N = 180°$$
$$40° + 90° + \angle N = 180°$$
$$130° + \angle N = 180°$$
$$130° - 130° + \angle N = 180° - 130°$$
$$\angle N = 50°$$

16. Base angles of isosceles triangles are equal.
Therefore, $\angle A = \angle B$.
$$\angle B = 180° - 121° = 59°$$
$\angle A = 59°$ because $\angle A = \angle B$

GED Practice: Geometry Word Problems (pages 82–86)

1. (5) 156 ft.
Add 2×7 ft. to each side of pool.
$$P = 2l + 2w$$
$$= 2(32 + 14) + 2(18 + 14)$$
$$= 2(46) + 2(32)$$
$$= 92 + 64$$
$$= 156 \text{ ft.}$$

2. (3) 600 sq. ft.
$$A = lw$$
$$= 32 \cdot 18 = 576 \text{ sq. ft.}$$
600 sq. ft. is the next larger size to 576 sq. ft.

3. (4) 48 sq. in.
$$A = \tfrac{1}{2}bh$$
$$= \tfrac{1}{2}(12)(8) = \frac{96}{2} = 48 \text{ sq. in.}$$

4. (1) $(15 \times 20) + (15 \times 20)$
Total Area = Area A + Area B
$$= (15 \times 20) + (15 \times 20)$$

5. (4) $1,500
Total Area = Area A + Area B
$$= (15 \times 20) + (15 \times 20)$$
$$= 300 + 300 = 600 \text{ sq. ft.}$$
$c = nr = 600 \times \$2.50 = \$1{,}500$

6. (4) 196 cu. cm
$$V = \tfrac{1}{3}bh$$
$$= \tfrac{1}{3}(7^2)(12)$$
$$= \tfrac{1}{3}(588)$$
$$= \frac{588}{3} = 196 \text{ cu. cm}$$

7. (2) $3.14 \times 345 \times 345$
Determine total radius:
radius of center = $\tfrac{1}{2} \times 450 = 225$ ft.
3 tracks each 40 ft. wide = 120 ft.
Total radius = $225 + 120 = 345$ ft.
$A = \pi r^2 = 3.14 \times 345 \times 345$

8. (1) 2,166.6 ft.
Determine diameter.
Diameter is twice the radius found in Item 7:
$$2 \times 345 \text{ ft.} = 690 \text{ ft.}$$
OR lanes + center + lanes =
$$120 + 450 + 120 = 690$$
$c = \pi d = 3.14 \times 690 \text{ ft.} = 2{,}166.6 \text{ ft.}$

9. (4) 452.16 sq. in.
Radius is $\tfrac{1}{2}$ of the diameter of 24.
Radius = 12 in.
$A = \pi r^2 = 3.14 \times 12 \times 12 = 452.16$ sq. in.

10. (3) 4239
$$V = \tfrac{1}{3}\pi r^2 h$$
$$= \tfrac{1}{3}(3.14)(15^2)(18)$$
$$= \tfrac{1}{3}(3.14)(225)(18)$$
$$= \frac{12{,}717}{3} = 4239 \text{ cu. m}$$

11. (2) 46
$V = \pi r^2 h = 3.14 \times 11 \times 11 \times 28$
$$= 10{,}638.32 \text{ cu. in.}$$
$10{,}638.32 \div 231 = 46.05$ rounds to 46 gallons

12. (3) 9 in.

Large Picture   Smaller Picture

$$\frac{\text{width}}{\text{length}} = \frac{\text{width}}{\text{length}}$$

$$\frac{12}{16} = \frac{x}{12}$$

$$16x = 144$$

$$x = 9 \text{ inches}$$

13. (4) 1:4

rise:span

5:20

1:4

14. (3) $37\frac{1}{2}$ ft.

$$\frac{\text{pole height}}{\text{shadow}} = \frac{\text{tree height}}{\text{shadow}}$$

$$\frac{6}{4} = \frac{x}{25}$$

$$4x = 150$$

$$x = 37\frac{1}{2} \text{ ft.}$$

15. (2) 54 ft.

$$\frac{\text{seedling height}}{\text{shadow}} = \frac{\text{tree height}}{\text{shadow}}$$

$$\frac{3}{4} = \frac{x}{72}$$

$$4x = 216$$

$$x = 54 \text{ ft.}$$

16. (4) 25 ft.

First find AB.

$$\frac{AB}{BC} = \frac{2}{3}$$

$$\frac{AB}{15} = \frac{2}{3}$$

$$3\overline{AB} = 30$$

$$\overline{AB} = 10 \text{ ft.}$$

10 ft.
+15 ft.
25 ft.

17. (2) similar

Proportional triangles are similar.

18. (2) 60 ft.

Use the Pythagorean relationship.

$$c^2 = a^2 + b^2$$
$$c^2 = 48^2 + 36^2$$
$$c^2 = 2,304 + 1,296$$
$$c^2 = 3,600$$
$$c = \sqrt{3,600}$$
$$c = 60 \text{ ft.}$$

19. (2) 40 ft.

$\triangle ABC$ and $\triangle CDE$ are similar. Thus,

$$\frac{AB}{BC} = \frac{DE}{CE}$$

$$\frac{8}{10} = \frac{x}{50}$$

$$10x = 400$$

$$x = 40 \text{ ft.}$$

20. (5) 1,000 miles

$$1\frac{7}{8} + \frac{5}{8} = 1\frac{12}{8} = 2\frac{4}{8} = 2\frac{1}{2} \text{ inches}$$

Change $2\frac{1}{2}$ to 2.5

$$\frac{2.5}{x} = \frac{0.25}{100}$$

$$0.25x = 250$$

$$x = 1,000 \text{ miles}$$

21. (3) 20 cm

Since the triangles are similar,

$$\frac{AC}{AB} = \frac{EC}{EF}$$

$$\frac{36}{40} = \frac{18}{x}$$

$$36x = 720$$

$$x = 20 \text{ cm}$$

22. (4) 5

The perimeter of the bulletin board is $2(12) + 2(18) = 60$. Change inches to feet.

$$\frac{60}{12} = 5 \text{ feet}$$

23. (3) 9 in.

$$a^2 + b^2 = c^2$$
$$a^2 + 12^2 = 15^2$$
$$a^2 + 144 = 225$$
$$a^2 + 144 - 144 = 225 - 144$$
$$a^2 = 81$$
$$a = \sqrt{81} = 9$$

24. (3) $\sqrt{3^2 + 4^2}$

Look at the right triangle formed by the roof. The width of the roof is the hypotenuse (c) of this triangle. The height is given as 4 ft. The base is $\frac{1}{2}$ the width of the shed, or 3 ft. These are the legs of the right triangle.

Thus, $c = \sqrt{a^2 + b^2} = \sqrt{3^2 + 4^2}$

25. (4) $\sqrt{225 - 121}$

$$a^2 + b^2 = c^2$$
$$11^2 + b^2 = 15^2$$
$$b^2 = 15^2 - 11^2$$
$$b = \sqrt{15^2 - 11^2} = \sqrt{225 - 121}$$

26. (4) 15 ft.

$$c^2 = a^2 + b^2$$
$$c^2 = 5^2 + 12^2$$
$$c^2 = 25 + 144$$
$$c^2 = 169$$
$$c = \sqrt{169} = 13$$

The ladder must be 13 ft. + 2 ft. or 15 ft. long.

27. (3) 40 ft.

$$c^2 = a^2 + b^2$$
$$c^2 = 24^2 + 32^2$$
$$c^2 = 576 + 1024$$
$$c^2 = 1600$$
$$c = \sqrt{1600} = 40$$

UNIT 4

28. (3) 60°
The angles of a triangle total 180°. Let x = the missing angle.
$$30° + 90° + x = 180°$$
$$120° + x = 180°$$
$$x = 60°$$

GED Review: Geometry (pages 87–89)

1. (1) 392 sq. in. (area)
First find the width.
$$P = 2l + 2w$$
$$84 = 2(28) + 2w$$
$$84 = 56 + 2w$$
$$84 - 56 = 56 - 56 + 2w$$
$$28 = 2w$$
$$14 \text{ in.} = w$$
$$A = lw = 28 \times 14 = 392 \text{ sq. in.}$$

2. (4) 94.2 sq. in. (volume)
$$V = \frac{1}{3}\pi r^2 h$$
$$\frac{1}{3}(3.14)(3^2)(10)$$
$$\frac{1}{3}(3.14)(9)(10)$$
$$\frac{282.6}{3} = 94.2 \text{ sq. in.}$$

3. (1) 24 cm (area)
Area of a rectangle = lw
$$24(8) = 192$$
Area of a triangle = $\frac{1}{2}bh$
$$192 = \frac{1}{2}(16)(h)$$
$$192 = 8(h)$$
$$h = 24$$

4. (4) 139 cu. ft. (volume)
Change 9 in. to $\frac{3}{4}$ ft.
$$V = lwh$$
$$= \left(14\frac{1}{2}\right)\left(12\frac{3}{4}\right)\left(\frac{3}{4}\right)$$
$$= \left(\frac{29}{2}\right)\left(\frac{51}{4}\right)\left(\frac{3}{4}\right)$$
$$= \frac{4437}{32} = 138.7 = 139$$

5. (3) 14 sq. ft. (area)
$$A = bh$$
$$= 7(2)$$
$$= 14 \text{ sq. ft.}$$

6. (2) $\frac{1}{3}(18^2)(36.5)$ (volume)

7. (4) II and III only (angles and lines)

8. (3) 42 ft. (triangles)
$$\frac{AC}{AB} = \frac{XZ}{XY}$$
$$\frac{21}{7} = \frac{x}{14}$$
$$7x = 294$$
$$x = 42$$

9. (5) 1.39 in. (circles)
$$\begin{aligned}27.14 &\quad \text{outer diameter}\\ -24.36 &\quad \text{inner diameter}\\ \hline 2.78 &\quad \text{thickness of 2 walls}\end{aligned}$$
$$\frac{2.78}{2} = 1.39 \text{ in.}$$

10. (2) 1:8 (volume)

Original	Doubled dimensions
$V = lwh$	$V = lwh$
$= 2 \times 3 \times 4$	$= 4 \times 6 \times 8$
$= 24$ cu. in.	$= 192$ cu. in.

Original:New
$$24:192$$
$$1:8$$

11. (5) 30 in. (triangles)
$$c^2 = a^2 + b^2$$
$$c^2 = 18^2 + 24^2$$
$$c^2 = 324 + 576$$
$$c^2 = 900$$
$$c = \sqrt{900} = 30$$

12. (2) 30 sq. ft.
Use the formula chart to find the area of a trapezoid:
$$A = \frac{1}{2} \times (\text{base1} + \text{base 2}) \times \text{height}$$
$$= \frac{1}{2} \times (12 + 8) \times 3$$
$$= \frac{1}{2} \times (20) \times 3$$
$$= \frac{1}{2} \times 60 = 30 \text{ sq. ft.}$$

13. (3) $(15 \times 15) - (7 \times 9)$ (area)
$$A = lw$$
(Area of Section I) − (Area of Section II)
$$(15 \times 15) - (7 \times 9)$$

14. (3) $2(15 + 15) - 2(7 + 9)$ (perimeter)
$$P = 2(l + w)$$
(Perimeter of Section I) − (Perimeter of Section II)
$$2(15 + 15) - 2(7 + 9)$$

15. (4) 18 ft. (perimeter)
$$P = 84$$
$$l = 24$$
$$P = 2l + 2w$$
$$84 = 2(24) + 2w$$
$$84 = 48 + 2w$$
$$84 - 48 = 48 - 48 + 2w$$
$$36 = 2w$$
$$18 = w$$

16. (2) $19\frac{1}{2}$ ft. (perimeter)
Change 20 feet 6 inches to $20\frac{1}{2}$ feet.
$$P = 2l + 2w$$
$$80 = 2(20\tfrac{1}{2}) + 2w$$
$$80 = 41 + 2w$$
$$80 - 41 = 41 - 41 + 2w$$
$$39 = 2w$$
$$19\tfrac{1}{2} = w$$

17. (3) 125 cu. ft. (volume)
The face of a cube is a square. If the area of the face is 25 sq. ft., 5 feet is the measurement of each side. Therefore, since all sides of a cube are equal:
$$V = lwh$$
$$= 5 \times 5 \times 5$$
$$= 125 \text{ cu. ft.}$$

18. (2) 65° (triangles)
$$\angle a + \angle b = 180°$$
$$115° + \angle b = 180°$$
$$115° - 115° + \angle b = 180° - 115°$$
$$\angle b = 65°$$

19. (5) $\angle g$ (triangles)
$\angle c$ corresponds with $\angle g$.
$\angle c$ and $\angle b$ are vertical angles.
$\angle c$ and $\angle f$ are alternate interior angles.
$\angle c = \angle g = \angle b = \angle f$

20. (4) 14 ft. (triangles)
Use the Pythagorean relationship to find the height of the triangle.
$$a^2 + b^2 = c^2$$
$$a^2 + 8^2 = 10^2$$
$$a^2 + 64 = 100$$
$$a^2 + 64 - 64 = 100 - 64$$
$$a^2 = 36$$
$$a = \sqrt{36} = 6$$
Add the height of the triangle to the height of the side of the barn. Since 6 ft. + 8 ft. = 14 ft., the height of the center of the roof is 14 ft.

SIMULATED TEST A
Part I (pages 102–106)

1. (1) $9.28 (Number Sense and Operations)
Sale price = 100% − 40% = 60% = 0.60
Sales price = $144 × 0.60 = $86.40
Sales tax = $86.40 × 0.05 = $4.32
Total cost = $86.40 + $4.32 = $90.72
Change = $100.00 − $90.72 = $9.28

2. (4) 5 × 1.5 (Number Sense and Operations)
Divide the dimensions by 10 to see how many of the $\frac{1}{2}$-inch segments you will need for each side. Since there are 3 ten-foot segments in 30, then 3 times $\frac{1}{2}$ will be $1\frac{1}{2}$. The other dimension is 100, for which there are 10 of the ten-foot segments. $10 \times \frac{1}{2} = 5$.

3. (4) 12 (Algebra)
$$y - 14 = 10 - y$$
$$y - 14 + 14 + y = 10 + 14 - y + y$$
$$2y = 24$$
$$\frac{2y}{2} = \frac{24}{2}$$
$$y = 12$$

4. $15\frac{1}{4} = \frac{61}{4}$ or 15.25 (Number Sense and Operations)
$$3\tfrac{1}{2} + 7\tfrac{3}{4} + 4 = \frac{7}{2} + \frac{31}{4} + \frac{4}{1} = \frac{14}{4} + \frac{31}{4} + \frac{16}{4} = \frac{61}{4} = 15.25$$

5. 24 (Number Sense and Operations)
To find the rate, think of the first time interval, which is two hours (from noon to 2). During this time interval the temperature rose 18 degrees (from −12 to +6). This gives a rate of 9 degrees in 1 hour. Applying this rate to the time from 2 PM to 4 PM gives 18° above the 6° at 2 PM. Then 6 + 18 = 24.

6. **(1) 1,200** (Data Analysis)
   $3,600 - 2,400 = 1,200$
   or $6(600) - 4(600) = 2(600) = 1,200$

7. **(2)** $\frac{9(600)}{3(600)}$ (Data Analysis)

8. **(5) Not enough information is given.**
   (Geometry)
   To determine the size of angle y, the size of angle x would be needed.

9. **(4) 110°** (Geometry)
   Since the measurement of $\angle ABC = 68°$ and BF bisects $\angle ABC$, then the measurement of $\angle EBC = \frac{1}{2}(68) = 34°$. Since the measurement of $\angle ACB = 72°$ and $\overline{CD}$ bisects $\angle ACB$, then the measurement of $\angle ECB = \frac{1}{2}(72) = 36°$.
   $34° + 36° = 70°$
   $180° - 70° = 110°$

10. **(5) (0.05)(380)** (Number Sense and Operations)
    The word "of" means to multiply. Percents are changed into decimals by moving the decimal point two places to the left, so multiply 380 by 0.05.

11. **(1) $705** (Number Sense and Operations)
    Transactions (a) and (d) are additions. Transaction (b) and (c) are subtractions.
    $\$630 - \$125 - \$50 + \$250 = \$705$

12. **175** (Algebra)
    Insert the values for each letter in that letter's place in the equation.
    $x = 7(y - 2z)^2$
    $x = 7(9 - 2[2])^2$
    $x = 7(9 - 4)^2$
    $x = 7(5)^2$
    $x = 7(25)$
    $x = 175$

13. **42** (Algebra)
    Let x = number of points scored by Jim.
    Let $3x$ = number of points scored by Bill.
    $x + 3x = 56$
    $\quad 4x = 56$
    $\quad\quad x = 56 \div 4 = 14$
    $\quad 3x = 3(14) = 42$

14. **(2) 256** (Data Analysis)
    $40 + 90 + 204 + 10 = 344$
    $600 - 344 = 256$

15. **(1) A** (Algebra)
    $-7.8 + 1.6 + 1.2 = -5.0 =$ point A

16. **(3) C** (Geometry)
    The formula for the volume of a cylinder is given on the formula page. Since $\pi = 3.14$ is used in all the calculations, you can leave it out. So, in each case, multiply the height by the radius by the radius. Looking at each cylinder:
    A = 4(2)(2) = 16
    B = 8(1)(1) = 8
    C = 1(8)(8) = 64

    Although these numbers are not the real volumes, they have the same relationship as the volumes, so you can see that C would hold the most water.

17. **(0, −3)** (Algebra)
    The equation is of the form $y = mx + b$, where m = the slope and b = the y-intercept. Therefore, the line must cross the y-axis at the point $(0, -3)$

18. **(2)** $\sqrt{36}$ (Number Sense and Operations)

$\sqrt{1} = \sqrt{1^2}$
$\sqrt{4} = \sqrt{2^2}$
$\sqrt{9} = \sqrt{3^2}$
$\sqrt{16} = \sqrt{4^2}$
$\sqrt{25} = \sqrt{5^2}$

The square of 6 is 36: $\sqrt{6^2} = \sqrt{36}$

19. **(5) ∠4 and ∠5 are alternate interior angles** (Geometry)

20. **(3) $3.55** (Number Sense and Operations)

After paying $1.15 for the first three minutes, there are 20 minutes left to pay for at the rate of 12 cents for each minute, or $2.40. $1.15 + $2.40 = $3.55

21. **20** (Geometry)

Use the Pythagorean Theorem and draw a right triangle.
$c^2 = (12)^2 + (16)^2$
$c^2 = 144 + 256 = 400$
$c = \sqrt{400} = 20$

22. **$1,350** (Measurement)

If you split the 50 yards into 5 pieces of 10 yards each, you would get 5 free yards, and have to buy 45 yards. 45 x $30 = $1350

23. **(4)** $(2\frac{1}{2} + 3\frac{1}{2} + 1\frac{1}{2} + 3) \div 10$ (Data Analysis)
Add the four distances, then divide by 10 to find the miles covered per hour.

24. **(4)** $\frac{2}{20}, \frac{32}{64}, \frac{15}{18}, \frac{28}{32}, \frac{32}{36}$ (Number Sense and Operations)

$\frac{2}{20} = \frac{1}{10} = 0.10$

$\frac{32}{64} = \frac{1}{2} = 0.5$

$\frac{15}{18} = \frac{5}{6} = 0.8333$

$\frac{28}{32} = \frac{7}{8} = 0.875$

$\frac{32}{36} = \frac{8}{9} = 0.8888$

25. **(2) It has one-half the fat of whole milk.** (Data Analysis)

According to the chart, whole milk has 8 grams of fat; 2% milk has 4 grams of fat, or half the fat.

Part II (pages 110–114)

26. **(4)** $\frac{6}{10} = \frac{x}{8}$ (Number Sense and Operations)
Remember in setting up proportions to compare corresponding parts.

27. **(4) 528,815** (Data Analysis)
Arrange in order from smallest to largest.

383,000
493,509
509,386
548,244 ⎫— middle values
903,084 ⎭
3,164,632

Add the two middle values:
509,386 + 548,244 = 1,057,630
Find the average of the two values:
1,057,630 ÷ 2 = 528,815

28. **(5) 2,781,632** (Data Analysis)
3,164,632
− 383,000
2,781,632

29. **(2) Base path *AB* is parallel to base path *CD*.** (Geometry)
Parallel means an equal distance apart at all points.

30. **(4) 5** (Algebra)

$3x - 6 = x + 4$
$3x - x - 6 + 6 = x - x + 4 + 6$
$2x = 10$
$x = 5$

31. 41.75 (Number Sense and Data Analysis)
First find the total mileage.
135 + 172 + 198 + 127 + 203 = 835 miles
Divide the total mileage (835) by the number of miles covered for each gallon of gas used (20) to find the number of gallons of gas needed.
835 ÷ 20 = 41.75 gallons

32. (2) 9,000 (Data Analysis)
The parts of the circle graph show occupations of wage earners in a city by percent. The entire circle is equal to 100%. 100% of the wage earners is 180,000. Transportation wage earners are 5% of the total.
0.05 × 180,000 = 9,000

33. (2) $40 (Algebra)
The difference in the percent is 0.2%, or 0.002 when changed to a decimal.
$10,000 × 0.002 × 2 years = $40

34. (4) Bad News Blues sold 65,000 copies in August. (Data Analysis)
This is the only correct response.

35. (4) $40,800 (Number Sense and Operations)
(60,000)(0.02)(34) = 40,800

36. (2) positive (Algebra)
The line slants upward to the right so the slope is positive.
Check: $m = \frac{y_2 - y_1}{x_2 - x_1} = \frac{4 - 0}{0 - (-5)} = \frac{4}{5}$

37. (Algebra)
Remember that the x-value is first and the y-value is second. The x-value is –3 and the y-value is 4.

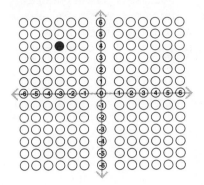

38. (3) $562.50 (Number Sense and Operations)
The breakfast cost would need to be multiplied by 5 days per workweek and then multiplied by 50 weeks per year.
$2.25 × 5 × 50 = $562.50

39. (2) 3 (Measurement)
Convert yards to feet.
$2\frac{1}{3}$ yards × 3 = 7 ft
7 yards × 3 = 21 ft
Multiply the radius, $3\frac{1}{2}$ feet, by 2 to find the diameter of the cover, 7 feet.
The fabric can fit 3 circles (21 ÷ 3 = 7).

40. (1) acute (Geometry)
2x = 1st angle
3x = 2nd angle
4x = 3rd angle
2x + 3x + 4x = 180°
9x = 180°
x = 20°
2x = 2(20°) = 40°
3x = 3(20°) = 60°
4x = 4(20°) = 80°

41. (2) $1,461.28 (Number Sense and Operations)
$2,185.60 − $434.99 − $199.89 − $89.44 = $1,461.28

42. (1) A > B (Geometry)
It is not even necessary to calculate the volumes, but just to set them up to see the relationship. Remember that the radius is half the diameter.
V = π(5)(5)(4) for container A
V = π(2)(2)(10) for container B
Not counting π, since it is common to both, you can see that A is 100, while B is 40, so A is larger than B.

43. $\frac{5}{19}$ (Data Analysis)

The purse contains $6 + 5 + 8 = 19$ coins. Five coins are dimes.

Probability = $\frac{\text{number of successful outcomes}}{\text{number of possible outcomes}}$.

In this case, there are 5 successful outcomes since there are 5 dimes. The number of possible outcomes is 19 since there are 19 coins in all. Thus, $P = \frac{5}{19}$.

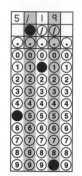

44. (3) $\angle DAB$ (Geometry)

45. (2) supplementary (Geometry)
$\angle 2 + \angle 3 = 180°$. Two angles whose sum equal $180°$ are supplementary.

46. (1) April and July are equally rainy months. (Data Analysis)
Choices 4 and 5 have nothing to do with the graph. Choice 1 is the only true statement.

47. (5) $3,150.00 (Data Analysis)
The chart gives the cost per $1,000 of insurance. There are 100 of these thousands in $100,000, so the premium has to be multiplied by 100.

48. (2) Greater than 9 and less than 10 (Geometry)
Substituting in the formula for the Pythagorean relationship gives the following:
$x^2 + 4^2 = 10^2$
$x^2 + 16 = 100$
$x^2 = 84$

Since $9^2 = 81$ and $10^2 = 100$, the answer (the square root of 84) is greater than 9 and less than 10.

49. (5) 5 ft. 4 in. (Algebra/Geometry)
$\frac{\text{Amanda shadow}}{\text{height}} = \frac{\text{Statue shadow}}{\text{height}}$
$\frac{4}{x} = \frac{12}{16}$
$12x = 64$
$x = 5\frac{4}{12}$
Since 1 foot = 12 inches:
$\frac{4}{12}$ foot = 4 inches
$5\frac{4}{12}$ feet = 5 feet 4 inches.

50. (5) 105 (Algebra/Geometry)
$\frac{\text{minutes}}{\text{gallons}} = \frac{\text{minutes}}{\text{gallons}}$
$\frac{15}{45} = \frac{35}{x}$
$15x = 1,575$
$x = 105$

SIMULATED TEST B
Part I (pages 120–124)

1. (2) $2\frac{1}{2}$% (Number Sense and Operations)
part ÷ base = percent
$30 ÷ 1,200 = 0.025 = 2\frac{1}{2}$%

2. (4) $\frac{1}{4}$ (Data Analysis)
Since there are two desired outcomes out of 8 possible outcomes, the probability is $\frac{2}{8}$ or $\frac{1}{4}$.

3. (1) $\frac{1}{2} = \frac{5}{10}$ (Number Sense and Operations)
$\frac{1}{2} \overset{?}{=} \frac{5}{10}$
$1 \times 10 \overset{?}{=} 2 \times 5$
$10 = 10$

4. 1365 (Data Analysis)
When you add the four calorie values, you get 5,460. Dividing this by 4 gives an average of 1,365 calories.

5. 24 (Number Sense and Operations)

If the gauge shows $\frac{1}{3}$ full, then the tank is $\frac{2}{3}$ empty.

$\frac{2}{3}$ of the tank = 16 gallons

$\frac{1}{3}$ of the tank = $\frac{1}{2}$(16) = 8 gallons

$\frac{3}{3}$ of the tank = 3(8) = 24 gallons

6. **(1) −34°** (Data Analysis)
The reading for a 12-quart cooling system with 6 quarts of antifreeze is −34.

7. **(4) $\frac{3}{10}$% of 70** (Number Sense and Operations)

$6\frac{3}{4}$% of 50 = 0.0675 × 50 = 3.375

8% of 90 = 0.08 × 90 = 7.2

50% of 100 = 0.50 × 100 = 50

$\frac{3}{10}$% of 70 = 0.003 × 70 = 0.21

$\frac{3}{4}$% of 240 = 0.0075 × 240 = 1.8

8. **(5) parallel** (Geometry)

9. **(5) 20** (Number Sense and Operations)

$\frac{\text{newspapers}}{\text{time}} = \frac{\text{newspapers}}{\text{time}}$

Change $1\frac{1}{4}$ to 1.25

$\frac{125}{1.25} = \frac{2,000}{x}$

$125x = 2,500$

$x = 20$ hours

10. **(5) 20.0%** (Number Sense and Operations)
Percent can be written: Part × $\frac{100}{\text{whole}}$. The part that is changed is 2.5 − 2.0 = 0.5. The whole is the original, 2.5, so 0.5 × $\frac{100}{2.5}$ = 20%.

11. **(4) 50** (Geometry)
$c^2 = a^2 + b^2$ (Pythagorean relationship)
$c^2 = 30^2 + 40^2$
$c^2 = 900 + 1,600$
$c^2 = 2,500$
$c = \sqrt{2,500}$
$c = 50$

12. **1** (Number Sense and Operations/Measurement)
Set up the proportion $\frac{16}{1} = \frac{x}{8}$, knowing that x will be in ounces because the 8 is in ounces. Solving for x gives $x = 8(16) = 128$ ounces. Since one gallon is 128 ounces, one gallon is the answer.

13. **11** (Algebra)
Let x = points scored by Jack.
And $x + 7$ = points scored by Ben.
And $x − 2$ = points scored by Paul.
$x + x + 7 + x − 2 = 38$
$3x + 5 = 38$
$3x + 5 − 5 = 38 − 5$
$3x = 33$
$x = 11$

14. **(2) 2.5 liters** (Measurement)
800 ml + 500 ml + 1,000 ml + 200 ml = 2,500 ml = 2.5 liters

15. **(5) $8** (Data Analysis)

If we add the amounts given

$11 + $6 + $5 + $40 + $30 = $92

This leaves $8 for profit.

16. **(3) $1,640** (Algebra)

Let $(x + $640)$ = student leader's money

Let x = $ for each of the other four students

$$(x + $640) + 4x = $5,640$$
$$5x + 640 = $5,640$$
$$5x + $640 - $640 = $5,640 - $640$$
$$5x = $5,000$$
$$x = $1,000$$
$$x + $640 = $1,000 + $640 = $1,640$$

17. **(5,–2)** (Algebra)

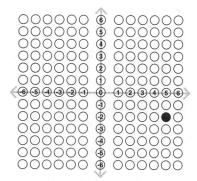

x-coordinate is 5; y-coordinate is –2

18. **(2) $x < 7$** (Algebra)

The open circle with the arrow pointing left means all numbers less than 7 are in the solution set.

19. **(5) $\angle H$** (Geometry)

$\angle A$ and $\angle H$ are alternate exterior angles and are equal.

20. **(3) 100°** (Geometry)

$$\text{Let } x = \angle G$$
$$\text{Let } x + 20° = \angle E$$
$$x + (x + 20°) = 180°$$
$$2x + 20° = 180°$$
$$2x + 20° - 20° = 180° - 20°$$
$$2x = 160°$$
$$x = 80° = \angle G$$

Substituting:

$$\angle E = x + 20° = 80° + 20° = 100°$$

21. $14\frac{3}{4} = \frac{59}{4}$ **or 14.75** (Geometry)

To find the width of the lawn, divide the area by the length.

$$302\frac{3}{8} \div 20\frac{1}{2} = \frac{2419}{8} \div \frac{41}{2} = \frac{2419}{8} \times \frac{2}{41}$$
$$= \frac{59}{4} \times \frac{1}{1} = \frac{59}{4} = 14.75$$

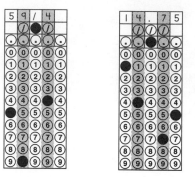

22. **50** (Number Sense and Operations)

$$\text{Percent of increase} = \frac{\text{new amount} - \text{old amount}}{\text{old amount}}$$

$$\frac{48,000 - 32,000}{32,000} = \frac{16,000}{32,000} = 0.50 = 50\%$$

23. **(4) 27,500** (Data Analysis)

According to the graph the population in 2000 was midway between 25,000 and 30,000.

$$25,000 + 30,000 = 55,000$$
$$55,000 \div 2 = 27,500$$

24. **(3) 1998 and 1999** (Data Analysis)

According to the graph the population in 1998 was 20,000 and in 1999 it was also 20,000.

25. **(2) 60 ft.** (Algebra)

$$\frac{\text{Lester's height}}{\text{shadow}} = \frac{\text{street light's height}}{\text{shadow}}$$

$$\frac{6}{4} = \frac{x}{40}$$
$$4x = 240$$
$$x = 60$$

Part II (pages 128–132)

26. **(4) $96,000** (Data Analysis)
40% of the total expenses of $240,000 went for labor.
40% = 0.4
0.4($240,000) = $96,000

27. **(2) $24** (Number Sense and Operations)
20% of $120 = 0.20 × $120 = $24

28. **(4) 55 $2 books and 45 $3 books** (Algebra)
Let x = $2 books
100 − x = $3 books
(2)x + (3)(100 − x) = 245
2x + 300 − 3x = 245
−x = −55
x = 55 and 100 − x = 45

29. **(5) 135°** (Geometry)
∠y + 45° = 180°
∠y + 45° − 45° = 180° − 45°
∠y = 135°

30. **(2) $1,000** (Data Analysis)
Meat department sales = $2,500
Dairy department sales = $1,500
Difference = $1,000

31. **16** (Number Sense and Operations)
10% + 25% + 30% + 15% = 80% passing papers
20% had failing papers (100% − 80% = 20%)
20% of 80 = .20 (80) = 16 failing papers

32. **(3) $6 \times 2(63 + 48) \div 36$** (Measurement)
One window $P = 2l + 2w$
$P = 2(63 + 48)$ inches
Six windows = Multiply by 6.
$6 \times 2(63 + 48)$ inches
There are 36 inches in a yard, therefore, divide by 36.
$6 \times 2(63 + 48) \div 36$

33. **(4) $25.53** (Measurement)
$6 \times 2(l + w) \div 36$
$6 \times 2(63 + 48) \div 36$
$6 \times 2(111) \div 36$
$6 \times 222 \div 36$
$1,332 \div 36 = 37$
$.69 \times 37 = 25.53

34. **(1)** $\frac{1}{4}x - \frac{1}{6}x = 18$ (Algebra)
Let $\frac{1}{4}x$ = first number
Let $\frac{1}{6}x$ = second number
$\frac{1}{4}x - \frac{1}{6}x = 18$

35.

(1) (Data Analysis)
You are looking for a graph that shows both variables increasing. Choice (1) is the only graph that shows this.

36. **(3) 3, 6, 9, 12, 15** (Geometry)
The distance from the middle of the target to its outer edge is 15 inches. There are 5 circles, so each one has a value of 3. Starting at the center, a 3-inch string makes the 6-inch bullseye, a 6-inch string makes the next circle, and so on.

37. **(−2, −5)** (Algebra)

Remember the x-value is first and the y-value is second. The x-value is –2 and the y-value is –5.

38. **(1) 40°** (Geometry)
First find the measurement of ∠ABD. ∠ABD is vertical to ∠CBE; therefore, ∠ABD = 50°
∠ADB + ∠ABD = 90° + 50° = 140°
Subtracting from the number of degrees in a triangle:
180° − 140° = 40° for ∠DAB

39. (4) 130° (Geometry)

$\angle DBC$ is the supplementary angle to $\angle CBE$; therefore, $180° - 50° = 130°$.

40. (5) 20 (Algebra)

$3x - 1 = 11$
$3x = 11 + 1 = 12$
$x = 12 \div 3 = 4$
$x^2 + x = 4^2 + 4 = 16 + 4 = 20$

41. (1) $\sqrt{6^2 + 10^2}$ (Geometry)

Check the formula page for the Pythagorean relationship ($c^2 = a^2 + b^2$). This problem is an application of that relationship, in which the length of the rod is the hypotenuse (the side across from the right angle). In order to find the length of the rod (c), you must use the square root.

42. (1) $\frac{x}{15} = \frac{50}{20}$ (Geometry)

This is a similar triangles problem, so you can use a proportion. The tree height is to 15 as the big triangle's base of 50 is to the smaller triangle's base of 20. This gives the proportion $\frac{x}{15} = \frac{50}{20}$.

43. 4 (Algebra)

$2a^3 - 3ay = 2(-1)^3 - 3(-1)(2)$
$\qquad\qquad = -2 + 3(2)$
$\qquad\qquad = -2 + 6 = 4$

44. (2) The daily average use in March was 250 gallons. (Data Analysis)

45. (1) $\frac{9}{19}$ (Data Analysis)

$\text{Probability} = \frac{\text{number of successful outcomes}}{\text{total number of outcomes}}$

In this case, there are 9 girls who could have been called upon. The total number of students who could have been called upon was 19. Probability $= \frac{9}{19}$

46. (5) −16 (Algebra)

$x = (n + 5)(n - 5)$
$x = (-3 + 5)(-3 - 5)$
$x = (+2)(-8)$
$x = -16$

47. (3) 40° (Geometry)

Since the measurement of $\angle ACB = 90°$, and the measurement of $\angle CAD = 40°$, then the measurement of $\angle B = 180° - 90° - 40° = 50°$. In $\triangle BCD$, the measurement of $\angle CDB = 90°$, and the measurement of $\angle B = 50°$. Therefore, the measurement of $\angle DCB = 180° - 90° - 50° = 40°$.

48. (3) 6a + 4b (Geometry)

To find the perimeter of a figure, find the sum of the lengths of its sides.
$(2a) + (a + b) + (2a + b) + (a + 2b) = 6a + 4b$

49. (3) $n^2 + n + 4 = 60$ (Algebra)

Let n = the number
Then n^2 = the square of the number
And $n + 4$ = the number increased by 4.
The equation is $n^2 + n + 4 = 60$

50. (1) $360 (Number Sense and Operations)

6 dozen $\times$ $7 = 72 \times $7 = 504
140% of cost = sales of $504
$1.4x = 504
$x = 504 \div 1.4$
$x = 360

Name: _____ Class: _____ Date: _____

○ Simulated Test A   ○ Simulated Test B

Part I

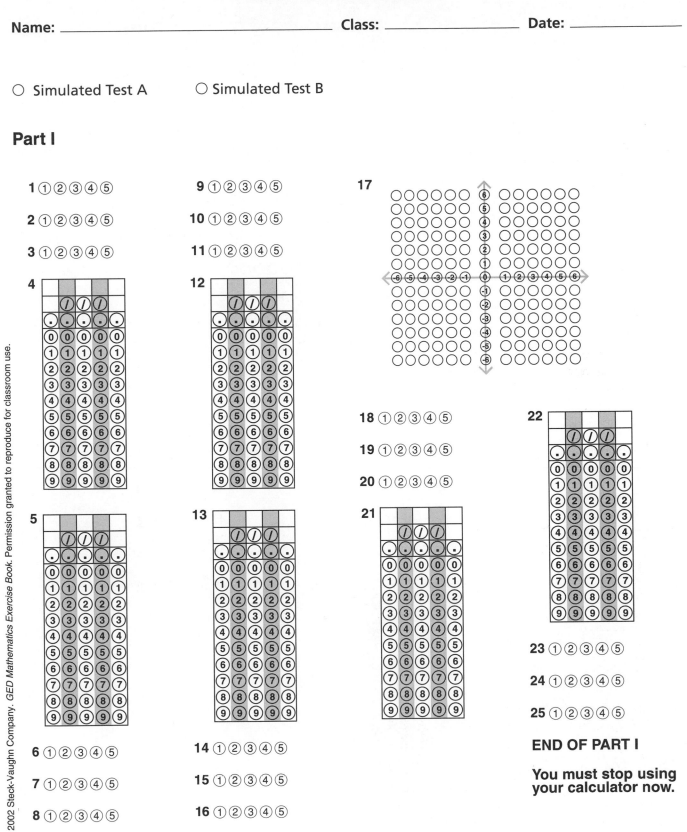

END OF PART I

You must stop using your calculator now.

Name: _____ **Class:** _____ **Date:** _____

○ Simulated Test A   ○ Simulated Test B

Part II

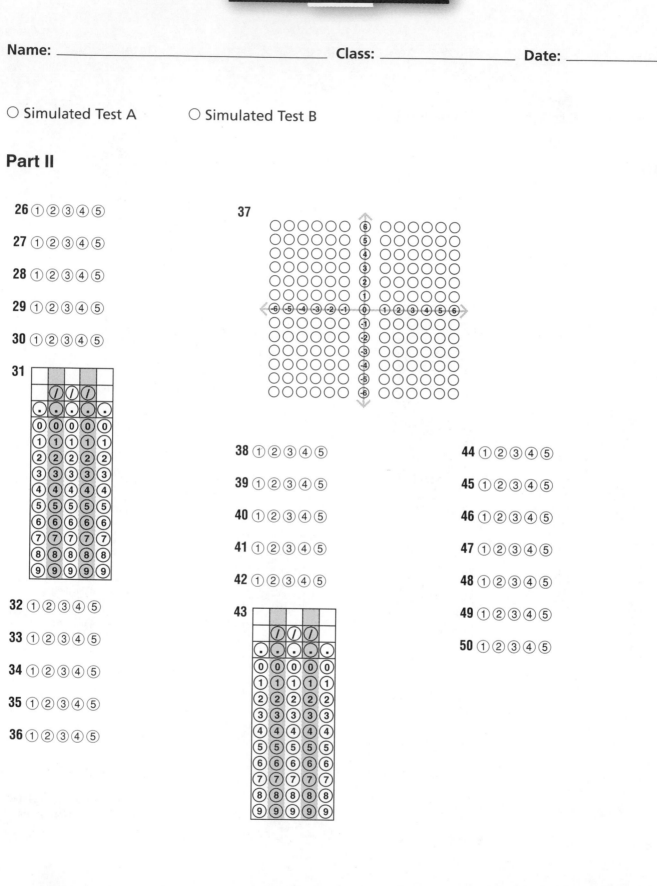

© 2002 Steck-Vaughn Company. GED Mathematics Exercise Book. Permission granted to reproduce for classroom use.